A Taste of Provence

A Taste of Provence

Francie Jouanin

KÖNEMANN

© 2005 Tandem Verlag GmbH
KÖNEMANN is a trademark and an imprint of Tandem Verlag GmbH

Art Director: Peter Feierabend
Project Management: Sabine Baumgartner, Isabel Weiler (revised edition)
Assistance: Stefanie Rödiger
Editing: Britta Rath, Astrid Roth
Design: Sabine Vonderstein
Cartography: Studio für Landkartentechnik Detlef Maiwald

Based on an idea and original concept by Ludwig Könemann
General Adviser: André Dominé

Original Title: *Provence. Mini Culinaria*
ISBN of the original German edition: 3-8331-1297-2

© 2005 for this English edition:
Tandem Verlag GmbH
KÖNEMANN is a trademark and an imprint of Tandem Verlag GmbH
Translation: Susan Ghanouni and Elaine Richards in association with First Edition Translations Ltd
Editing: Lin Thomas in association with First Edition Translations Ltd
Typesetting: The Write Idea in association with First Edition Translations Ltd
Project Management: Mine Ali for First Edition Translations Ltd, Cambridge, UK
Project Coordination: Nadja Bremse-Koob

Printed in Germany

ISBN 3-8331-1458-4

10 9 8 7 6 5 4 3 2 1
X IX VIII VII VI V IV III II I

MONTÉLIMAR, LES BARONNIES, AND CHÂTEAUNEUF-DU-PAPE

This is where the real south of France begins: Bit by bit, the vegetation loses its northern character. The beech trees, oaks and hornbeams are all gradually replaced by Aleppo pines, olive trees, and broom.

The sun is hotter, the light more luminous, the rhythm of speech more musical. This is the Drôme region: a landscape of undulating heathland, buffeted by the mistral, and famous for its rosemary and truffles.

Route 7 passes through Montélimar. This used to be the main route to the South of France before the *Autoroute du Soleil* (highway to the sun) replaced it.

The Drôme region is fragrant with the herbs that give its cheeses their distinctive flavor. Dieulefit is home to *picodon*, a goat milk cheese, while grapes ripen on the surrounding slopes of the Tricastin vineyards.

Farther south at the Château de Grignan, the largest Renaissance castle in southern France, you might catch an echo of the dying breaths of Madame de Sévigné – who was one of the most cultured women of Louis XIV's reign. Suze-la-Rousse is almost submerged in the sea of vineyards surrounding the citadel, which today is home to the renowned wine university of the same name.

The outline of the Baronnies Ridge is visible on the horizon, a region of green hills and lush vegetation. The Baronnies – the name conjures up the peace and quiet of ancient, sun-bleached villages and the lively bustle of market days. Nyons, amidst its olives, linden trees, and herbs, celebrates its "Olivades" festival in July at which you can sample olives of every conceivable variety. Buis-les-Baronnies celebrates its own festival of linden trees, lavender, and olive trees the same month.

Continuing your journey toward the south, you will encounter further sources of delight. There are green vineyards which stretch across the whole countryside, only occasionally relieved by a splash of color that marks a village. The road meanders through the vineyards of famous and world-renowned Côtes du Rhône estates – a veritable cornucopia of fruits, vegetables, olives, honey, almonds, and wine. Land of abundance: This is Provence.

Even though not actually typical of the region, sunflowers nevertheless symbolize the light and sun of the south.

ALMOND CULTIVATION

The beneficial properties of almond oil and its derivatives were already recognized in ancient times. Even the Hanging Gardens of Babylon boasted this legendary tree and its fruit is mentioned in the Bible as a valuable food source: rightly so, for almonds are rich in vitamins B and E, calcium, potassium, phosphorus, and magnesium. Almond trees, which originated in Asia Minor, were first introduced into the Mediterranean region by the Arabs in the 5th century, but it was not until the 16th century that Olivier de Serres (1539–1619) – an innovative farmer, who had previously introduced beets and corn to France – began cultivating almond trees in southern France in a serious fashion.

This tree, which thrives in barren, sun-drenched soil and wind, has made itself thoroughly at home in Provence. Olive trees, vinestocks, and lavender are often found growing in its vicinity: singing cicadas inhabit its branches. Van Gogh, too, is known to have been captivated by the silvery shimmer of the almond tree, its unique shade of green, its tender branches, and its fruit, whose hard exterior conceals a soft kernel of proverbial softness and sweetness.

It is virtually impossible nowadays to imagine the hilly Mediterranean hinterland without the almond tree. Its lifespan is rarely longer than 60 years and it bears fruit from its third year onward. It is at its most productive between its 10th and 20th year.

The weather is still cold when the almond buds first begin to open in February. It is the earliest fruit tree to come into blossom and its flowers compete with the primroses. It treats us to quite a spectacular show when the blossoms start to unfurl on its delicate

Summer has arrived and the green almonds in their velvety shells are waiting to be picked.

branches, and spring throws out a final delicate pink challenge to persistent winter. The delicacy of the blossom is at odds with the robust appearance of its knotted twisted trunk. Depending on the species, the blossom can be either red, pink, or white. Only 30 percent continues to develop into fruit, the rest drop from the tree, where they form a *coulure*, a carpet of blossom adorning the ground.

Van Gogh loved fruit trees in blossom. He painted orchards full of peach trees, almond trees and sweet chestnuts.

Seed and fruit, the almond is both at once. It is a hard-shelled fruit which has an edible kernel and is also propagated by that same kernel. Almonds from wild almond trees are bitter and generally unsuitable for eating. The blue acid they contain forms a dangerous compound in contact with water. On the

Green almonds still on the tree, waiting to be harvested.

The almonds are carefully sorted, usually by hand – a very time-consuming job for the growers.

The almonds are then extracted from their shells. This, too, is often done by hand.

The shells are broken upon a hard, mortar-like base.

At this point, the growers are able to judge the quality of the harvest.

The final stage of the harvest, when the almonds are placed in boiling water to remove the skin.

other hand, almonds that have been cultivated are deliciously sweet.

Delicate female qualities have always been ascribed to the almond – hence we find names such as "Sultana," "Princess," "Lady of the Languedoc," "Round Lady," or "Pointed Lady."

The harvesting of "green" almonds gets underway at the beginning of summer when the young almonds are still encased in their velvety, delicate green shells. They are knocked from the tree either by hand or with the aid of machines. Only strong teeth can bite their way through the somewhat bitter outside to reach the milky succulent fruit. The "dry" harvest is not until the almonds drop from the tree by themselves. The shells are then completely removed and the almonds are either dried in the sun or fan dried, depending on whether a traditional or a rather more modern approach is preferred.

Finally, the almond kernels are dropped into boiling water to skin them. Once this last stage is completed, they are used in the manufacture of famous candies, such as nougat, *calissons* (lozenge-shaped candies made of ground almonds), burnt almonds, sliced almonds, and macaroons. Tossed in honey, sugar, butter, or chocolate, they are guaranteed to tempt anyone with a sweet tooth.

Green almonds have to be knocked from the tree whereas ripe almonds drop to the ground by themselves.

The soft texture of the *calisson*, a specialty of Aix-en-Provence, the pink coating of burnt almonds, the featherlight macaroon – utterly delicious! And on a summer's evening, the almond's slightly salty and smoky flavor is the perfect complement to a summery drink, such as *mauresque*, that mildly bitter-tasting liqueur made from pastis and almond milk syrup which is a classic among classics in Provençal bars and cafés.

Montélimar Nougat

version is certainly very convincing since nougat is a harmonious blend of sugar, honey, and egg white, that is flavored with vanilla and studded with almonds.

Early in the morning, the *nougatiers* heat up the copper cauldrons. Into these they pour the lavender honey: it takes about 55 pounds (25 kg) of honey to make 220 pounds (100 kg) of nougat. The honey is beaten by a mixer for two to three hours in a bain-marie heated to over 212 °F/100 °C until the water content is reduced. The next step is to add 165 pounds (75 kg) of sugar and glucose syrup, 1 ¼ pounds (800 g) egg white – the equivalent of 300 eggs – confectioner's sugar and 12 cups (3 liters) of water. The temperature to which the syrup is heated determines how soft or hard the nougat will be.

Finally, a further 11 pounds (5 kg) of honey, some natural vanilla, and two most important ingredients are added: 62 pounds (28 kg) of almonds that have been peeled, and no more and no less than 4 ½ pounds (2 kg) of uncooked, untoasted Sicilian pistachio nuts. The lavender honey, and top quality almonds and pistachios are what have earned this sweet its Appellation

The streets of Montélimar are just one big shop window displaying the town's specialty, nougat. It is virtually impossible to leave the place without buying a little bag of the stuff since this delectable delicacy is simply everywhere. In the vicinity of the factories, the very air is full of its scent.

Nougat was introduced into Provence during the Middle Ages, but it was not until the 16th century that Montélimar became the center of nougat production. Experts claim that the name derives from the Latin *nux gatum* – (nut cake) – but tradition has it that it originates from the expression *tu nous gâtes* – (you spoil us). Whichever theory you prefer, the second d'Origine Contrôlée (AOC) label and made Montélimar nougat so highly sought-after.

Black nougat and praline varieties do not contain any egg white since this would give them too light a color. They are made instead with blossom honey, which turns dark when heated to very high temperatures, and toasted unskinned almonds, which have a stronger flavor than skinned ones.

After being made in the morning, the nougat mixture is poured into rectangular pans lined with rice paper and left to dry. By afternoon, it is ready to be cut up (usually by machine) and wrapped. It is ready for despatch to the candy stores the same day.

White or black, pink or blue, with hazelnuts (filberts) or candied fruits, nougat is delicious at any time and goes wonderfully well with coffee, for example.

The process of modernization which characterized the 1980s also filtered through to the nougat manufacturing industry. The copper pans have been largely replaced by time-saving pressure cookers: some of these so-called "flash cooking processes" take no more than a mere 15 minutes.

Nevertheless, Montélimar is still home to small workshops such as the Chaudron d'Or, for example, where nougat is made in the traditional way by hand.

Sugar and honey, glucose syrup, egg white, confectioner's sugar, and water,

thoroughly blended together, form the basic ingredients of nougat.

Just a little more honey, then it is time to add the almonds to the mixture.

The nougat gradually acquires the right consistency, color, taste, and shape.

Perfect nougat, in which the almonds or almond bits are visible, is a delectable

type of candy that is popular in countries all over the world.

La "Table de Nicole" in Valaurie

The D 541 from Montélimar to Valréas has another gastronomic treat in store for the traveler. A short detour off the main road into the countryside beyond will lead you to the gates of a country inn, "La Table de Nicole." The present owners have converted this former silkworm farm, with its profusion of wild roses and its shady terrace, into a charming hotel restaurant.

Guests quickly feel right at home here as Nicole's enthusiasm for good food and natural products is something she has inherited from her family's background in farming: her recipe for wild plum jam was handed down to her by her grandmother. You will not find anything exotic or artificial in her kitchen; her dishes consist entirely of regional products and are based on traditional recipes. "Just like home," she is fond of saying, and you only need to taste her rabbit stuffed with *tapenade,* or sample her desserts or mature cheeses to realize this is indeed so. It is the seasons that dictate which fresh products go into the pot. The approach of winter heralds the start of the truffle season. Nicole's preference is to serve them fresh with just a little olive oil, with salt, or as a *brouillade*. However, truffles do appear on the restaurant menu all year round, wrapped in puff pastry and served on a bed of liver pâté.

The fully ripened cheeses are chosen carefully by Nicole: robust homemade cheese, Saint-Marcellin and a choice of goat cheeses. Nicole's crowning glory for every meal is her selection of desserts: warm apple pie, chocolate

As delightful as her cuisine – Nicole and her selection of hors d'oeuvres.

soufflé, vacherin – a dessert consisting of meringue, ice cream and whipped cream – or nougat with fresh fruit.

Mostly wines from the Rhône valley are to be found on the wine list. As a foretaste of the culinary delights to follow, Nicole recommends a rosé rounded off with a hint of orange as an aperitif.

The restaurant is on the terrace, surrounded by flowers, herbs, the scent of lavender, and the whirring sound of cicadas.

La brouillade selon Nicole
Nicole's scrambled eggs with truffles

Serves 2

6 eggs
1 truffle, weighing at least 1 oz/30 g
A pinch of salt
Pepper
4 tsp/20 g butter
Olive oil
Coarse-grain sea salt

Carefully brush the truffle clean and place it with the eggs, still in their shells, in a firmly sealed preserving jar. Refrigerate for two days before use. Whisk the eggs. Grate the outer skin of the truffle and add this to the eggs. Finely dice half of the truffle and carefully cut the other half into wafer-thin slices. Season with a little salt and pepper.

Melt the butter in a saucepan over a low heat. Add the eggs and stir the mixture continuously using a wooden spoon until light and creamy. Make sure the mixture does not stick to the saucepan and burn. Place the sliced and diced truffle on a plate, sprinkle with oil and a little salt. Pour over the scrambled eggs and serve immediately.

Selection of Provençal hors d'oeuvres

Provençal broiled peppers, melon, pistou soup, tellins (tiny clams), fresh anchovies, marinated in various kinds of vinegar, herbs, and the best olive oils of the region – the gourmet here can run the gamut of this mosaic of colors and tastes, and range from traditional Lyonnaise cuisine to the aromatic dishes of the Drôme. Herring fillets are an essential accompaniment to potato salad and chicken or turkey liver paté is always served with onion cream. The onions used to make the cream are lightly sautéed and soften the strong taste of the pâté. A bundle of small, green asparagus is served with a vinaigrette dressing. *La cervelle de canut* – curds with onions – is a specialty from Lyon, while *caillettes* –small herb vol-au-vents – are a typical Provençal dish.

La cervelle de canut à la drômoise
Drôme-style curds with onions

Serves 3

1 lb/500 g fresh,
full cream goat cheese

Salt, freshly milled pepper

Small bunch of chives

1 clove of garlic

Walnut oil

Allow the cheese to drain, then beat with a whisk until it reaches a smooth consistency. Season with salt and pepper. Chop the herbs and garlic and add these to the cheese mixture, together with a dash of walnut oil. Serve with potatoes boiled in their skins.

Parfait de foies de poulet (ou canard)
Chicken (or duck) liver pâté

Serves 3

½ lb/250 g chicken or duck liver

3 cloves of garlic

½ cup/113 g butter

Salt and pepper

1 tsp Armagnac

Cook the liver for eight to ten minutes in boiling water. Allow to cool. In the meantime, peel and crush the garlic. Divide the butter into small pieces. Place the liver, butter, and garlic in a food processor and blend until very smooth. Add the Armagnac and season with the salt and pepper. Serve on toasted rustic bread as an appetizer or with lentil salad as a starter.

19

RICHERENCHES, "CAPITAL OF THE BLACK GOLD"

Richerences, a town steeped in history and situated a few kilometers southwest of Valréas off the D 941 to Nyons, is well worth a detour. It boasts the medieval ruins of the former headquarters of the Knights Templar, the most well-preserved in all Provence. Nowadays, Richerenches is also known as the truffle capital: At the beginning of the century, the region's vineyards were almost completely wiped out by an outbreak of phylloxera. The vines were replaced with oak trees, which provide the perfect growing environment for truffles. Consequently, Richerenches now finds itself at the center of a major truffle-growing area.

If you have not smelt a fresh truffle, you can have no idea how enticing its unusual aroma is.

The truffle market

Each Saturday from November 15 to March 15, the village is gripped by a strange kind of fever: It is market day, but this is no ordinary Provençal market. The visitor will not find any goods on display here, nor will he encounter bustling throngs of people. Instead, the whole business is conducted in a very low-key manner with the aid of a set of hand scales and a pencil, but with every sense fully primed. This market is a meeting place for the initiated who communicate using a minimum of words or gestures.

The Richerenches truffle market is the largest in France, handling 15 to 25 percent of the country's truffle production. Truffle producers and dealers from neighboring *départements*, and sometimes even from Périgord, assemble here for a kind of secret ceremony:

There is a glitter of desire in the eyes and something mystical in the gestures of those buying and selling the "black gold."

Truffle producers bring their valuable crop to market in a plastic bag or shoulder bag. Dealers and restaurateurs stand by the open trunks of their cars eagerly awaiting their arrival. The truffles are felt, scratched, sniffed, weighed, and paid for. A short discussion, a not particularly pleasant aroma as the truffles are extracted from the sack, and a little earth scratched under the fingernail are all that is needed to assess the quality. These deals represent many thousands of Euros, the exact amount varying, depending on the year, but reflecting the cost of around 1,300 pounds (600 kg) of *rabasses*. Cash and truffles

Black and white marbled coloring characteristic of the *rabasse* truffle.

Easy to dig up with the aid of a strong twig or a screwdriver.

The truffles are cleaned of their earth and then sold at market. They are

quickly weighed on old-fashioned scales before changing hands.

Not only pigs but dogs too are adept at helping the truffle hunter in his search. The dog stops in his tracks: He has picked up the scent of a truffle which he knows will earn him a reward.

Mini guide to truffles

Tuber melanosporum or *magnatum, aestivum, unicatum* – these are the scientific names for the truffle, this dirty-looking fungus, the taste of which is superior to that of any other wild mushroom. There are approximately 30 types of truffle, including the:

• Périgord truffle (*Tuber melanosporum*) – otherwise known as *rabasse* in Provence; it is black on the outside, has black and white marbling on the inside and an intensive aroma;

• white Piedmont truffles (*Tuber magnatum*), which, to the chagrin of neighboring countries, are only found in Italy and are extremely aromatic;

• the heavy, black summer truffle (*Tuber aestivum*), common in Provence, but relatively uninteresting as far as taste is concerned, and lastly

• the Burgundy truffle (*Tuber unicatum*) which is extremely delicate despite its weak aroma.

The Périgord truffle is not, as its name suggests, only found in the southeast or southwest of France, but in Spain and Italy as well. In Provence, it grows around the base of the holm oak and, less frequently, near hazelnut bushes, Aleppo pines, linden trees, and rockrose shrubs.

The Périgord truffle prefers a sandy soil, but also does well in the stony ground in the area around Mont Ventoux. The rocky soils of this Provençal giant provide nourishment for small, delicate truffles (care must be taken when digging them up!) which have a strong aroma and unforgettable flavor.

To smell is to enjoy! A very simple gesture, but enough to make your mouth water.

for truffles. Collecting truffles is hard work, demanding patience and a keen eye. More than this, it is a science, an encounter with one of the closely-guarded secrets of nature with the promise of an almost divine harvest. This exquisite and wild mushroom is, after all, well hidden in the earth and not very easy to find. Animals can provide invaluable assistance when searching for truffles.

The crown of laurels must go to the pig as the oldest truffle hunter of all. It is still used for this purpose in the Haut-Var district and in the Alps of Haute-Provence. It pokes around in the earth with its snout, exposing the truffles. Occasionally, however, it gobbles up the truffles it unearths with the result that its position as truffle hunter par excellence is gradually being usurped by the dog, which does not have quite such a fondness for truffles and is easier to control.

No one breed of dog is better suited to truffle hunting than another. Dachshunds are used sometimes because their short legs place them so near to the ground that they can more easily sniff out the truffles. Whatever the breed, dogs need careful training before they are able to be effective and fill their owners' baskets.

change hands discreetly. There is, however, nothing illegal about it as the producers are paid flat rates. These are not laid down by the government but instead are determined by supply and demand.

Sometimes, the sale is effected companionably in a café. The transaction is carried out in hushed tones and rounded off with an amicable drink, accompanied by a *brouillade*, lightly scrambled eggs with truffles, or even more simply, truffles with salt.

The market is an experience in itself and perpetuates this ancient trade as a local tradition.

The search for "black gold"

Truffle devotees are transported into a state of near-euphoria once they embark on a hunt

There is one other way to find truffles: Certain species of flies lay their eggs where truffles have reached an optimum degree of maturity. Digging around in such places will uncover them. They should be dug out very carefully as they are very delicate and difficult to spot covered in soil. Take heed, however, since not every swarm of flies marks a truffle trove.

Beware of impostors

Buying truffles is something best left to the experts. There is a great temptation for charlatans to make big profits from inferior products.

Some dealers have been to known to color the truffles to improve their appearance or pass summer truffles off as black truffles. If you are inexperienced in the art of buying truffles, you should stick with proven quality: Apt, Carpentras, Richerenches, Uzès, and Valréas are all, without exception, famous truffle markets subject to strict control.

The simple history of a complex fungus

Preserving

Truffes de première ébullitio on the label means that the truffles have already been boiled once (two to three hours at 230 °F/112 °C) which will have seriously impaired their quality. Often, the juice is collected and sold separately – this is invariably so if they are boiled a second time. If they have been cooked twice, the truffles are seldom eaten as they are but used, instead, to enhance sausage or poularde in this rose, they end up being boiled yet again which inevitably gives rise to the question as to whether this highly prized so-called black gold is, in fact, anything more than costume jewellery.

Essence of truffle

There are, to be sure, good truffle oils and concentrates available on the market which really do simulate the unique aroma of truffles and are perfect for flavoring various dishes. The only and not inconsiderable drawback of this is that you miss the pleasure of actually experiencing this subterranean diva's unique taste and crumbly, compact texture.

Beware of artificial aromas: only the words *arômes naturels de truffe* (natural truffle aroma) on the label guarantee that the product derives from genuine truffle extract.

How to store truffles

Bought fresh from a truffle producer, they will keep for up to ten days in the refrigerator or six months in the freezer. Prior to use, they should be rinsed off, brushed clean, and patted dry. Wrapped in aluminum foil and preserved in an airtight container, they can then be used straight from the freezer.

Truffle oil is another product which is easy to make yourself. Season a few deciliters (say, 1 pint) of oil with the outer casing of the truffles, filter the liquid after two weeks before bacteria have time to develop and make the oil unpalatable. The aromatized oil should be used without delay and is delicious in a dressing to go with mesclun salad.

"LA BEAUGRAVIÈRE"

Yes, you heard right, truffle ice cream! No joking! There really is such a dessert. At Guy Jullien's restaurant in Mondragon, the Périgord truffle is truly the undisputed queen of a culinary art, which revolves almost entirely around the subtle flavor of this fungus.

"La Beaugravière" on Route 7 treats truffle enthusiasts to an unforgettable gourmet experience. This restaurant on the outskirts of the village has been run for the past 20 years by Guy Jullien. His one overriding

desire has always been to introduce his guests to the regional products of the area, thereby inspiring in them an enthusiasm to match his own. With all the passion of a true truffle fanatic, this master chef and native son of Provence offers a variety of dishes with three different menus in tribute to the "black gold." As a very well-known truffle specialist, Guy

"La Beaugravière" truffles are served fresh and are accompanied by an excellent wine or they can be served as a dessert in the form of truffle ice cream.

Jullien passionately supports an Appellation d'Origine Contrôlée being introduced for the Tricastin truffle. He is equally vehement in condemning the modern commercialism which is damaging the very qualities that make the *Tuber melanosporum* so special: This includes canned and artificially colored truffles, which have become all too common. He does not even like freezing truffles, but this is the only way he can offer a few of his world-famous specialties throughout the summer.

He is an artist of his profession with a fine instinct for creating dishes which are pleasing to the eye, paying attention to the tiniest detail of color harmony. He contrasts the truffle in its mantle of black with golden pastry, with yellow "Ratte" potatoes – a firm, waxy-fleshed potato – choice olive oil, or white rice.

The attraction of the "La Beaugravière" restaurant for the truffle enthusiast lies in the very simplicity of its cuisine: pumpkin soup, turnip purée, scallops, or lightly scrambled eggs merely serve to enhance the delicate flavor of the truffles.

A daring truffle-based ice cream provides the finishing touch to any meal taken at the restaurant. In Guy Jullien's opinion, "this combination of egg and milk forms the perfect complement to the black gold."

Guy Jullien loves his truffles because they are so simple to prepare, yet so complex in their subtleties of taste.

Truffes fraîches en salade sur lit de pommes de terre Charlotte tiède
Fresh truffle salad on a bed of warm "Charlotte" potatoes

8 medium waxy-fleshed potatoes
1 clove of garlic
4 oz/120 g good truffles
Coarse-grained sea salt
Freshly milled pepper
"Vin vieux" wine vinegar
Truffle oil

Peel the potatoes and cut into slices, measuring about 1 inch (2.5 cm) across and 3 inches (8 cm) lengthwise. Sprinkle with salt and cook. Keep warm.

Rub a plate with the two halves of the garlic clove. Slice the truffles and arrange them on the plate. Sprinkle with salt, pepper, a few drops of vinegar, and a little truffle oil. Cover with aluminum foil and set aside.

Arrange the potato slices in a circle on warmed plates, sprinkle with salt, pepper, and truffle vinaigrette. Cover with the truffle slices and serve warm.

Nyons, Home of the Olive

Le Nyonsais lies between the Drôme and Vaucluse. The winding Eygues river meanders its way across the Tricastin plain before flowing beneath the Roman bridge of Nyons with its charming ogee arches. Nyons is situated at the foot of the mountains, protected from the mistral and its icy blasts.

They say that the sun shines more here than on the Côte d'Azur. Considering how many kinds of exotic plants flourish here this must indeed be the case. What is more, the town has become a center for cultivating the sun-loving olive tree. Oil mills, an olive oil cooperative, an olive tree museum and a *scourtinerie* – a factory for sisal-type matting – these are, and have for a long time been, major features of the town.

The olives grown between the Baronnies and Nyonsais are the only ones to boast an Appellation d'Origine Contrôlée quality control label. These olives are called *tanche* and it is only the black ones that are eaten.

Tree of the gods and legends

It was the Greeks 2,500 years ago who first introduced the olive tree, *Olea europea* being its Latin name, to the

A small country house hidden in an olive grove – a typical sight in the Provençal countryside. An ideal spot to read a book in peace and quiet or enjoy a picnic with friends.

island of Corsica, Italy, Sicily, Sardinia, and Gaul. It retained its importance in Provence well into the 19th century: Its wood was used in many different ways, the fruit consumed or turned into oil. It was a perfect commodity to trade with other countries.

The olive tree is simultaneously the symbol of immortality, peace, wisdom, light, and of purity. According to legend, it was created as a result of a disagreement between Athena and Poseidon. The goddess Athena is said to have planted the first olive tree near the source of Athens, thus taking possession of the city, which Poseidon was also claiming for himself. Many myths and legends depict victors with crowns of olive leaves on their heads. The bible tells of a dove bringing Noah an olive branch as a symbol of the flood being over. Even today, people still associate the olive tree with various virtues – reason enough in itself to continue to nurture and cultivate it.

It took a great deal of effort on the part of the farmers to clear the dry ground of scrub, terrace it, and dig it over. Years of hard work, patience, and persistence have gone into planting the olive groves. A long wait was involved until the

Olive trees growing in the land of sunshine: warmth and light is what the "eternal tree" needs to nourish its fruit.

olives could finally be harvested since it takes years before an olive tree repays all the efforts that go into its cultivation.

It bears only a small amount of fruit as a young tree, its growth is slow and, depending on variety, can grow to between 10 and 50 feet (3.15 m) in height. It reaches its maximum growth after 35 years. Considering that an olive tree can reach an age of several hundred or even a thousand years, this is still very young. In February 1956 winter returned unexpectedly and temperatures dropped to minus 4 °F (-20 °C). The sap rose early in the olive trees of Provence that year. The cold snap, which held the whole of France in its grip, caused the wood to split.

One million trees died, entire olive groves disappeared, Provence lost its most valuable commodity. The olive tree, however, has for thousands of years been too firmly rooted in the Mediterranean region, is too closely associated with the barren and sun-baked soil to give up the ghost that easily.

Olive trees awake from their winter rest in March and come into bloom from May onward. From then on, their fruits grow, greedy for light and the warmth of the sun. The olive's journey from the tree to the palate of the gourmet is an extremely labor-

The olive groves are draped with nets when the olives begin to ripen. The decision has to be made as to whether to wait until they drop from the tree of their own volition, whether to pick them by hand, or whether to knock them off with a pole. The important thing is not to damage the fruit so that it remains in perfect condition.

The fruit of the olive branch – symbol of peace and wisdom – does not taste pleasant until it has been treated. After being sorted and washed, the olives are ground by granite mill wheels. The fruit is crushed and then ground into a paste, the aroma of which permeates the whole mill.

The paste is pressed and the resulting liquid separated by centrifugal force into oil and juice. The olives being reserved for the table are kept in giant vats of brine for several months. This helps counteract their somewhat bitter taste. Aromatic herbs are also added to the olives to improve their flavor.

intensive one – the fruit in its fresh state has a bitter taste. The olive harvest begins in September and continues until February, depending on whether the fruit is to be picked while green or when it is black. A green olive remains firmly attached to the branch, whereas a black one drops off easily. To reach an optimum degree of ripeness, olives have to be left long enough to experience the first frosts of winter.

This oil press, part of it made from oak-tree trunk, is from Gallo-Roman times. It can be admired by visitors at Les Bouillons.

The methods used by the olive-grower to harvest the fruit have remained unchanged since time immemorial. Either he uses a ladder to pick the fruit by hand or uses a rake, collecting the olives in a canvas bag or wicker basket. This way he can select the choicest specimens in order to save them for the table. Alternatively, he can knock the branches with a hazel pole so that the ripe fruit drops onto sheets spread out on the ground. Next, the olives are sorted: the smallest – with the exception of the Niçoise, which are a small variety – and any imperfect olives are sent to the mill where they are weighed and stored for not more than two to three days at 68–77 °F (20–25 °C). They are then rinsed clean in cold water and finally crushed under enormous granite wheels. The mill stones grind the fruit into a thick paste.

The pulp is then layered on disks of sisal or hemp matting (synthetic material is more commonly used nowadays). Eighty of these are stacked on top of one another and then hydraulically pressed. The matting acts as a sieve, separating the flesh and stones of the olives from the liquid. The hydraulic pressure forces out the juice which consists of olive water and 30 to 45 percent oil. As soon as it leaves the press, this mixture is separated by centrifuge. The oil, extracted and filtered by this chemical-free procedure, is given the label: *Huile d'Olive Vierge, produit naturel, 1ère Pression à froid* – Virgin olive oil, natural product, first cold press. The larger, better quality olives undergo a special procedure to extract their bitter flavor and they have to be handled very carefully in order to avoid even the tiniest amount of damage. Once they have been cleaned and the leaves removed, they are left in brine to mature for five months. Olives quickly absorb the flavor of herbs and are particularly enhanced by bay leaves, fennel, savory, thyme, or basil. Sometimes, they are stuffed with a sardine fillet, red pepper, or an almond, depending on whether a strong or mild flavor is required.

THE OLIVE OILS OF PROVENCE

Olive oil forms the basis of Mediterranean cuisine: *tapenade, aïoli,* or *pistou,* broiled fish and bell peppers, marinades, or simply tomato salad with mozzarella – all these dishes would be inconceivable without olive oil. No two oils produced in the numerous olive mills are ever the same. With a fruity aroma of dried fruits or plants, the intensity of flavor varies, depending on composition and the region in which they were grown.

The black *tanche,* for example, smells of green apples and freshly cut hay, the *verdale* is reminiscent of artichokes, and olives from Baux have a distinctive aniseed bouquet. Olive oil made from green olives is more bitter and keeps longer than oil from black olives.

And since olives, just like grapes, experience good and bad years, it is a good idea to establish a small "oil cellar" in the home (olive oil is sensitive to light): mild olive oil for vegetables and broiled dishes, a light one for green salads, and a more strongly flavored oil for fish, meat, and pasta.

There are several mills and a museum in the vicinity of Nyons which are open to visitors:
• Moulin Dozol Autrand
Olive oil from the Dozol Autrand mill has a slightly fruity flavor. The best way to taste it is on a slice of rustic bread, rubbed with fresh garlic: it is delicately flavored with a suggestion of hay.
• Vieux Moulin
Experience the lovingly preserved, traditional method of olive oil production in a 16th-century mill.

"Taste it, it's like fruit juice" – is the simple slogan Maître Farnoux uses to advertise his olive oil.
• Musée d l'olivier
The best place to learn more about the history of olive oil, a combination of nostalgia and poetry.

Tapenade, a paste made from olives, garlic, and anchovies, is sold at olive stalls in markets throughout Provence. This purée, otherwise known as "Marseille caviar," is a vital ingredient for flavoring delicate salads. With a dash of added vinegar, it can be used as the basis for a dressing or mixed with fresh pasta. Spread on toast, it makes a popular snack to serve with an aperitif and is a perfect accompaniment to poultry or rabbit.

Tapenade
Olive paste

Serves 3

1 lb/500 g green or black olives
2 anchovy fillets
2 tbsp capers
1 clove of garlic
2 basil leaves,
according to taste

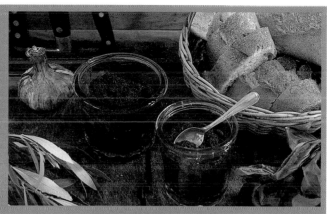

Stone and finely chop the olives. Pound the fillets of anchovy into a paste with a pestle and mortar. Mix in the capers, garlic, and finely chopped basil. Mix well and slowly dribble in a trickle of olive oil until the mixture reaches a spreadable consistency. Season with salt and pepper to taste. *Tapenade* can be stored for several days in the fridge if covered with a thin layer of olive oil.
Serve on slices of toast.

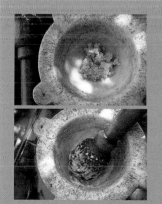

Aïoli
This amazing mixture of olive oil and garlic is said to have been invented by the Romans, although the Catalans likewise claim the credit for it. No matter who is responsible for its existence, *aïoli* is an integral part of any Provençal family celebration or summer party. It is an excellent accompaniment to dried cod, fried fish, lamb, braised vegetables, or potatoes cooked in their skins. Other vegetables, such as artichokes, zucchini, cauliflower, carrots, broccoli, raw or blanched, are delicious when they are served with this piquant and extremely tasty garlic mayonnaise.

Aïoli
1 whole garlic bulb
1–1¼ cups/ 250–300 ml olive oil
Salt
Lemon

Separate and peel the individual garlic cloves, cut into small pieces then pound to a paste with a pestle and mortar or purée in a blender.
Add the oil by drop, stirring continuously, then increase the oil to a thin stream as the mixture begins to set. Season with salt and, if desired, a few drops of lemon juice.

"Rendezvous over an aperitif"

The first hint of sunshine is the signal for umbrellas to appear on the café terraces. As soon as the church bells toll the midday hour, it is time to settle down for a chat. It is aperitif hour in summertime Provence. Beneath shady plane trees around village squares and in café bars all over the region, the ritual gets underway to the accompaniment of clinking ice cubes and sounds of laughter. Sometimes, a mere gesture, a brief glance on the part of a regular, is all that is needed for a "pastis," that little yellow drink, to be brought straight over. A small bowl of olives helps the appetite along. Too soon, the church bell strikes half past noon, signaling the end of the short midday break.

In the evening, people get together again, perhaps to play a game of boules. Life slows down and people take time out. The cafés, terraces, and squares fill up again.

The people in rural areas get together with their neighbors for an aperitif outdoors, either in the garden amid the wisteria blossoms, in a summerhouse, outside their houses, or even along a tree-lined road: a stone seat, a hastily erected table, and a little bit of room to play a game of boules are all that is needed.

Some Provençales like to drink what is almost

A few olives, toasted bread dribbled with a little olive oil or rubbed with fresh garlic, a "pastis" or a "Ricard" – these are the essential ingredients for a pleasant evening.

an obligatory glass of "51" (Pastis 51) or Ricard. Others favor the Moorish tradition and take a glass of *casa* (Casanis) made from almond milk syrup. These are always accompanied with a carafe of cold water, tinkling with ice cubes. Some prefer a homemade brandy, made to a secret recipe with fruits and herbs.

Somewhat lighter than pastis are the golden Muscat and sweet amber wines. Those who prefer a stronger flavor will choose a well-chilled rosé wine or a Picon beer.

The idea of an aperitif without olives, whether they be mild or strong, to enhance the respective drink is simply inconceivable. However, radishes, cherry tomatoes, cauliflower florets fresh from the garden and simply sprinkled with a little salt also make an excellent accompaniment. Equally delicious is the sliced sausage with olives, rosemary, or with goat cheese. A slice of melon with raw ham is an ideal snack for a hot day in high summer. As the day draws to a close and twilight begins to fall, the olive is all that remains of an hour or so filled with such pleasant conviviality.

A glass of wine cements friendship: The people of Provence like to take time out for a chat, a bit of a laugh and generally enjoy life. A small dish of olives is an essential part of this.

Les Baronnies

As you approach the Baronnies on the D64 from Nyons , the vegetation begins to change: Here the lime, or linden tree, with its distinctive perfume and healing properties, rules supreme.

Buis-les-Baronnies made its fortune from the silkworm trade. Set amidst fields of lavender and mint, this old town has all the charm typical of the small villages of Provence's Drôme region.

The town's main claim to fame, however, is its annual linden blossom market on the first Wednesday in July, an essential port of call for anyone dealing in this commodity.

When the region's silkworm breeding and dye industry fell into decline back in the 19th century, the linden tree was brought out of the forests where it had grown wild since time immemorial and cultivated in plantations. It was grafted and pruned and is nowadays subject to strict selection procedures. The linden trees of the Baronnies region are of the highest quality and have brought fame to Buis and its environs.

The linden tree: king of the Baronnies

The *Tilia platyphyllos* thrives in the sunny Baronnies with its temperate climate and moderate rainfall since it likes neither excessive heat nor heavy frosts.

It takes six years before a young tree produces its first blossom. After that, it will bloom each

Picking begins in June and has to be done quickly since the blossoms will not wait.

The harvest is often an excuse for a family get-together with lively conversation and laughter.

Sackloads of blossom are taken to the market in Buis-les-Baronnies.

One handful of linden blossom is sufficient to make a soothing tea. The blossom can be boiled in water or simply left to infuse.

year, producing an ever increasing number of blossoms. Around 88 pounds (40 kg) of blossom can be picked from a tree of moderate age in 10 to 20 hours. This represents 22 pounds (10 kg) in dried weight.

The pickers cannot waste any time when the crop is ready in June since the blossoms only last a couple of days. They collect the blossom by hand using ladders. It is hard work and demands considerable care but once it is completed, the workforce gathers beneath the trees for a lively celebration.

The blossoms must be left to dry for a week after being picked – stored away from the light on the barn floor or on a screen. The delicate fragrance and almost eggshell fragility of the *Tilia de Baronnies* is a world removed from the crushed, rather bland-tasting lime or linden blossom which can be bought in tea bags.

Once it has been harvested and dried, pharmacists and practitioners of alternative medicine descend upon the Buis les Baronnies market where the blossom is sold in sacks. Renowned for its high quality, the *Tilia platyphyllos* is very popular and is used to treat a wide range of ailments.

Linden blossom tea and health

This medicinal tea is renowned for its fragrantly mild yet full aroma. It is made from linden trees of the Baronnies region, which contain more essential oils than others of their kind. Apart from its pleasant taste and its soothing, sleep-inducing properties, it also has many other virtues.

A herbal remedy with surprising qualities

• For migraine, digestive problems, attacks of dizziness, and arterial sclerosis: Place 40 blossoms in a saucepan of boiling water, remove from heat, cover and leave to infuse for 15 minutes.

• For rheumatism and onset of arthritis: Place 1 oz/30 g lime, or linden, tree bark (second bark) in a saucepan with two pints (one liter) of water and boil until the liquid has reduced to three-quarters of its original volume. Drink two glasses of this during the course of each day.

• For a relaxing bath: Infuse four handfuls of blossom for 20 minutes in around four pints (two liters) of boiling water. Strain and pour into the bath water which should be heated to approximately 95 °F/35 °C. Take two baths a week, each lasting 20 minutes.

THE LINDEN BLOSSOM MARKET

Buis, the historical linden blossom capital, is *the* meeting place for producers and traders. The calming properties of linden blossoms are of no effect against the "feverish trading" that takes place on the Promenade du Prince de Monaco and on the banks of the Ouvèze. The farmers start arriving at 7 a.m., emptying the contents of their *bourras*. It is from these fully stuffed, gigantic jute sacks that the sweet-scented blossoms, only a few of which are required to let the sun rise from our steaming cups, tumble out. The traders wander from pile to pile, touching, smelling, comparing, and haggling over prices until the gong sounds. The market is officially opened 8 a.m., and the year's basic price is set. There follows renewed checking of the produce and price bargaining before the deals are clinched. The blossoms are weighed in the traditional way on Roman scales, and then change hands. In some years, the approximately 30,000 linden trees of the Drôme valley have produced up to 450 tons of blossoms, contributing 90 percent of France's entire production. However, economic circumstances and competition from abroad have led to a decline in the trading price. Even though the linden blossom harvest is today just a source of additional income, this old tradition is still maintained.

Some traders at the market also offer lavender in addition to linden blossoms.

Séguret

To reach Séguret, follow the D5 in Quvèze valley to the impressive Cliff formations of the Dentelles de Montmirail. Séguret, perched on the hillside, appears to rise out of the cliff. With its narrow streets and arched passageways, this village is one of the prettiest in France.

Winery and restaurant – there can be no better combination. Whether indoors or outside on the lovely terrace, the food and wines on offer at "Domaine de Cabasse" are delicious.

Dining at the foot of the Dentelles de Montmirail

After Séguret, follow the route des vins towards Sablet. A lavender blue easel outside the entrance to the "Domaine de Cabasse" restaurant gives details of the petite carte de midi, the lunch menu. Suggestions for lunch are written in chalk on a big slate: sandwiches or salads, ratatouille, and melon. The wine menu sounds slightly more impressive with a list of "our Domaine de Cabasse wines" as well as "Séguret wines made by fellow vintners" and Roaix-Séguret wines.

The history of the "Domaine de Cabasse" can be traced back to the 14th century and it probably owes its name ("Casa Bassa" in Italian) to the Italian popes who resided in Avignon in the 14th century. The name roughly means "house below the village." The property today comprises of a charming hotel with its own pool, and a beautifully laid out garden. It is a quiet and inviting place. It is also ideal for getting to know the great wines there, and, accompanied by the cellar master, the cellars of "Domaine de Cabasse" can also be visited.

The wines of the "Domaine de Cabasse"

The wine-growing estate is the property of Marie-Antoinette and Alfred Haeni. They moved to France fifteen years ago from Switzerland in the hope of finding themselves a vineyard. Alfred was quick to spot the potential and outstanding quality of the Cabasse vineyards. He had

The board lists a promising menu of Mediterranean dishes, including melon, salads, and goat cheese.

always been interested in living in the country: His family were farmers and he spent 20 years in agricultural research investigating viral diseases. He has now gone back to rural life in Cabasse where he can put the results of many years of research to good use.

Their first grape harvest was in 1990 when they won their first medal. From the beginning, Alfred Haeni worked in close collaboration with Noël Rabot, a wine expert from Sorgues, and Eric Michel, a vintner in Mondragon.

Alfred Haeni is either to be found tending his vegetable garden with the utmost care or looking after his vines

and watching over his developing wines. His day alternates between sun and shade, warmth and cold.

Since the very first vintages, his *Cuvées Casa Bassa* and *Garnacho Séguret* have been widely applauded not just by wine enthusiasts but by wine experts as well. Alfred Haeni likes to cultivate the sort of wine which is good for laying down. By blending his wines from several varieties of grape, he succeeds admirably in producing wines which reflect the rich diversity of the distinctive Côtes du Rhône region. As a wine grower, he applies very strict standards to every stage of cultivation, from the hard pruning the vines receive, to the pressing of the grapes. After every harvest, he personally sorts the fruit grape by grape. "All the grapes pass through my hands," says Alfred Haeni. Up to five percent of the fruit is rejected – no matter how slight the imperfection may be – since this could affect the fermentation acids or the color of the wine. Eventually, around 100 tons of

hand picked and personally checked grapes will go to be pressed.

Alfred Haeni has opted for a traditional method of wine growing. The *Cuvée Garnacho* and *Gigondas* are left to mature in large barrels, while the *Casa Bassa*, made from Grenache and Syrah grapes, goes into smaller *barriques* (barrels). Aware that great caution has to be exercised with new wood, which might adversely affect the flavor of the wine, he chooses the barrels with the utmost care, ordering them only from the very best coopers. Haeni has handed down his philosophy to his son Nicolas, who is now in charge of the vineyard. Together they have created *D'Eux*, a *Cuvée* produced two thirds from Syrah and one third from Grenache. *D'Eux*, the first fruit of their cooperation, matures for 18 months in barrique barrels before being bottled without filtration.

Care and hard work in the vineyards is rewarded by 100,000 bottles of wine per year, 75 percent of which are destined for export, mainly to Switzerland, the USA, Canada, and Germany. These highly prized wines, which are increasingly appearing on the wine lists of France's best restaurants, are worth a detour. *Les Primevères*, a 2004 white wine, is especially fresh with rich aromas reminiscent of spring, the 2004 Rosé de Marie-Antoinette is an ideal wine for summer evenings, while the cellar wines *Cuvée Garnacho* 2001, *Cuvée Casa Bassa* 2001, and *Gigonadas* 2001 accentuate a refined, elegant and lasting presence on the palate.

From the vegetable garden onto the plate

It is not only the "Domaine de Cabasse" wines that delight the visitor: The restaurant is equally famed for its extremely delicious food. The menu changes daily, but whether you choose from the ordinary menu or the more extensive "menu of the day," the emphasis is on vegetable dishes in which herbs always feature prominently.

Marie-Antoinette Haeni draws up the week's menus with the help of Chef Michel Ducellier: The dishes are based on the traditional and unfussy cuisine of southern France. The restaurant's own garden produces eggplants, tomatoes, and zucchini for the table. These are combined with home-made olive oil and herbs. Only homegrown or fresh market produce is used. Zucchini

The vegetable garden at its best. Raw or cooked, in their natural state or enhanced with herbs, the vegetables of Provence bring sunshine to your plate.

flowers are stuffed, beans with tapenade are served as a salad, herbs find their way into ravioli, and tomatoes are steamed with pistou – summer in province is revealed in the innumerable variations of an imaginative, refreshing, and light cuisine. Lovers of meat can enjoy *agneau en trois façons*, a combination of braised leg of lamb, cannelloni stuffed with meat from the shoulder, and broiled lamb chops. Or one can try the delicious saddle of rabbit stuffed with tapenade.

A cool glass of "Domaine de Cabasse" rosé complements a summer salad beautifully.

Michel Ducellier likes to cook with fish. Lotte fried with bacon and served on a mild garlic cream, broiled cod marinated with pistachios, or salmon roll with cucumber and hazelnut oil speak volumes about his culinary passion. A light, fruity red wine goes down especially well with these dishes! To satisfy the smaller appetite, Marie-Antoinette recommends a summer salad, the ingredients of which can change from day to day according to their availability: home-grown cherry tomatoes, fresh goat cheese and rocket; or you can have an open sandwich consisting of a crisply toasted slice of rustic bread topped with light, easily digestible fresh cheese that is exquisitely combined with tender lettuce leaves. The lettuce has naturally been picked from the garden.

When the sun is at its zenith, what could be better than sitting in the shade of these hundred-year-old trees.

Le délice de Cabasse
Cabasse delight

Serves 2

| 2 slices of rustic bread |
| 1 ½ oz/40 g truffles |
| Olive oil |
| Coarse-grain sea salt |

Lightly toast the bread so that it remains soft on the inside and crisp on the outside. Sprinkle with a little olive oil. Cut the truffle into wafer-thin slices using a sharp knife and arrange them on the toast. Pour over a little more olive oil and sprinkle with salt.
Serve with a rosé wine, well chilled between 46 and 50 °F (8–10 °C).

Elisubeth Bourgeois, Marie-Antoinette Haeni's advisor, has shared the following recipe with us from her cookery book La cuisine provençale du Mas Tourteron *(Editions du Chêne). The dish is not only delicious but also very easy to prepare:*

Lasagne de courgettes au cabillaud
Zucchini lasagna with shellfish

Serves 6

| 8 medium-sized zucchini |
| 1 ¼ lbs/600 g shellfish |
| 6 anchovy fillets in oil |
| 1 cup/200 g freshly grated Parmesan cheese |
| 1 clove of garlic |
| 2 cups/½ liter fish stock |
| Salt and pepper |

Béchamel sauce

| ⅛ cup/25 g flour |
| 2 tbsp/30 g butter |
| 1 cup/¼ liter milk mixed with 1 cup/¼ liter fish stock |
| Salt and pepper |

Poach the shellfish in the fish stock for eight minutes. Remove the shellfish, leave to cool, then strain the stock through a fine sieve. Remove the skin and bones from the shellfish and cut into pieces.
Heat the fish stock and milk
Melt the butter in a saucepan, add the flour, and stir with a wooden spoon. As soon as the mixture begins to foam, remove the saucepan from the heat and add the milk and fish stock a little at a time, stirring continuously.
Return to the heat, add the anchovies and season with pepper.
Wash and dry the zucchini and cut lengthwise into thin slices. Rub the inside of a baking dish with garlic and butter and place a layer of sliced zucchini on the bottom. Cover with chopped shellfish, pour over some of the béchamel sauce, then sprinkle with Parmesan. Repeat these layers until all the ingredients are used up, finishing with a layer of zucchini. Sprinkle the whole dish with Parmesan. Bake the lasagna for 15–20 minutes in a pre-heated oven at 430 °F/220 °C.

WINES FROM THE SOUTHERN CÔTES DU RHÔNE

Wine has been grown on the Côtes du Rhône since Roman times. The Côtes du Rhône vineyards today stretch more than 120 miles (200 km) between Vienne and Avignon, where they are blasted by the mistral winds, drenched in sun, and rooted in limestone. The Rhône valley produces outstanding grape vines, some clinging to steep hillsides, others growing on the plains. Underestimated and disregarded for a long time, these wines are now at home in the best restaurants.

The Côtes du Rhône wines with their ancient tradition are France's second main Appellation d'Origine after Bordeaux. They include an extraordinary variety of wines, suitable for any occasion, as an aperitif or with dessert – a moment's pleasure or rapturous delight, depending on the vintage and origin. As you make your way south, there will always be a Côtes du Rhône well worth making a detour for. The grape varieties along the northern Côtes du Rhône, predominantly the varieties of Syrah and Viognier, are grown on small, steep, and sunny terraces. Names that are famous throughout the world appear all along the route: *Côte Rôtie, Condrieu, Château-Grillet, Crozes-Hermitage, Saint-Joseph, Cornas,* and the sparkling *Clairette de Die.*

Gigondas is proud not only of its wines, but also of its beautiful, historic town center.

Another 30 miles or so (50 km) farther south, however, between Montélimar and Avignon, the Côtes du Rhône really begin to dominate the landscape. From the slopes of Tricastin to the Costières de Nîmes, terraced vineyards stretch as far as the eye can see, basking in the sun. Nature suffers at the hands of the strong mistral winds and dry Mediterranean climate. It is hot and the air carries the scent of neighboring Provence, of herbs and the dry *garrigue* region. Strong fragrances fill the air and scent the earth, giving the land a pleasant Mediterranean feel.

The road winds through typical Provençal villages, the very names of which are enough to stir up longing in travelers with a passion for good wines and historical villages: Gigondas, Vacqueyras, Cairanne, Séguret, Sablet, Rasteau, Vinsobres, Visan, and Beaumes-de-Venise, to name but a few, are all jewels of the Côtes du Rhône. Wine tasting goes on everywhere, promising to expand the connoisseur's knowledge of this noble juice. Medieval villages, bleached by the sun and surrounded by vines, whose twisting alleyways and wine cellars could no doubt tell countless stories.

It was in 1937 that the winegrowers in this part of France, where the Alps had deposited their detritus on the clayey soil of the valley, first obtained the Appellation Côtes du Rhône, after agreeing to a strict regulating procedure limiting the yields of the grapes.

The range of southern wines comprises no less than 13 different types of grape. Generally speaking, the red wines are a blend of Grenache Noir, Syrah, Mourvèdre, and Cinsault; Grenache Noir, Camarèse, Cinsault, and Carignan are the grapes that go into the rosé wines and Clairette, Roussanne, Bourboulenc, and Grenache Blanc constitute the white wines. The sublime *Châteauneuf-du-Pape* may, in theory, contain all of the 13 permitted grape varieties but in actual fact consists of only eight, preferably from Grenache. The vineyards on the right-hand side of the Rhône have a much more modest reputation.

Châteauneuf-du-Pape, its very name is full of great promise. After becoming the popes' summer refuge in the 14th century, agriculture has blossomed in the region.

Nevertheless, they can still boast several Appellations of outstanding merit. The red Lirac wines, a perfect accompaniment to main courses of white meat, are often very full-bodied and fruity. The Tavel rosé wine is in a class of its own. This particular wine, an Appellation d'Origine Contrôlée, was apparently a favorite at the courts of the French kings Francis I and Louis XIV.

Gigondas and Vacqueyras

The Romans, who settled here over 2,000 years ago and took a great liking to the place, called it "jucunditas" – meaning joy and pleasure. Thanks to its Roman origins and later efforts by men of the cloth, Gigondas has always been associated with winegrowing. Unfortunately, a phylloxera outbreak in the 19th century devastated the vineyards. Olive trees were planted instead but these also succumbed to hard frosts in the winter of 1956. Fresh attempts at winegrowing got underway in the 1960s and, since 1971, the wine has carried the "Gigondas" label of origin. The vines are only grown in the Gigondas district where, sheltered by the nearby mountains and rooted in the stony clay deposits of the limestone slopes or wide terraces, they manage to withstand the mistral and draw their nourishment from 2,800 hours of sunshine each year.

Gigondas produces an average of 1,056,000 gallons (40,000 hectoliters) of high-quality wine each year. About 40 producers, including Château Raspail, the Domaines des Pesquier, Pallières, Saint-Gayan, and Vignobles Amadieu, own the 2,965 acres (1,200 ha) of vineyards between them. The Gigondas wines are mainly reds made from Grenache Noir, Syrah, and Mourvèdre although some smooth, delightful rosé wines do exist, together with a handful of white wines. After a lengthy fermentation process, the red wines are drawn off into barrels made of old wood where they reach 12.5 percent proof. Their deep ruby red color sparkles in imitation of the sun – the same sun which these grapes have been soaking up all summer. They have a fruity bouquet which, in the case of more mature wines, includes subtle overtones of undergrowth. A typically strong and full-bodied Gigondas is an ideal accompaniment to red meat, game, and cheese, but does not like sharing the table with other wines.

The Gigondas rosé wines have to be drunk young. The reds, on the other hand, take

longer to mature and are ideal for laying down. The following years were good vintages: 1990, 1991, 1994, 1995, 2001 and 2002 to name but a few. The 40 producers of this Appellation store their wines in the "Caveau de Gigondas" in the village square, where the previous two years' wines can be sampled and bought.

The neighboring village of Vacqueyras was a great favorite with the famous

Gigondas – worth visiting for its medieval streets as well as its wines.

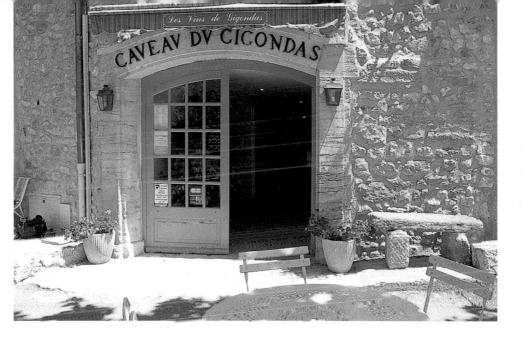

actress Sarah Bernhardt. She loved wandering through the village's narrow, winding streets. Similarly, Frédéric Mistral, a native poet, also succumbed to its charm. Vacqueyras has over 1,700 acres (700 ha) of vineyards that stretch as far as Sarrians at the foot of the Dentelles de Montmirail. In 1990, Vacqueyras wine at last was awarded its own Appellation d'Origine.

The sandy-clayey soil, abundant sunshine, generous rainfall, and traditional grapes of the Vacqueyras region combine to produce elegant, full-bodied, predominantly red wines. The albeit good-quality rosés and white wines do not go very far. The deep reds, delicate golden rosés and pale yellow

The wines produced by the Appellation's 40 vintners can be tasted at any time in the *Caveau de Gigondas*, the cellar in Gigondas' main square.

white wines all exude a distinctive floral bouquet redolent of ripe fruits and spices.

A five- to seven-year-old red Vacqueyras which is served at a temperature of 61 – 64 °F (16 – 18 °C), is the perfect accompaniment to simple, well-cooked food. Its two contemporaries, the Vacqueyras whites and rosés, however, do not improve with age but will grace any occasion if served well-chilled.

The cellar of the Vacqueyras vintners is well worth a visit, as are the La Fourmone, La Garrigue, Le Sang des Cailloux, and Le Château des Roques vineyards…

Cairanne, Séguret, Sablet, and Rasteau

The red wines can be stored for two to six years, but the others are at their best when drunk young.

Séguret, whose houses of unhewn stone rise up out of the hillside, is not only one of Provence's prettiest villages, but it also embodies the region's passionate dedication to winegrowing.

In 1966, it was awarded the "Côtes du Rhône Village" label of quality. This small winegrowing area, encompassing around 250 acres (100 ha) of clayey slopes, produces some very pleasant red wines which form an excellent accompaniment to Provençal cuisine. The rosé wines are an ideal companion to sausage, while the whites are perfect with fish, shellfish and goat cheese.

Sablet has its own small wine growing area, covering about 200 acres (84 ha) Its red wines, with their blackcurrant flavor, are good for laying down whereas the whites with their aroma of apricots do not keep for very long. The rosé wines are, in any case, best drunk when young.

The winegrowing region around Rasteau likewise goes back a long way. It is renowned

Winegrowing began in Cairanne in Roman times and became more widespread in the Middle Ages under the Knights Templar. Little by little, cultivation spread to neighboring slopes and the wine absorbed its distinctively robust, full-bodied character from the red clayey soil.

It is often said that nothing complements a Cairanne wine better than roast beef with pepper sauce and a good cheese. It is a powerful wine, the color of deep red garnets, and brings to mind the dry *garrigue* landscape and ripe fruits. Be they red, rosé, or white, the Cairanne wines go particularly well with spicy dishes and hearty cuisine.

mainly for its sweet red and white wines, the *Vins Doux Naturels*, consisting almost entirely of Grenache grapes These make a delicious accompaniment to sweet Cavaillon melon, raw mountain ham, or a chocolate dessert.

Valréas and Vinsobres

The Côtes du Rhône wines are so numerous that you could meander from one winetasting to another. Valréas, on the boundary between the Vaucluse and Drôme *départements*, produces fiery wines. Most of the local wine producers have banded together to form a cooperative.

The Vinsobres vineyards in the Drôme region stretch for just over four miles (7 km) around a hill. Rocky outcrops protect the dry alluvial terraces and stony slopes from the mistral and other alpine winds. Vinsobres produces mainly big red wines, deep red to purple in color, which are best served at 61–64 °F (16–18 °C) in order to do justice to their intense, fruity flavor They go very well with Mediterranean dishes which are not too heavily spiced. The wines mature well and can easily be laid down for a period of five to ten years. In 1633, the Archbishop of Vaison-la-Romaine, when referring to the wine of Vinsobres, gave the advice: "Drink it in moderation."

Séguret's narrow streets and alleyways have been lovingly restored; a wander around the village is the best way to see its traditional architecture.

"Beaumes-de-Venise" Muscat Wine

Beaumes-de-Venise where France's best Muscat wine, is produced.

A few miles farther on from Gigondas is Beaumes-de-Venise, a small village situated in the foothills of the Dentelles de Montmirail where it is sheltered from the mistral. Like their famous Vaucluse neighbors, the wine producers here also boast very good wines.

Beaumes red wines, sold in their characteristic "Venetian"-style bottles, are often fiery and full-bodied. The sweet rosé and white wines of Beaumes also deserve a mention: Their forefathers are said to have tempted the Papal Court in Avignon into worldly pleasures. The outstanding Muscat wines of Beaumes-de-Venise have to this day lost none of their magic; they still lend a certain *je ne sais quoi* to a dessert. Only small, white Muscat grapes are used to produce this Muscat wine. It should be stored for no more than four years. It takes on an apricot- or peach-like scent, with a suggestion of roses and sometimes a hint of orange. It is intoxicating without being heavy. It is an intense wine, yet surprisingly fruity so that you do not necessarily notice its 15 to 20 percent alcohol content. Its color is unique: shimmering gold, amber, or yellowy orange – just like the sun as it advances through the day.

As an aperitif, it is drunk almost ice cold. It is also a delicious accompaniment to toast served with Roquefort cheese, a *medaillon foie gras* or alongside a starter such as

Perfect harmony: Sliced apple and a glass of Beaumes-de-Venise perfectly complement the delicate flavor of duck liver pâté.

A thoroughly delectable dessert: velvety apricots in a crunchy biscuit shell, served with a glass of Muscat.

chilled melon. Muscat wine goes exceedingly well with desserts, such as ice cream, apricot tart, or fresh fruit.
A chat with friends over *petits fours* beneath a shady linden tree becomes even more agreeable with a delicious *Muscat de Beaumes-de-Venise* to sharpen the senses.

The inhabitants of Beaumes-de-Venise are justifiably proud of the riches produced by their region: the black and green olives, Muscat wines, as well as red, white, and rosé wines.

His Excellency, the Wine of Châteauneuf-du-Pape

They are red, they are white, they are famous. They have a picture of the pope on their label: the papal coat-of-arms of Avignon is a reminder of the fact that in the 14th century, popes used to spend the summer months in Châteauneuf.

The seven popes who successively chose to escape to Châteauneuf for the summer to escape the scorching heat of Avignon were gourmets and bon vivants with a natural interest in wine growing: Popes Clement V and John XXII, in particular, were largely responsible for the cultivation of the vineyards which now stretch across the whole district and even cover land belonging to neighboring villages. Vines stretch in neat rows as far as the eye can see, covering nearly 7,400 acres (3,000 ha) of very stony, clayey, and dry soil. The stones retain the day's heat, releasing it again overnight, thus accelerating the ripening process. This region, which is subject to a unique microclimate and singular geographical

7,400 acres (3,000 ha) of vineyards, visible for miles. Some days, the vines are blasted by the strong mistral winds.

The dry, stony soil stores up the sun's heat during the day so that the grapes continue to ripen during the night.

Châteauneuf-du-Pape goes back a long way: here and there, ruins bear testimony to its history.

conditions, is traditionally allowed to cultivate 13 different varieties of grape, although only eight are actually grown nowadays. Some of the vines have reached a grand old age and are pruned hard so as to be better able to withstand the mistral. The rigid regulations that govern production have influenced French legislation apropos the Appellation d'Origine Contrôlée. The grapes must be sorted on the vine, and five percent of the crop, regardless of the vintage, has to be extracted. The annual

These are some of France's most aristocratic wines: The papal coat of arms indicates a Châteauneuf-du-Pape wine – credit, where credit is due.

production tops 2,640,000 gallons (100,000 hectoliters), 96 percent of this being red wine and a mere four percent being white wine. There are many outstanding châteaux and vineyards: Château de Beaucastel, Rayas, Mont-Redon, des Fines Roches, Clos des Papes, Domaines de Beaurenard, du Vieux Télégraphe, de la Solitude… Referring to this most famous of all Côtes-du-Rhône wines, the 19th - century French writer Alphonse Daudet called it "The wine of kings and the king of wines."

THE VINTNER AND HIS VINEYARD

Châteauneuf-du-Pape is exposed all year round to strong winds and in summer to the scorching hot sun. The stony vineyards stretch for miles and famous wine producers with equally famous labels have settled in their midst.

Prior to the 18th century, Châteauneuf-du-Pape wines tried in vain to establish a name for themselves and were relegated to the role of being used to improve the local Bourgogne wines. This was something of an affront to these delightful wines of the Rhône valley. For a long time, they were regarded merely as the poor relations of French wine as their sole *raison d'être* was simply to enhance the Bordeaux wines.

It took the far-sightedness and persistence of one vintner, Baron Le Roy, to help to restore the vineyards to their appropriate position of strength and quality.

The year 1923 may be seen as the dawn of a new age for Châteauneuf-du-Pape wines. What was important was to draw up a kind of charter in order to retain the local Appellation, thus introducing specific standards of quality control. The charter contained strict regulations governing production and cultivation methods, grape varieties, and alcohol content. It also prescribed that five percent of the harvest be systematically extracted and, at the same time, prohibited the production of rosé wines. It was also decreed that a "Châteauneuf-du-Pape" label could not be granted until the wine had been subject to a wine-tasting test.

In 1929, the Châteauneuf-du-Pape wines were granted their Appellation d'Origine Contrôlée seal. This in itself represented a well-deserved triumph in finally being admitted to the elite band of AOC-wines, but, in fact, it meant even more than this. It brought a sense of satisfaction, and it meant reaping the reward and finally gaining recognition for the ceaseless efforts which had gone

The combination of wind and sun ensure that the grapes enjoy optimum growing conditions.

It's time for the grape harvest: this means the start of several weeks of hard work for the grape pickers.

The grapes are picked pannier by pannier until all the vines are stripped. Sweet and juicy, the grapes hold the

promise of delicious wine. Once the hard work is over, the grape pickers can look forward to a lively celebration.

into the production of what are now highly prized Châteauneuf-du-Pape wines.

Cultivating the vineyards in this region of France is very hard work since three-quarters of the soil is covered with stones and some of the slopes are very difficult to reach. What is more, the grapes require a great many hours of sunshine.

There are 320 winegrowers all producing wine with this label of origin and many of these rely on organic methods. They are aided in this by the cold air of the strong mistral winds which sweep through the Rhône valley, protecting the vines from disease.

Thanks to the strict regulations governing wine cultivation, Châteauneuf-du-Pape has managed to create a special class of wine with a reputation all of its own. An

excellent exhibition showing the traditions of this interesting winegrowing region around Châteauneuf-du-Pape is on display at the Père Anselm museum. Plows, pruning equipment, panniers, a 16th-century press, and a 14th-century barrel illustrate the development of viniculture in this region. The museum is not just devoted to the past, however, but includes a special exhibition room dedicated to the present where the visitor can learn all there is to know about modern winegrowing methods and its attendant problems and achievements.

The basic principles of wine production have withstood the test of time; the photo shows a 16th-century press.

THE ALPILLES
AND THE CAMARGUE

Situated right in the heart of Provence are the Alpilles, the "little Alps," a landscape of jagged limestone cliffs, pockets of trees and bushes surrounded by vineyards, and by fields of vegetables, almond, olive and cypress trees. The writer Rainer Maria Rilke was so impressed by the Alpilles that he wrote: "…mountains, rising at an angle one behind the other, springboards, as it were, from which three last angels took a terrified running jump."

To the south of Arles, the Rhône splits into two, its two arms encircling the tip of Provence, an area known as "Petite Camargue" (Little Camargue). The "Grande Camargue" comprises the eastern Languedoc region and part of the Crau plain. Both parts of the Camargue consist of vast, uncultivated plains, dunes, and swamps with their own unique flora and fauna. It is a wild place which still clings to the traditions of the herdsmen and their cattle and horses, a place of pilgrimage and festivals.

The bulls roam freely over an area of almost 99,000 acres (40,000 ha) of grazing land – 3.7 acres (1.5 ha) of this land represents grazing for just one animal.

Strict breeding programs for the Brave and Camargue breeds of cattle ensure that the meat from these animals, with its AOC seal of quality, is of a very high standard.

The best way to discover and understand the Camargue is to travel through it, absorbing all its sights and sounds. You have to be prepared to stop and watch the flight of a heron, stand and gaze at a flock of pink flamingos, or unhurriedly admire the rice fields, a waving sea of green, or be awed by the dignity of the black bulls and the beauty of the white horses. Listen to an enthusiastic aficionado describing a bullfight and perhaps you, too, will be tempted to attend a *course camarguaise*. The Camargue experience is a feast for the senses and any visit to the area must include a *feria* and a drink in a *bodega*.

The Camargue is a lively region that is characterized by a strong sense of tradition and fighting spirit, and is open to anyone who is ready to appreciate it.

The Camargue boasts some magical scenery: a picture book landscape exuding tranquility.

THE ALPILLES

The wines of Les Baux-de-Provence

The Les Baux-de-Provence Appellation d'Origine Contrôlée covers seven districts of the Alpilles region: Fontvieille, Saint-Etienne du Grès, Saint-Rémy de Provence, Mouriès, Maussane, Le Paradou, and Les Baux. The vineyards are situated over 300 feet (about 100 m) above sea level and cover around 840 acres (340 ha) of dry, stony clay soil at the foot of the Les Baux limestone plateau. There are only 13 winegrowing estates in this region, which is not only blessed with more hours of sunshine than any other in the Bouches-du-Rhône *département* but also benefits from effects of the wind. It produces altogether 370,000 gallons (14,000 hectoliters) of wine, in other words, the equivalent of

The fortress of Les Baux with its 13th-century dungeons is built on top of a rocky precipice and towers over the actual town like part of the cliff itself.

around 1,867,000 bottles. The grapes consist mainly of Syrah, Grenache, and Mourvèdre varieties, as well as some Cabernet-Sauvignon. Depending on the vintage, the wine develops to its full potential after three to ten years. The rosé wines are also enhanced with additions of Cinsault. Unlike the whites, which can be laid down for a good four to five years, the rosés should be enjoyed young. Most of the white Les Baux wines are made almost entirely from white Sauvignon and Rolle varieties of grapes.

The Alpilles region is not only a paradise for wine enthusiasts. Drive along the winding roads, meandering through vineyards, and you will inevitably succumb to the magical Mediterranean quality of light and landscape. Here and there, you will glimpse an isolated *mas*, as Provençal farmhouses are called – Van Gogh immortalized the Mas de la Dame in one of his paintings – or a *bastide*, a fortified country house that is typical of the Provence region.

The best way to find out more about any of the region's wines – often organically produced – is to visit different wine cellars and go to winetastings. One wonderful example of what makes this winegrowing region unique is the Château Romanin with

its wine cellar resembling an underground cathedral. This is the ideal, but no means the only, place in which to get acquainted with the locally produced wine.

The red wine of Château Romanin, which lends itself to medium- or long-term storage, consists mainly of Cabernet and Grenache grapes. It goes well with game birds and red meat. The 1998 vintage promises to be one of the best of the decade. The crisp rosés are also an excellent accompaniment to roast meat, the white wines, whose bouquet is reminiscent of white dog roses, are heavier and more complex and go particularly well with shellfish and marinated fish. All the wines of this Appellation can be sampled throughout the summer at the "Maison des Vins," the house of wine, in Les Baux-de-Provence.

The great vineyard of Château Estoublon is one of the most famous in the Alpilles region.

Beautiful Nature and Naturally Produced Wines

The harsh landscape of the Alpilles produces some wonderful wines.

One way or another, most of the Les Baux wines are organically produced.

As long ago as 1989, the Château Romanin estate decided to switch to organic wine production. In other words, winegrowers must now endeavor to respect and conform to the region's naturally prevailing conditions. The vineyard is seen as a living microcosm which has its own natural balance, subject to the influences of earth and sky. Soil type, water, warmth, as well as air, are regarded as basic elements which must find their own natural balance. This equilibrium will then be reflected in the land and the plant itself.

Organic cultivation, therefore, forbids the use of synthetically manufactured chemicals, depending instead on isopathic methods. These are based on the theory that every organism can produce its own defense mechanisms to enable it to fight disease. In very much the same way that inoculation works for humans, these obviate the need for toxic chemicals without harming the environment. The lunar calendar is also considered an important factor in this organic approach to working the soil, tending the vines, and harvesting the grapes. The Mas de la Dame estate has opted for a form of organic production whereby the vines are treated with natural substances: trace elements and home-produced compost. In this way, the winegrowers of Mas de la Dame have come up with a practical compromise between solely profit-oriented wine production and the somewhat restrictive methods of organic farming in order to maximize the crops of fruit.

The Domaine Terres blanches estate has also gone over to organic wine production. Its vintners use neither chemical fertilizers nor herbicides or pesticides. The only substance used is the so-called "Bordeaux mixture,"

Once work in the vineyards is finished, the terrace at Mas de la Dame is an inviting place to relax.

consisting of sulfur, marine algae, and plant extracts in powder form, which protects the vines from mildew and other diseases. In autumn, the space between the rows of vines is spread with vegetable compost and grain, which eventually gets mixed with vine cuttings. This produces a green manure which, like fertilizers made from animal manure, straw, and foliage, provides the soil with nutrients right into the following summer. This natural compost is also a home for earthworms, ladybugs, and birds which, in turn, help keep down the vineyard pests.

It is quite impressive to see how well nature can look after herself.

The start of the grape harvest at Château Estoublon: juicy grapes hold great promise. The vintner will have been taking repeated readings of the Öchsle degrees and will know from experience whether it is a good, very good, or an outstanding vintage. The full, ripe grapes are picked and... it is a good year.

Oil from the Moulin Jean-Marie Cornille

The Les Baux citadel towers above the plain with its countless olive groves, shimmering in a silvery haze. Fruit from the 377,000 trees produces an outstanding olive oil. There is also a special oil mill close at hand.

Maussane-les-Alpilles is a quiet and unassuming place. Thankfully, this typical Provençal village has so far avoided becoming a mecca for tourists. If you do happen to visit, however, you should take time to enjoy a coffee in the shade of the plane trees in the square behind the village church. The peaches and melons in the fruit and vegetable store across the way look decidedly tempting. The main recommendation for stopping off in Maussane, however, is the Jean-Marie Cornille oil mill located nearby on the main street. This is France's most important oil mill, producing an outstanding olive oil, which was awarded a gold medal in Paris for being the one of the best in France. This velvety smooth oil with its unusual flavor of dried fruits and almonds and slightly dull greenish-gold color is perfect for use in fresh summer salads. In hot dishes, it is

Reading the label

The less acid an oil contains, the better it is. The oleic acid content is classified as being between 0.5 and 4 percent. *Huile d'olive extra vierge* (extra virgin olive oil from the first cold press) has a maximum of 1 percent oleic acid, often as little as 0.5 percent – a true delight.

Huile d'olive vierge or *fine vierge* (fine virgin olive oil from the first cold press) contains up to 2 percent acid – also very good to the taste.

Huile d'olive vierge courante (semi-fine virgin olive oil, usually from a second cold press) contains up to 3.3 percent acid and is ideal for everyday use.

The best Provençal olive oils (other than the Cornille oil) are: the yellow Château Estoublon olive oil with its green shimmer and aroma of herbs, hay, artichokes, and almonds; Moulin des Pénitents olive oil with its fragrance of green apples, straw, and hazelnuts and the fruity Moulin de la Balméenne oil.

Olives can be used in a variety of ways. Superior quality oils promote good health – and inner beauty. They can also be beneficial to one's outward appearance: soaps that contain olive oil are particularly good for the skin. They are attractively packaged for despatch and are sold in high quality stores.

superb for bringing out the flavor of fish, meat, and vegetables. It has such a strong aroma that no more than a few spoonfuls are needed. It is worth trying it on just a piece of bread or goat cheese, allowing its intense yet delicate flavor to unfold on the tongue.

The *salonenques, grossanes, beruguettes, verdales,* and *picholines* olives used for this oil come exclusively from olive groves in the Les Baux valley. After being harvested, they are stored for a while at the mill where they begin to ferment gently. This allows them to develop additional aromas.

The oil is produced by hand in a single cold pressing; 11 pounds (5 kg) of fruit produces about two pints (one liter) of oil. Subsequent filtering is not necessary as the suspended particles settle by themselves. The oil from the Moulin Jean-Marie Cornille can justifiably be labeled a "natural product."

Olive oil from Maussane is decanted into either simple little carafes, or elegant little bottles sporting a deep gold label. Its dark green color and its abundant aroma will evoke a breath of the Provence region when you are back home again.

Olives from the Baux valley are delivered to the Jean-Marie Cornille mill to be pressed into one of the best olive oils in France.

"LA REGALIDO" – A RURAL INN

Approximately six miles (10 km) west of Maussane on the D 78, four windmills still stand like sentinels watching over the charming village of Fontvieille. After a sharp bend in the road, the traveler suddenly comes face to face with an old 18th-century oil mill: all the aromas here epitomize Provence. Virginia creeper climbs up the walls and cascades down from the eaves, seemingly trying to merge with the garden which, depending on the season, is filled with hollyhocks, lavender and oleander.

Situated under the arches is a restaurant that offers original Provençal cuisine. Occupying pride of place on the menu are, according to season, a salad with fresh truffles and olive oil from "Domaine du Grand Sevran," fried scallops and giant prawns with aniseed, wolfish, fried skin side down, on braised cubes of tomato. Traditional dishes can also be found on the menu – *aigo sau*, a fish stew consisting of vegetables and orange peel, aioli, anchoiade, creamed anchovies, or *pieds et paquets*, a specialty made from lamb's feet and sheep's stomach. They bring to life the scents of the countryside. The menu *de la semaine* (of the week), the menu *de saison* (of the season, as well as the menu *tout à l'huile d'olive* (everything with olive oil), are tributes to the produce and flavors of the Mediterranean: Alpilles lamb with garlic and thyme, *brandade de morue*, a purée of braised stockfish with black Fontvielle olives, a fish platter combining various fillets of fish, shellfish, scampi, fresh shrimp, and calamari in fish stock, while red mullet is served on bread with a green *tapenade* and a small fennel salad – to name just a few of the restaurant's specialties. It goes without saying that "La Regalido's" wine list includes a selection of the region's best wines, chosen to complement the dishes on offer.

In the heart of the garden, all you can hear is the sound of birdsong and chirruping crickets.

Tranches de gigot d'agneau en casserole et à l'ail
Braised leg of lamb steaks with garlic

Serves 4

4 thickish slices of leg of lamb,
unboned
(about ½ lb/300 g each)

Thyme leaves
1 ½ tbsp olive oil
12 unpeeled cloves of garlic
Salt and pepper
4 tbsp/60 g butter

Rub the lamb steaks the day before with a tablespoonful of olive oil and a handful of thyme. Store in the fridge in a sealed container or wrapped in plastic wrap until required.

Place the unpeeled cloves of garlic in a small microwaveable bowl with the remaining oil and a little thyme and cover. Heat in the microwave for about five minutes. The garlic should be soft to the touch.

Heat a large skillet over a high heat without adding any oil or water. As soon as the base is really hot, quickly sauté the lamb on both sides. Season with salt and pepper, add the butter and remove from the heat. Toss the steaks so that they are coated with butter on both sides, then add the pre-cooked garlic.

Return the skillet to the hob just before serving and toss the meat in hot butter once more, adding a few drops of water to dissolve the meat juices off the base of the skillet.

Arrange on a serving dish.

"La Regalido's" excellent coffee is always served with little meringues, chocolate, or small cookies but do not let this deter you from trying one of the delicious desserts, such as green apple tartlets, which are glazed with sugar and olive oil.

If you want to take a bit of Provence home with you, just follow your nose. Emma's Boutique on the ground floor is redolent with the seductive fragrances of Provence. This is not just a place for satisfying culinary needs, however. Although the shop does indeed sell gourmet jams, *tapenade*, and Fontvieille olive oil, there are also longer-lasting souvenirs on sale here. Anyone with a nostalgic bent might be unable to resist the embroidered lingerie or romantic children's clothing or decide on a memento to adorn the home. A wide variety of antique treasures, old lamps and fine old porcelain make it almost impossible to leave the store empty-handed.

Arles

Arles with its glorious past that is reflected first and foremost by the Roman amphitheater, is the gateway to the Camargue. The city attracts many visitors with its Ferias and sites of interest.

Arles the city of light

The small city of Arles, nestling on the banks of the Rhône, flooded in light, and shaped by its Gallo-Roman past, was not build for modern traffic. A network of narrow streets and alleyways crisscross the buildings of the old town that almost appear to be supporting each other. The name of the city is derived from "Areleate," meaning "city in swampland." The origins of the city are Roman, and its ancient builders achieved something so remarkable that the city today form part of UNESCO's world heritage. Magnificent residences were later added between the 16th and 18th centuries. But Arles has not rested on the laurels of its shining past.

The Arles of today holds the *Rencontres internationales de la Photographie* every year in July. The city is given up to the tourists during the hot hours of the summer. However, the most pleasant and relaxing hours can be experienced when evening arrives. People readily gather at the Place du Forum, cap-

The historic and romantic city of Arles. The Place du Forum, once a favorite haunt of van Gogh, now plays host every July to photography enthusiasts.

tured by van Gogh's brush and oil paints on a starry night, to eat a small salad or while the evening away over a glass of rosé.

Arles certainly knows how to celebrate a festival. The city comes awake in spring with the Easter Feria. 500,000 visitors, including 60,000 aficionados, pour into the city each year, becoming intoxicated with the bullfights and singing and dancing to the sounds of the penas. At night, the bodegas are full with revelers succumbing to the heady properties of the sangria.

Arles once again becomes quieter later in the year. That is, with the noted exception of the Provencal market held on Saturdays. This

Glossary of terms for the Camargue

AFICIONADO:
bullfight enthusiast

ABRIVADO:
arrival of the bulls in a town, driven by riders on horseback

BODEGA:
small café, typical of Provence

BOUVINE:
herd of free-roaming Camargue cattle

CAPELADE:
parade and salute of the *razeteurs* before every *course camarguaise*

COURSE CAMARGUAISE:
a spirited and playful confrontation that takes place between man and beast in the arena – without a fatal outcome for the bull

ENCIERRO:
letting the bulls loose in the town

The torero, an unmounted bullfighter, takes the salute in the arena

FERIA:
traditional festival with bullfighting

FERRADE:
branding the young bulls with their owner's mark

GANADERIA:
bull breeding

GARDIAN:
traditional cowboy, who looks after the herds of cattle and horses

GARDIANNE:
Bull Meat in red wine. A traditional Camargue dish served at every local feast.

MANADE:
herd of bulls all bearing the same brand

MULETA:
red cape of the torero

PENA:
brass and percussion band

RAZETEURS:
participants in a *course camarguaise*

SANSOUIRE:
salt flats of the Camargue

famous and renowned market lures gourmets to its stalls where olives, fruit and vegetables, spices, rice, and all things characteristic of the Camargue are offered for sale.

A typical *gardian*, riding proudly through the town.

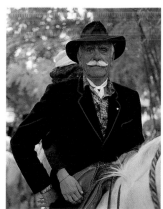

The "Queen of the Carmarque" is an ambassador of Carmarque culture.

"Saucisson d'Arles" and other specialties

A sausage is a sausage. Or is it? Not only do the flour-dusted sausages hanging from hooks in butchers' shops come in all shapes and kinds, ranging from round, long, or coiled, to coarse or finely ground, but, what is more, not all of them come from the pig. They can be made from beef or even donkey or corrida-bull meat, thus widening the choice of sausages to include flavors that are largely unknown beyond the regions of Arles and the Camargue.

There are three specialty sausages: the *saucisson d'Arles*, and sausages made from bull meat and donkey meat – all three traditionally encased in natural beef intestine without any artificial coloring. These sausages form an integral part of the Camargue's culinary traditions.

The *saucisson d'Arles* is the town's most famous culinary

specialty and has been popular since the 17th century. It is said to have been created by Sieur Godard on July 6, 1655 in honor of Louis XIV's visit to Arles. This royal sausage consists mainly of lean ham and beef, as well as bacon fat.

Only regionally produced meat is used. The meat that goes into the sausages is cleaned of sinews, cut into small pieces, ground, marinated in white wine, seasoned, stuffed into the intestines, and hung to dry for four to six weeks in a drying chamber before being sold.

The sausages made from donkey and bull meat are also made from lean meat, with the addition of bacon fat.

The individual seasonings and ingredients remain a carefully guarded secret. Anyone discovering the original recipe is very lucky indeed!

Many delicacies can be found in the small and inviting streets of Arles.

The *saucissons* look very appetizing: a chunk of baguette with thin slices of sausage – delicious!

Ox roast

The sort of bull used for this traditional dish weighs between 330 to 440 pounds (150–200 kg) and provides enough meat for 2,000 people. The animal is skewered on an enormous spit, its flesh rubbed with crushed garlic, doused with salt water, brushed with aromatic olive oil, and roasted throughout the night. The spit is continuously rotated

440 pounds (200 kg) of bull on a spit! The feast can now begin; the band plays traditional music far into the night.

over the embers to ensure that the meat is evenly cooked, layer by layer, without becoming too dry. Beech and oak are preferred as firewood since this gives the meat its distinctive flavor. Eventually, music from George Bizet's opera "Carmen" signals the start of the festivities and the guests at this opulent feast all rise to their feet in appreciation when the roasted hunks of meat, cut into slices, are borne in on great platters that have to be carried by several men.

Olé! The spectators jump to their feet: The torero fixes the bull with a menacing stare.

The bull is decorated with a cockade for the *course camarguaise*. The *raze-teurs* have to try and snatch it off.

Abrivado in Aigues-Mortes: Men on horseback drive the bulls into the arena, pinioned between the horses.

The first *corrida* to be held in France was during the 19th century. It was originally called a *course espagnole*, a term which covered all kinds of bullfighting.

The rules governing this clash between man and beast vary from region to region. In the Spanish version, the bullfight usually ends with the death of the bull, but there are also courses provençales or courses landaises or even just taunting with the cape. The Ligue Française des Droits de l'Animal ('French Animal Rights League) is at great pains to emphasize

the difference between the Spanish *corrida* and the French version, the *courses provençales* and *courses landaises*, in which the bull is generally unharmed.

In the Camargue today, there are approximately 6,000 head of the Brave black longhorn cattle, the stock favored for bullfighting. The female and male animals can weigh between 440 pounds (200 kg) and a mighty 1,430 pounds (650 kg).

During the *ferrade*, the young yearlings, the *anoubles*, are branded. The bullherders pin the animal to the ground with

their tridents and burn the respective breeder's brandmark onto the animal's left rump. The *ferrade* always culminates in a big festival with cattle-running, riding displays, and bullfights.

AIGUES-MORTES, A TOWN STEEPED IN TRADITION

Two kilometers before you reach the town on the D 38, you come to the Carbonnière Tower that dates from the 13th century. It is well worth climbing this unique fortification since it provides an excellent view over the flat and watery landscape to be found around Aigues-Mortes.

St Louis, King Louis IX of France, who believed he had a calling to spread the Gospel, decided one day that Aigues-Mortes would be the springboard from which to launch his Seventh Crusade. The name Aigues-Mortes is derived from the Latin *aquae mortae*, meaning "dead waters."

The French king wanted a port on the Mediterranean and the town's geographical location fitted the bill perfectly. To protect the coast, the port, and the town itself, he had a mighty tower built, the Tour de Constance, one of 15 towers incorporated into the battlements encircling the town.

The fortifications surrounding Aigues-Mortes, today such a peaceful town, are a magnificent example of medieval architecture. You feel as if you have stepped back in time. Once you have passed through one of its gateways, however, you will find yourself in the relaxed atmosphere of a thoroughly modern town, full of cafés and art galleries.

En route to recapture Jerusalem, Louis IX, in 1249, seizes the Egyptian port of Damietta. Historical illustration.

The town is a good center from which to explore the canals and rivers of the Petite Camargue and delight in the flora and fauna of the region, or visit a herd of bulls and ride out with the cowboys. It is also an area where grapes and asparagus are cultivated, where reeds are grown, and salt extracted.

Salt extraction in Aigues-Mortes dates back to early Christian times when Peccius, a Roman engineer, was given the task of organizing the extraction of salt. By the 17th century, there were 17 small salt pans. Salt, an essential dietary requirement for both humans and animals, is nowadays produced by the Compagnie des Salins du Midi, formed in 1856, at the rate of 450,000 tons a year for both domestic use and export.

Salt and the salt workers

Sodium chloride, NaCl, otherwise known as "salt," has not always been regarded as everyday seasoning, but used to be considered a precious commodity.

For several centuries, it represented a valuable trading commodity. Roman legionaries were paid a major part of their wages, their "salarium," in the form of salt.

Among Aigue-Mortes' most impressive sights are the fortified city walls with their imposing towers. They conceal a lively town, full of charm and tradition.

From the 14th to the 18th century, people in France had to pay a salt tax: The "gabelle" was levied on salt producers as well as ordinary citizens who needed salt. This was eventually abolished in France in 1945 but in Germany it continued in force until 1993.

Salt was used to rub into leather before tanning, as well as in enamel and soap manufacture. Today, there are over 14,000 potential uses for salt in private households, industry, and chemical manufacture. You only have to remember some of your grandmother's household tips. salt whitens silk, sets textile dyes, removes stains…

So many beneficial uses does salt have that the sea would have kept it for itself if man had not been so determined to extract it. The main objective of the salt worker, the "farmer of the sea," is to ensure top-quality salt. This requires at least five years' experience. He learns how to utilize this gift from the sea, while at the same time respecting and protecting the natural environment on which his livelihood depends. Defense barriers have

been constructed to prevent waves from damaging the salt pans, and a nature reserve, the Parc Naturel de Camargue, has been created to protect the region's flora and fauna. For many wild animals, the Camargue is the one remaining habitat in France where they can live and roam freely.

Always time for a chat: People enjoy a get-together on the streets of Aigues-Mortes.

The salt pans of Aigues-Mortes stretch across an expanse of roughly 27,000 acres (10,800 ha). In other words, the area forms a rough square, measuring just over 11 miles (18 km) north to south, and eight miles (13 km) east to west. This area could easily accommodate the whole of Paris. This endless expanse of flat, peaceful wilderness is criss-crossed by 220 miles (355 km) of roads and tracks.

Great black-backed gulls, black-headed gulls, coots, and flamingos live all year round in the salt marsh while Belon shelducks are seasonal visitors in the breeding season. There is also a colony of rare terns in the area, nowhere more popular than in the Camargue. *Dunaliella salina*, a tiny species of algae, thrives in the ponds, providing food for small crabs. These are consumed in turn by the flamingos. It is the carotene in these crabs which gives the flamingos' legs and feet their pink color.

A salt pan is technically defined as "a flat, level area of impermeable ground into

Despite their lanky legs, flamingos still manage to move gracefully through the shallow waters of the Camargue.

which sea water is pumped or collects naturally over as wide an area as possible to a depth of about two feet (60 cm)." The "salt gardens" of the Camargue cover 18,500 acres (7,500 ha) of uncultivated land, comprising 136 "ponds" protected by 280 miles (450 km) of dikes.

The rainfall decreases from March onward while natural evaporation increases. This is the time to switch on the pumps which pump in seawater along a canal at the rate of about 70 cubic feet (2 cubic m) per second. In this way more than 1,600 million cubic feet (45 million cubic m) of water is pumped from the sea each year.

Vast horizons, shallow water, and white *camelles* – mountains of salt: This is where the sea is forced to relinquish one of its greatest treasures, its salt.

The seawater pumped into the salt gardens also contains sole, eels, crabs, mussels, and algae. These are removed later.

The seawater, two pints (one liter) of which contains around one ounce (29 g) of salt, is circulated around the salt garden. In order for the salt to crystallize, the sun, the mistral and tramontane winds must join forces to bring about the evaporation of nine-tenths of the original volume of water. The salt workers keep channeling the water further along into other pools, depending on the salt concentration in each.

By the end of three-and-a-half months, the water will have completed its journey through the pans and will have reached a salt concentration of about nine ounces (260 g) per two pints (liter). It is then channeled into salt chambers, 50 square-shaped basins measuring from 12 to 27 acres (5–11 ha) each. Here, the saturated salt water covers the Aigues-Mortes salt pans with a pink coating, further evidence of the presence of the alga *Dunaliella salina*.

By September, when the relentless sun and wind of the summer have finally evaporated the constantly replenished sea water, and the salt concentration has reached the required level, all that is left is a layer of salt about three and a half inches (9 cm) thick: The "white gold" has finally become a "cake" of salt – the fruit of a whole year's labors.

Salt – a vital substance

Bread and salt are ancient symbols of peace and welcome. Nowadays people use salt almost without thinking, sprinkling it into the palm of their hand, into boiling water, or, if there is too much of it, simply rinsing it away down the sink. In actual fact, it merits a closer look.

A daily salt intake of up to a quarter ounce (4–7 g) protects us from dehydration and, thanks to its iodine and fluoride content, helps to fight tooth decay. It also plays a vital role in ensuring that the heart, brain, and stomach function properly. In other words, it is essential to life.

The salt harvest

The salt is collected once a year before the heavy autumn rains can start to dissolve the salt crystals again. Lifting the "cake," in other words the layer of salt, is done in the same way as you would serve a slice of cake: A machine-operated metal plate slides underneath the layer and lifts it. The salt is removed piece by piece. Salt "harvested" in this way is particularly pure and has a sodium chloride content of 99.5 percent. The somewhat gray color of the *gros sel*, or salt, comes from the clay bed of the salt pans.

Trucks, or so-called "dumpers," take it to be washed and cleaned of impurities. It is then transported by conveyor belt to where forklift trucks stack it into salt mountains, up to 70 feet (22 m) in height: these are the so-called *camelles*, which, from a distance, resemble snow-covered mountains.

The next step involves the almost balletic maneuvering of the bulldozers whose task it is to remove the daily quotas of salt for transportation. Once again, the white gold is washed, dried, and graded according to the size of the crystals. This marks the last of the salt's contact with the endless expanse of the sea, from which it was wrested a few months earlier. It finally reaches the consumer packaged in small bags, cardboard boxes, or miniature saltcellars.

"La fleur de sel"

In summer, once the mistral and tramontane winds have abated, millions of fine, light particles form on the surface of the salt pans. When the wind picks up again, this fine salt is wafted to the edge of the basins where it collects in clumps of natural white salt. The "salt flowers," *fleurs de sel* as they are known, are gathered by hand using a kind of large scoop and simply left to dry in the sun for a few hours. This work requires considerable skill and dexterity.

For use as a seasoning, take a small pinch of *fleur de sel* and rub it between your fingertips, sprinkling it over the food. The grains with their mild salty flavor and slightly damp quality impart an incomparably delicate flavor to grilled fish, fresh salad, and to dishes consisting of grilled meat, seasoning the meal appropriately.

"White gold" mountains along the edge of the salt pans.

The superior quality of *fleur de sel* is reflected in the small size of the container in which it is sold.

Fish Recipes from the Camargue

Brandade, a delicious dish made from stockfish, or dried cod, is purported to have originated in Nîmes but, whatever its origins, it is now one of Provence's best-known dishes. Cod has long been considered the king of the sea, providing a source of food to rich and poor alike all over the world. It is mainly found in northern waters but is nevertheless an important ingredient in the culinary traditions of the Antilles. Portugal boasts 365 ways of preparing it, one for each day of the year. *Brandir* means "to swing," hence the name *brandade*, referring to the back and forth movement of the wooden spoon: the constant stirring motion needed to mix the fish, oil, and milk together, making the dish as delicious and creamy as possible.

It can be made from fresh, salted, or dried fish and eaten hot or cold.

Freshly caught, it is called cod, once it is salted it becomes stockfish and is the basis for one of the most economical fish dishes.

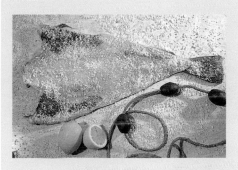

La brandade chaude
Hot creamed cod

1 dried cod, scales removed
2 ¼ tbsp/35 ml milk
⅔ cup/150 ml olive oil
3 tbsp extra virgin olive oil
2 cloves of garlic
Pepper

Poach the dried fish for a few minutes in boiling water with two teaspoons of milk added, then drain. Carefully remove the bones and skin, then mash with a fork. Heat the remaining milk and the ⅔ cup of olive oil separately in two small saucepans.

Peel and crush the garlic. Heat the extra virgin olive oil in a small saucepan, adding the garlic and fish. Stir briskly with a wooden spoon, alternately adding the heated milk and oil a little at a time. Stir for a good 15 minutes until the mixture reaches the consistency of creamed, puréed potatoes.

Season with pepper and then serve the creamed cod hot on slices of toasted bread.

A common variation of this dish is to mix the cooked fish with four potatoes, which have been boiled then mashed with olive oil.

La brandade froide
Cold creamed cod

½ lb/250 g salted stockfish (dried cod)
Thyme, bay leaf
2 cloves of garlic
2 tsp/10 ml olive oil
5 tbsp/75 g crème fraîche (or yoghurt)
Salt, pepper
Lemon juice to taste

Soak the stockfish in lots of water the night before, changing the water several times.

Drain the fish and cut into pieces, place in a saucepan with the thyme and bay leaf and cover with water. Bring to the boil and simmer for eight minutes. Drain the fish once more and mash with a fork. Set aside.

Peel and crush the garlic with a pestle and mortar. Add the olive oil a drop at a time, forming a creamy paste. Heat the mixture in a small saucepan over a low heat, gradually adding the fish and crème fraîche a little at a time, stirring vigorously the whole time. Season with salt, pepper, and the lemon juice.

Anchoïade
Anchovy paste

Serves 4

¼ lb/100 g desalted anchovies
4 cloves of garlic
1 tbsp capers, chopped
⅔ cup/150 ml olive oil
1 tbsp vinegar
Salt and pepper

Anchovy paste, or *anchouiado*, as it is called in Provence, is made as follows: Finely dice the anchovies and peel and crush the garlic. Mix the two together with the capers, adding some oil and vinegar. Season with salt and pepper. Serve on toast with crudités, such as cauliflower florets, slices of carrot or cucumber, mushrooms, raw slices of bell pepper, or small artichokes. It is delicious when served with an aperitif.

If stored in a cool place in a sealed container, anchoïade will keep for several days at a time.

Anchouiado
Provence-style anchovy paste

7 to 8 whole anchovies in brine
2 tbsp olive oil
Pepper
3 cloves of garlic
Vinegar
1 large white loaf

Wash and rinse the anchovies several times in cold water to remove the salt. Fillet the fish, pat dry, and place on a plate. Sprinkle with olive oil, season with a little pepper, and sprinkle with finely minced garlic. Sprinkle with a little vinegar, if desired. Cut the loaf into slices just under one inch (2 cm) thick, dividing each slice into three (reckon on one piece per person). Cut enough pieces for all the guests. Lay one anchovy fillet on each piece of bread. Cut the remainder of the loaf into cubes, first removing the crust. Soak up the remaining oil with these bread cubes, then use them to squash the anchovies on the slices of bread so that the bread soaks up more and more of the anchovy paste. Toast the bread briefly – ideally over a charcoal fire. This dish tastes best cooked and eaten outdoors amidst the scents and sea breezes of Provence.

The anchovy

Measuring no more than six inches (16 cm), with a large mouth out of all proportion to its body, the anchovy lives in deep water, swimming together in great shoals, their slim silvery-blue bodies shimmering as they migrate from place to place, consuming huge quantities of plankton.

The fishermen put to sea at night in brightly colored, floodlit boats. The anchovies, attracted by the light, get caught in the nets. Once back on shore, they are sold fresh at the market. They are delicious barbecued like sardines. Alternatively, they can be salted as soon as they are caught. They are gutted and then cleaned and the heads removed before being placed in layers, each one sprinkled with salt. They are left to mature in weighted barrels for three months where they develop their distinctive aroma. Before going on sale, the anchovies are washed, put in glass jars, and covered with brine.

Anchovies are a common feature of Mediterranean cuisine. They are popular as a pizza topping or wrapped around a caper or an olive. Anchovy paste is also frequently used to stuff green, stoned olives. It is rare for this little fish to be overlooked since its characteristic aroma, which is unmistakable, tends to make itself noticed.

Anchovies are sold or cooked fresh from the sea.

They are kept cool in ice until they are eventually placed in vinegar.

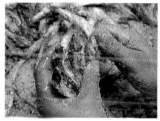

Unless they are to be eaten straight away, they are covered with salt.

The heads are removed and the fish filleted before being layered in barrels.

The anchovies mature on a bed of coarse-grained salt for three months,

after which they are washed and bottled in brine ready for sale.

Rice from the Camargue

It is known as "arisi" in Tamoul, the language of the Berbers, and as "arruz" in Arabic. The cultivated rice that we are familiar with is thought to have come originally from Southeast Asia where it grew wild in the swamps around lakes and rivers. There are also wild varieties of rice in Africa and Asia. This uncultivated rice should not be confused, however, with what we commonly know as wild rice: The latter comes from a different species of cereal grass.

The cultivation of rice spread from East Asia to India, Iran, the Arab countries, and Spain until it finally reached southern France at the end of the 13th century. The Camargue now accounts for 70 percent of France's rice production. The rice fields are as much a part of the landscape as the black bulls, the pink flamingos, and the salt beds.

The story goes that it was Henry IV who instigated rice growing among the farmers of the Camargue – in an effort to find the ideal accompaniment to his *poule au pot*, his Sunday chicken. Accordingly, his Minister, Sully, drained the swamps of the Camargue and tried to stimulate the overall economy of the region by introducing rice as a growing crop. As it happened, this coincided neatly with his maxim that "fields and pastures are the two breasts of France." It was not until two centuries later, however, that rice cultivation really took off in France. In 1830, dikes were built as a defense against the devastating flooding caused whenever the Rhône burst its banks. Meanwhile, the salty groundwater posed a further problem for farmers. Rice cultivation seemed to offer a remedy for this since not only does rice thrive in salty soils but also helps to desalinate it by drawing the sodium chloride down, deeper into the earth. Three years later, this previously unproductive soil was nourishing vines, fruit, and vegetables.

Henry IV (1589–1610) was a popular king: His policies ended the Wars of Religion and led to a booming economy. His Minister, Sully, drained the marshes of the Camargue.

World War II, which halted rice imports for its duration, as well as the declaration of independence by Indochina, hitherto France's main rice supplier, resulted in domestic rice production being stepped up. Irrigation was necessary to quench the extraordinary thirst of the rice crops.

Wine was obliged to make way for rice, at that time considered the more important crop of the two. It is, after all, the staple food of over half the earth's population.

Up until the 1960s, rice fields covered around 81,500 acres

(33,000 ha) of the Camargue; today, rice growing is confined to around 62,000 acres (25,000 ha). Nevertheless, the 80,000 tons of white rice that is produced here represents one third of France's requirements.

View across the paddy fields: Rice plants require a maximum of 3 inches (10 cm) of water and a lot of sun.

Rice cultivation

Cultivating a rice field requires extensive irrigation planning and careful design: The area to be cultivated must be as flat as possible. Today's advances in technology mean that the land can be made almost completely level and the water levels in the rice fields controlled. The shallower the water – between one-and-a-half to three inches (5–10 cm) deep at most – the bigger the rice crop. Although it likes its roots in water, it also appreciates the warmth of the sun. The crop is sown four or five days before the waters of the Rhône flood the fields. To avoid

The Camargue has always been Europe's most northerly rice growing area. Its 62,000 acres (25,000 ha) produce one third of France's domestic consumption.

Arles, daughter of the Camargue, celebrates the rice harvest! The *Prémices du riz* are held in September with a *feria*, *corridas* in the bullrings, flower processions, and freshly prepared paellas at street stalls. Rice is one of the main agricultural products in this part of the world.

damaging the seeds, they are scattered on top of the ground rather than sown in the soil.

The individual sections of land, measuring about seven acres (3 ha), are separated from each other by earthworks, and are under water from April to September. This expanse of water has to be warmed by the sun – rice will not germinate below 50–60 °F (10–15 °C) – otherwise the seed will rot and the whole process will have to be repeated.

Rice can withstand very high temperatures. It flowers only once and only for two hours in August. If the flower fails to open fully, the husk will remain empty. Early varieties of rice can be harvested after 130 days, later ones after 150 days, provided that the ears are still enjoying temperatures over 58 °F (14 °C) at the onset of autumn. The ripened rice has a water content of 27 percent and has to be dried in special ovens to prevent the grains of rice rotting. Once its unpalatable outer skin, the husk, is removed, what remains is a grain of brownish, vitamin-rich whole grain rice. It often undergoes further processing and bleaching. Sometimes, it is glazed or parboiled to preserve some of the vitamins.

The rice fields are burnt after the harvest. This makes it easier to remove the remaining plant growth and, at the same time, enriches the soil with trace elements.

The paddy is threshed in this separating machine. The husks remain on top while the smooth wholegrain rice drops to the bottom.

After sorting, the rice is packaged. Long grain rice is increasingly taking the place of the traditional round grain rice of the Camargue.

Rice and its various stages of development

• *Paddy* is the term given to the unmilled rice immediately after harvesting, when it is still enclosed in its protective but inedible husk.

• *Cargo rice* or wholegrain rice is the term applied to the rice once the husks have been removed, while it still has its fine silvery skin, its seed, and, more importantly, its full complement of vitamins, proteins, and amino acids. Whole grain rice is an extremely healthy food.

• Once the rice has been divested of its second coat, it loses about 60 percent of its vitamins. It is then called white or polished rice.

• *Parboiled rice* is rice that is partially cooked by steaming, thereby preserving a good proportion of the vitamins by concentrating them in the grain's center.

Red rice is a specialty of the Camargue and is served as an accompaniment to traditional dishes.

Varieties of rice

The world's most popular rice varieties are the Japonica variety of short grain rice, which also includes Italian rice and the Camargue rice, as well as the Indica variety of long grain rice, which includes Basmati and Thai rice. There are many different types of rice nowadays which are typical of a country or which are needed for a particular dish. A particular Camargue specialty is red rice, which has been specially grown for about 15 years. Its aroma is reminiscent of hazelnuts or filberts. It is a naturally occurring hybrid of the native red cereal grass and white rice. Like the meat from the semi-wild bulls of the region, this nutritious red rice is an essential ingredient of cuisine in the Camargue area.

Rice can rise to any culinary occasion; it is equally at home as a side dish to savory dishes and as a key ingredient in sweet desserts.

Many countries have national dishes evolving around rice, these include paella in Spain, risotto in Italy, and many more. In addition to this, rice is also used in the manufacture of cornstarch and oil production and cattle are fed on its by-products of meal and straw.

"Lou Mas Doù Juge," Camargue Folklore and Good Food

On the road from Aigues-Mortes to Arles, there is a turnoff to the right signposted to the Petit Rhône (Little Rhône). If you take this road, you will suddenly come across a large billboard in the shape of a bottle.

As you turn into the road, you are likely to see a group of white horses, stirring up swirling clouds of dust. The *gardians* in their traditional black hats, ride around on their snorting animals, rounding up the bulls before herding them to the bullring. This is pure Camargue.

"Lou Mas Doù Juge" is more than just a country inn: It is a place which upholds the old traditions, to the great delight of nostalgic native inhabitants and tourists. Whenever a wedding is celebrated, the old-fashioned carriages are brought out of the barns and there is dancing to the strains of the *pena*, the traditional band.

You can also enjoy the experience of a *course camarguaise*, explore the estate's 320 acres (130 ha) riding on horseback, attend an *abrivado* or go to a lively *ferrade*. Romance and atmosphere are guaranteed.

Freedom for the horses before they are hitched to a carriage or mounted for a hack.

Renée Granier and her nephew Gilles were farmers in the Camargue before they decided to convert the family home into a guest house. For them, "Lou Mas Doù Juge" signifies pleasure and good food. The walls of the large dining room, formerly a sheep shed, are decorated with equestrian paraphernalia, stirrups, saddles, as well as stuffed birds. The enormous fireplace looks ideal for spit-roasting game when the weather turns cold.

The meal starts off with a homemade aperitif, of which you can drink as much as you like. Afterwards, the landlord leads all the guests in a *chanson sévillane*, a traditional folk-

song inspired by Spanish bullfights, which puts everyone in a relaxed mood and gets the party going.

Then come the delicious house specialties: The hors d'oeuvres include *anchoïade*, *rilletes*, soft pork spreading sausage with red bell peppers, bread with sheep cheese and garlic. These are followed by barbecued dishes: grilled zander, sea bass, turbot, fillet of scorpion fish with fruits de mer; small stuffed suckling pig, capon with zucchini pudding, rack of lamb with Mona Lisa Gratin and the inevitable *Gardianne* with fresh pasta.

There is no menu, the day's dishes depend on what is available at the market. From the main course to the cheese course and the homemade desserts, the meal is accompanied by a never-ending succession of carafes of wine, red, rosé, or white.

The highlight of the evening is when a donkey and a horse force their way into the dining room during the meal and try to beg a piece of bread. They say thank-you to the assembled company by yawning – or even by smiling – broadly!

The fireplace also serves as a barbecue, where fish, clamped within a specially designed metal holder, can be cooked directly on the embers, promising a delicious meal.

When evening falls in the Camargue, the *gardians*, tired from their day on horseback, sit down to dinner ready to enjoy the best of the region's dishes.

La gardianne des manadiers
Manadier gardianne

Serves 6

3 lbs/1.5 kg beef, leg or neck, cut
into large chunks
2 slices smoked bacon
1 clove of garlic, finely chopped
2 tbsp olive oil
1 small glass of cognac
3 tbsp flour
2 glasses of wine
Salt and pepper

Marinade

2 cups/½ liter red wine
1 glass wine vinegar
2 cloves of garlic
Thyme, bay leaf
3 cloves
2 onions
Parsley
Coarse-grained sea salt

Leave the meat to marinate for 24 hours.
Cut the smoked bacon into small pieces
and sauté in a casserole dish together with
the garlic.
Add the oil and the drained meat. Sauté
over a high heat until the meat is browned all over.
Heat the cognac, then pour it over the
meat and set alight.
Mix in the flour, then pour in the marinade and wine, stirring gently. Season with
salt and pepper. Cook for three hours over
a low heat, topping up the sauce with a
little water from time to time. Taste and
add more seasoning, if necessary.
Serve hot with Camargue rice, potatoes,
or fresh pasta.

Estouffade de taureau
à la provençale
Provençal-style beef stew

Serves 6

¼ lb/100 g lean piece of bacon,
cut into cubes
4 tbsp/50 g butter
2 lbs/ 1 kg diced braising steak
2 onions, quartered
½ cup/35 g all-purpose flour
1 clove of garlic, crushed
2 cups/½ liter of white wine
2 cups/½ liter of brown meat juices
1 cup/200 g chopped tomatoes
¼ lb/100 g mushrooms
½ cup/100 g black olives, pitted
Salt and pepper

Sauté the bacon in 2 tbsp (25 g) butter
until golden brown. In an ovenproof dish,
sauté the meat with the salt, pepper, and
onions. Add the bacon, flour and garlic.
Pour in the white wine and brown stock
and add the tomatoes. Bake in the oven
for two hours at 350 °F/180 °C.
Meanwhile, slice and sauté the mushrooms in the remaining butter. Once the
meat is tender, add the mushrooms and
olives and simmer for a further 15 minutes over a low heat. Serve piping hot with
Camargue rice.

From the Manade to the Ring

The *Manade*

Hundreds of acres of land, a ranch, bulls, horses, a registered name, a *gardian,* and a top-quality leather saddle: Welcome to the *manade*!

The word *manade* stems from the Latin "manus," meaning "hand," and the term encompasses both the breeding of bulls and horses in the wild as well as the herds themselves. What is also implicit in this term is man's natural dominance over the animals of the herd.

It is the *manadier*, or owner of a herd, who gives it its name and his crest and it is his initials that are branded onto each animal in the herd. The soul of the *manade* and symbol of the Camargue is the mounted *gardian*, immortalized by "Jou Marquès." The Marquis de Baroncelli-Javon, who lived at the beginning of the 19th century, was a passionate *manadier* and fervent defender of the Camargue's traditions and folklore.

With his broad-brimmed hat and three-pronged pole, the *gardian* patrols the *manade*, on the look-out for sick animals or selecting the bulls for the next bullfight. Since he spends hours at a time in the saddle, it must be chosen with the utmost care. It must guarantee him maximum comfort particularly with regard to its padding, back support, and pommel. It is usually left to the region's best saddleries to meet these requirements that are very exacting.

Beauty, poetry, and freedom are bound together in the landscape of the Camargue. But no matter how untamed the black and white herds, no matter how much the region is epitomized by wild gallops across the countryside or the sight of *gardians* roaming the region on horseback, the *manades* are subject to strict controls. These include the compulsory registration of one's name and brand mark in the register of the Camargue National Park. These regulations are also important for maintaining the ecological balance of the environment.

The horses of the Camargue

Like the saddle and the rest of the riding tackle, the stirrups of the *gardian* are made by hand. Great care is taken by the craftsman.

The Camargue horse is a descendant of the ancient Solutré race. They are stocky, tough animals – a fully grown stallion measures just under 14 hands (1.48 m) at the withers. It has a solid head and is very sure-footed. A new-born foal's coat is dark gray or has dark gray patches but later turns white. Its short neck has a thick mane. The Camarguais has a lively nature and great stamina: This robust animal has adapted to the marshes and has to cover great distances to find enough food – the salt beds are inhospitable and offer little

in the way of nutritious grazing. Since it has never been used to a stable, it is impervious to all kinds of weather, be it winter freezing over the watering holes, or the searing heat of summer and swarms of insects.

Camargue horses are mainly born out in the marshes and live in the wild, exposed only to the forces of nature. Once it reaches one year old, the day comes when the *gardian* eventually lassoes it so it can be branded with the *manade's* mark. After this, the young horse can roam the Camargue again for another two years, at which time it begins its apprenticeship in the stables where it is accustomed to the human voice and touch, the girth, saddle, and stirrups. It takes a lot of time, great patience, and an iron will on the part of the *gardian* in order to be able to

Symbol of freedom and a typical sight in the Camargue: Born in the marshes, the white horses fear neither the winter cold nor the summer heat.

subdue the independent instincts of a horse that will always remain semi-wild.

In the past, it was used to thresh corn in this difficult terrain which was inaccessible to machinery, or was hitched up to plows or carts. It was really born to canter, however, and is perfectly adapted to cope with the hours of riding involved in looking after the bulls, its companions in this vast emptiness of plains, lakes, and lagoons. It sometimes even accompanies them to the bullring through village streets high on *abrivado* fever. It is a very important part of all festivals; its agility and ability to do an about-turn and suddenly come to a complete standstill

It is a festival day and the *gardians* are assembling for the *course camarguaise*.

At the age of three, the bulls are allowed into the bullring for the first time. They have cockades tied around their

make the Camarguais an indispensable feature of all bullfights held in the region.

The bull

Between them, the 30 *ganaderias*, breeders, have approximately 6,000 head of cattle of the

Brave breed. They were introduced to the Camargue from Spain in 1870. They are predominantly black in color and have low-slung, forward-pointing horns. They tend to be aggressive and, bred for fighting, are best not approached in the wild. The female animals can weigh anything from 440 to 880 pounds (200–400 kg), the males from 880 to 1,430 pounds (400–650 kg). These bulls are killed in the bullring and used for their meat.

Smaller and more numerous than the Brave bulls are the Camargue breed cattle. There are currently around 100 breeders, each farming 10,000 to 12,000 animals. The cattle have dark coats with long, crescent

Ferrade: The *gardians* separate the young animals from the rest of the herd in order to brand them,

horns. The white-clad *razeteurs* try and get near enough to snatch off the cockades. If they succeed, they get a cash

prize. After the *course*, the bulls are released again, happy to return to their pastures.

or lyre-shaped, upward pointing horns. The bulls weigh up to 990 pounds (450 kg), the cows up to 595 pounds (270 kg). Bulls of the Camargue breed are bred exclusively for the *course camarguaise* and folk festivals. A bull only goes into the bullring every three weeks and once it has risen

to the rank of a *cocardier*, a fighting bull, then only six to seven times a year. When they reach the age of 15, the animals are "retired" and are returned to their herd. When they die, the animals are by tradition buried upright with their heads facing the sea.

The course camarguaise

1402: Louis II, Count of Provence, attended the celebrations held in his honor in Arles. These included, among other things, a fight between a bull and a man. This proved so popular with the populace that it still continues to this day. The *course camarguaise* is a gentler, but no less dangerous form of bullfighting. The contest does not involve *banderillas*, the spears used in other types of bullfighting, and the bull is not killed at the end. Bulls, chosen for their brave spirit and agility of movement, are led into the ring to the impatient applause of the *aficionados*. They have cockades, ribbons and tassels tied to their horns.

The *razeteurs*, whose task it is to snatch the cockades from the bull with a hook or *razet*, are so agile that they appear to fly over the barriers to safety if they are attacked. These white-clad men, armed with nothing but their courage, make their moves according to a set of fixed rules. While some try to divert the bull's attention, others approach it and try to grab its ribbons – a ballet involving man and beast to which Bizet paid tribute in his "Toréador" aria. The splendid spectacle of the *course camarguaise* takes place from April to October.

LES SAINTES-MARIES-DE-LA-MER

In order to reach Les Saintes-Maries-de-la-Mer, you have to cross the "Petite Rhône" on the Bac du Sauvage ferry. Each year, the Sinti and Roma people make a pilgrimage here on May 24 and 25. Outside the tourist season, Saintes-Maries-de-la-Mer is the epitomy of the true charm of the Camargue.

The tellin collector

Up until a few years ago, the town of Les Saintes-Maries-de-la-Mer used to dedicate two annual festivals to this "wonderful little shellfish." Paying tribute to the *Donax trunculus*, its scientific name, provided an excuse for the sort of public celebration that the Camargue excels at: *course camarguaises, ferrades, abrivado,* and the boules competition. The port, the tellins (tiny clams), and tellin collectors received a blessing and freshly caught clams could be sampled, raw or uncooked, all over Les Saintes. Unfortunately, this tradition has since been abandoned.

These small shellfish breed in the sea from March to May. Hidden in the sand, they are better protected from predators than oysters or common mussels, but do not keep as well. Tellins are collected all year round. Very early in the morning, the fishermen decide,

The clam collector is sorting his catch: Any small unwanted specimens fall through the grid.

depending on the wind direction, where the best harvest is likely to be found. They go about 100 to 200 yards (90–180 m) out into the sea, harnessed to their *tellinier* – a kind of net which drags along the seabed. They have to go a long way because the clams change their position depending on tide and current. Unlike common mussels which cling to rocks, they drift along, burying themselves in up to two to four inches (5–10 cm) of sand, when the weather is pleasant, and up to eight inches (20 cm) deep when it is bad. Not a day passes that the fishermen are not seen roaming up and down the coast, bent over the water like farmworkers, filtering the sand. They walk backwards, dragging the *tellinier* toward the shore, where they shake out the clams before going back out to sea. It is hard work, involving hours of ceaseless coming and going. The tellins are sorted as soon as they have been harvested, with the smallest of them, any stingfish, or other unwanted intruders being thrown back into the sea.

Fishing for these small pebble-like clams is subject to very strict regulations: The mouth of the *tellinier* may not be more than three

It is barely daybreak when the fishermen start work.

The job is easier if there is no wind because the tellins hide beneath the sand the moment the sea becomes rough.

The fisherman looks for a likely spot to drop his net. The catch is a good one.

The *telliniers* are full of pebble-like clams which will be shaken out onto the beach straight away to be sorted.

Then it is back out to sea to try and catch some more.

Donax trunculus clams are a prized catch which fishmongers are delighted to offer for sale.

feet (1 m) wide, the mesh must not be less than two-fifths of a square inch (1 sq cm), and the shells must measure at least one inch (2.5 cm) across.

The town is only just waking up when the fishermen return home with their catch, which is immediately sold to local hotels or fish merchants.

Tellins – tiny in size, big in flavor

They look like small pebbles, which the sea has ceaselessly polished to a smooth finish. They resemble small cockleshells, shiny, elongated triangles, shimmering gray and pink, with delicate blue veins. The tellin is also known as a "sea olive" or "sea bean." *Telinos* is the Greek word for bosom – and this tiny clam should be handled accordingly, with all the consideration and tenderness befitting such a sensual object. It is advisable to bite them in half slowly in order to fully appreciate the delicate iodine taste.

The tellin is a type of clam native to the Camargue: the Rhône delta provides it with a sandy bed in which it can roll to and fro. No matter how appetizing they seem, it is still quite a feat to transform them into a feast for the palate: Tellins are full of sand and salt and should be thoroughly washed in water – preferably, seawater – then rinsed several times under running water, at the same time giving them a good shake to make sure all the sand and salt is completely removed. After this, tellins can be prepared in various ways just like common mussels. Try these exquisite little clams as an accompaniment to an aperitif either raw or lightly marinated in lemon and white wine.

Work is over for another day: evening in Les Saintes-Maries-de-la-Mer.

Tellines marinées au citron et vin blanc
Clams marinated in lemon and white wine

Serves 2

2 onions

1 ⅔ cups/400 ml dry white wine

⅔ cup/150 ml white wine vinegar

1 lemon, thinly sliced

Approx. 2 lb/1 kg tellins (tiny clams)

Salt, pepper

1 tbsp freshly chopped coriander

Peel the onions and cut into thin slices. Add to the wine and vinegar in a pan and bring to the boil. This mixture should be allowed to simmer for ten minutes before adding the lemon. Set aside.
Clean the clams, cover, and bring to the boil over a high heat, shaking the pan until the shells open. Drain off the water, leave the clams to cool, discarding unopened ones, then extract the meat from the shells. Filter the marinade and add the clams. Season with salt and pepper and bring the whole lot to the boil. Leave to cool and set aside for six hours. Sprinkle with coriander and serve.

Tellines à la persillade
Clams with parsley

Serves 4

4 lb/2 kg tiny clams

7 tbsp/100 g butter

Juice of one lemon

3 finely chopped garlic cloves

1 bunch finely chopped flat-leaf parsley

Salt and pepper

Place the cleaned clams in a saucepan with a walnut-sized knob of butter. Cover and simmer at a steady heat until they open. Pour over the lemon juice, then turn everything into a skillet, adding the chopped parsley and mixing well. Sauté over a high heat and season with salt and pepper. Olive oil can also be used in place of butter and the clams served with *aïoli* or *rouille*, a hot peppery sauce.

Poêlée de tellines au fenouil
Clams with fennel

Serves 4

1 small head of fennel

1 onion

2 cloves of garlic

3 tbsp olive oil

4 lb/2 kg tiny clams

2 tsp parsley, finely chopped

Cut the fennel into thin slices and finely chop the garlic. Sauté everything together in a skillet with olive oil, then add the cleaned clams. Give them a shake until they start opening.
When they have opened, sprinkle with parsley and serve immediately.

From Mont Ventoux to Aix-en-Provence

Mont Ventoux, known as the "giant of Provence" rises 6,200 feet (1,909 m) above sea level. At any time of the year it appears to be snow-capped although in the summer it is actually the white limestone that produces this effect. Only in winter is it likely to be snow.

From the summit, you can see as far as Dauphiné, the Cévennes, Mont Sainte-Victoire and the Phare du Planier lighthouse off the coast of Marseilles.

Up here, the mistral can reach gusts of up to 120 mph (200 kph). Storms and heavy downpours are commonplace, but when the sun does shine, it is so intense that its heat can be almost paralyzing. Mont Ventoux looms over the high plateau of the Vaucluse and the Carpentras plain like some mythical sentinel – the Celts chose this spot to worship their wind god and the Romans built a shrine here. Although temperatures have been known to drop to minus 13 °F (-25 °C), the mountain still supports flora and fauna that are rare in Europe. UNESCO has consequently designated a large part of this region as a world heritage conservation area; almost the entire spectrum of vegetation zones are to be found here apart from eternal snow.

Mont Ventoux rises from a fertile plain. The Comtat with its wealth of fruit and vegetables stretches as far as the Luberon, which forms a natural protective ridge between the Alps and the Mediterranean. Between the Petit and Grand Luberon, as the the north- and south-facing slopes are known, this "poets' mountain," celebrated by Henri Bosco in the 19th century, has served as a muse to numerous artists thanks to the vast diversity of its natural landscape. Its caves and deep gorges, steep green slopes, and holm oak forest contrast sharply with the Mediterranean garrigue landscape with its broom, boxwood trees, and oak forests. Here you will find sun-drenched villages, old ruins and bories, early Celtic dry-stone huts, the cedars of Bonnieux and the ocher-colored rock formations of Roussillon.

This fruit garden of France is nourished and watered by the Durance river.

The Rhône river flows through Avignon beneath the 12th-century Pont Saint-Benezet. It was severely damaged when the river burst its banks in the 17th century.

Avignon

There are many faces to the Vaucluse and its capital, Avignon. The surrounding countryside is mainly agricultural land. More fruit and vegetables are produced here than in any other region of France. In the 14th century, the town became a summer residence for various popes. Their splendid papal palace and magnificent residences can still be seen to this day. The residents of Avignon also have something of a passion for the theater. Every summer since 1947, the town has played host to the Festival d'Art Dramatique, to which celebrities like Jeanne Moreau, Ariane Mnouchkine, to name a few, have lent their names. As a center of culture, Avignon in the year 2000 is a vibrant and lively town, full of charm – in summer it is the perfect place for lovers.

The "croquette Aujoras" – crisp and delicate at the same time

The year is 1920, Robespierre Square, Avignon: Aujoras, the baker, has just invented his famous *croquettes*. The recipe is so outstanding that even today the mere thought of it is enough to make a gourmet's mouth water.

A *croquette Aujoras* is a dry, golden brown cookie, about two inches (8 cm) in length, the thickness of two cigarettes and studded with almonds.

Are you likely to break your teeth on it then? No, on the contrary. Even the sound of its name does not imply hardness. The *croquette* is light and delicate and with a little patience will melt on the tongue, so you will not even need to dunk it in tea or coffee to reach its center. The gentle approach is the best way to appreciate fully the delicate flavor of almonds and the hint of lemon.

Flour, sugar, locally grown almonds, vegetable fat, and a few drops of natural lemon essence are mixed together in a traditional baking bowl. Between 550 and 660 pounds (250–300 kg) of this fairly stiff dough are produced each day. The dough is rolled out and, using a special roller, cut into strips the width of the *croquettes*.

The dough is left to dry until next day when it is cut into fingers and baked for 20 minutes. These golden brown, crisp *croquettes Aujoras*,

The bridge with the Palace of the Popes in the background: This fortified palace is considered to be an outstanding example of French Gothic architecture.

with an occasional toasted almond peeping out, emerge from the oven, ready to enhance a glass of tea, an ice cream, or even a glass of champagne.

For a long time, these cookies were the one specialty of the Croquette Aujoras cake store. Nowadays, however, they share this honor with other equally popular cakes and cookies made here. For example, the plain pastry ice cream boats, the soft macaroons made of honey and almonds, and the more elaborate Florentines that are made with glacé fruits. They are all products of the same confectionery traditions and are manufactured from local ingredients, like *garrigue* honey, almonds, or candied orange peel.

Then there are the *chardons*: small blue, green, or yellow balls of chocolate filled with liqueurs, such as Ventoux elixir of rosemary or extract of artemisia from Barcelonnette – a glass of cognac with your coffee and a chocolate treat all rolled into one.

Since 1920, the crispy *croquette* has been so popular that over 550 pounds (250 kg) of them are baked every day.

Every morsel is pure enjoyment: The *croquettes Aujoras* emerge crisp and golden brown from the oven.

The bakery is wreathed in the delicious aroma of burnt almonds: People cannot wait to get their hands on the

croquettes. They melt in the mouth with a delicate flavor of almonds and lemon.

CARPENTRAS

It never disappears from view, it is always standing sentinel in the background: The white summit of Mont Ventoux is visible all along the 15-mile (25-km) route from Avignon to Carpentras.

Since 1320, Carpentras has been the fortified capital of Comtat Venaissin, a fertile region of alluvial plains fed by the Durance, Rhône, and Ouvèze rivers.

The town is on a par with the grandiose natural monuments of Mont Ventoux – the Dentelles de Montmirail or the Nesque caves. Momentous historic events have left their mark on it. In the 13th century, this former Roman colony offered refuge to the Jews whom Philippe IV, known as Philippe the Fair, had expelled from the French kingdom. A 14th-century synagogue, the oldest one in France, still exists as testimony to their enforced exile.

The Carpentras weekly market is an important place to meet and see regional products on display.

From 1768, Carpentras profited from a growing demand for red madder dye. During the 19th century, the construction of a canal spur off the river Durance turned the Comtat's *garrigue* landscape into a fertile fruit growing area. This attracted numerous markets to the town as well as agricultural exhibitions, which, even today, attract a large number of visitors from near and far.

The weekly market in Carpentras

Friday morning in Carpentras: The town seems to be bursting at the seams, the sidewalks are overflowing with market stalls. The

Flowers and herbs from Provence as far as the eye can see. With its intense aroma, basil is a temptation almost impossible to resist.

streets seem to be full of hundreds of wicker baskets swinging from the arms of would-be shoppers.

The smell of pizza makes your mouth water. You quickly buy a small portion of Pizza Quattro Formaggi to stave off the pangs of hunger while you shop. Golden brown chicken legs roasted with herbs and honey, a gigantic paella, all help provide ideas for aperitifs in the summer house or an improvised meal with friends.

It is almost impossible to resist the delicious smell of freshly baked bread.

Freshly made or matured, natural or flavored: Goat cheese is an integral part of Provence.

You can get anything you want from the market: cheap clothing, crockery, and crafts.

The vegetable produce grown around Carpentras is picked fresh and sold at market.

Olives are the stars of the show. It is difficult to make a choice from the wide range of varieties on offer.

The floral patterns of the materials reflect the bright colors and sunshine of the Provençal countryside.

You can buy everything you need here, everything you put on your list that morning. However more often than not, it does not stop at the list. It is all too easy to succumb to the temptations afforded by the colorful and fragrant diversity of goods on sale at the market.

The throngs of shoppers under the plane trees in the Avenue Victor Hugo, spilling into every street, in fact, where the market traders have set up their stalls for a few hours, make it impossible to move along more than a few small steps at a time. It is like shopping in a giant open-air supermarket, bursting with stands of all descriptions, selling second-hand goods, material brightly patterned with olives and sunflowers, moderately priced household goods, lavender flowers, soap, essential oils, herb teas, and local crafts. Everything your heart could desire is likely to be on sale here. Apart from traditional items reflecting local color, there is also an abundance of fresh produce from the surrounding countryside, picked fresh or collected that very morning, and possibly even ready-prepared.

Carpentras market is a real experience in itself: It makes you want to touch the goods, feel them, smell the herbs. The colors intoxicate the senses and the fresh produce carries with it the anticipation of quite exquisite and delicate culinary delights to come. Such

Provençal cuisine makes the most of all nature's gifts: Snails are served with tomatoes and with lots of herbs.

sights involuntarily conjure up visions of all sorts of delicious dishes in the mind of the observer.

There is tempting garden arugula, tender oak leaf salad, strings of garlic, little Grelot onions, and fresh basil, which brings to mind *pistou* or tasty tomatoes with mozzarella. The choice of produce awakens cravings, followed by bewilderment: What on earth to choose for the evening meal...

The freshly baked bread with olives, made according to traditional recipes, sausages made by butchers from the surrounding villages, coated in herbs and pepper, freshly made or matured goat cheese, *crottins de chèvre* – all these products tell their own tale of an old bakery or a traditional sheep farm and reveal something of the region's culinary traditions.

The olive tree thrives beneath the skies of Provence – and olive oil, that noble and constant companion of Mediterranean cuisine, makes its proud appearance at local markets. The green bottles have an almost majestic appearance which cannot help but draw attention. They know and fear no rival. A few drops sampled on a slice of bread is enough to guarantee that the bottle will end up in your shopping basket, perhaps sharing the space there with a tub of fresh *tapenade* and a few handfuls of olives with delightful names such as *picholines, cassée-fenouil, niçoises.*

The truffle market – a friendly place with a hint of mystery

"Per la Glori dou terraire,
Vivo la rabasso dou Coumtat."
(May the Comtat rabasse truffle
ever bring glory to the region.)

Each year, on November 27, an unusual market is held in Carpentras. A visit is well worth the effort, even if the weather is already ice cold at this time of year. Cold weather is an indication that that the prized truffles are ready for harvesting.

The Vaucluse is France's main truffle-producing region – two thirds of domestic production hails from this area. On the plains of Carpentras, which provide exceptionally good growing conditions for this "black gold," the truffle can imbibe the forest air of the Comtat. The first truffle market of the year used to be held on Saint Siffrein's Day. For several years, however, the Carpentras truffle season has got underway a week earlier. Truffle markets are held at nine o'clock every Friday morning right up until the end of March. Unlike the market in Richerenches, during the half-hour before the market

Black gold: From November onward, numerous truffle specialties are available in the restaurants.

opens, smaller truffle producers have the opportunity to sell their modest pickings to private buyers.

In Carpentras as in Richerenches, the only hint of the day's business is the smell of truffles: The noisy bustle that is usually associated with market day is just not part of the truffle trade. On the first day of the 1999 Carpentras market, 682 pounds (310 kg) of truffles were sold. This amount would normally constitute the equivalent of an entire harvest for a rainy year. The extremely hot summer of 2003 led to a very small harvest about 110 lb:

One third of an ounce (10 g) of this superior fungus is sufficient to delight the palate. No matter how delicious it may be in an omelet or wrapped in pastry, the best way to savor it is to eat it uncooked. If you feel that fresh *Tuber melanosporum* is too expensive just to eat on a piece of rustic bread, sprinkled with coarse-grain sea salt, truffles can be bought more cheaply as a preserve. During the preserving process, in which it is cleaned and sterilized for three hours, the truffle loses up to 25 percent of its original weight; however, the juice produced by this process is ideal to use for cooking purposes.

Comtat has, for the past few years, held the record for producing the largest truffles, weighing as much as 14–30 ounces (400–900 g). It is home to numerous restaurants, famed for their truffle dishes.

The Duchess of Berry, who was the daughter of the Regent Philippe d'Orléans, continually shocked society with her scandalous behavior.

Truffles in history

Plinius described them as a "miracle of nature," the Romans ate them like candies during performances at the theater, Philippe the Fair in the 13th century was fond of *truffes en chemise* (truffles in their nightshirts), the popes at Avignon gave them pride of place at their banquets, Francis I ate them as comfort food while he was a prisoner of Charles V, the Duchess of Berry, who was beset by scandal, is said to have fed her husband truffles, so convinced was she of their aphrodisiac properties. During the 18th century, fashionable society used to eat them during the interval at the opera and by the 19th century, any elegant meal was considered incomplete without them.

The "berlingots" of Carpentras

Carpentras has yet another specialty to offer: the *berlingot* fruit candy. It is considerably cheaper, far more popular than the truffle and has become inextricably associated with Carpentras.

The *berlingot* is an elegant little candy with a surprising taste. It can be red, green, blue, transparent or opaque, with white stripes running through it. Hard on the outside, it dissolves slowly to reveal a center flavored with peppermint, aniseed, strawberry, or perhaps lemon.

The name of this unusual little candy is said to come from "berlingozzo" in Italian, a colorfully striped cake for special occasions. It has been made in Carpentras since the beginning of the 19th century.

It owes its originality to a thrifty candy manufacturer who was looking for a way to use

Attractive packaging adds to the temptation…

up the syrup left over from producing peppermint-flavored candied fruits. He eventually came up with the idea of turning the syrup into candies.

The *berlingot* became so popular in the 1950s and 1960s that 2,000 tons of them were consumed each year. Nowadays, they are produced more for the sake of tradition than anything else. These candies nevertheless have a very persistent sort of old-fashioned charm. Every morning, the candy-makers follow the same traditional ritual. They mix together sugar, glucose, and water in a copper pan, enough to make about 26 pounds (12 kg) in weight. Once this mixture is heated and has boiled for a time, it turns into a transparent caramel, which is poured carefully onto a marble slab. A few drops of flavoring and coloring are added and the mixture slowly turns into a *berlingot*. The color seldom bears any relationship to the flavor: A red candy does not – as you might expect –

taste of cherry or strawberry, it tastes, unusually, of peppermint.

As soon as it has cooled down, gloved fingers deftly fold the mixture over and over, shaping it into something resembling a long bolster. The confectioner cuts a fist-sized piece off the end of this, which he then pulls and stretches into long strands, looping them round a simple hook on the wall. The mixture loses its color during this procedure and becomes white. These long white strands are spaced at regular intervals around the outside of the "bolster" which is then rolled to and fro over the work surface, all the while being stretched and pulled until eventually it resembles a very large cigar. This is hot work for the confectioner, since the mixture becomes increasingly stiffer. Finally, the roll of candy mixture is fed into a machine which gives it the desired shape and cuts it into hundreds of *berlingots*.

Fresh batches of syrup are being boiled up all the time. This is exhausting work and the sweet smell can almost make you feel dizzy. If the syrup happens to be flavored with peppermint, the fumes are particularly intensive, so much so that red *berlingots* have to be dried separately so that their flavor does not overwhelm all the other candies in the selection. They are also packaged separately in a box all of their own as if in tribute to the fact that they were the first *berlingots* to be produced in Carpentras. The Mont Ventoux candy workshop opens its doors to the public each day so that candy lovers can watch it being made. The visit includes an opportunity to sample candied oranges and cherries, *chardons à la liqueur*, liqueur-filled chocolates as well as olive-shaped chocolate pralines.

Berlingots à gogo! The peppermint-flavored candies are packaged separately from the others.

The confectioner boils up the various flavors of syrup for the *berlingots* several times a day.

The hot mixture is poured from the copper cauldron onto a large worktop made of marble.

The mixture is carefully spread over the slab and left to cool.

The confectioner skillfully lays the white strands along the "bolster" of setting syrup.

The zebra-striped mixture is rolled constantly back and forth, getting longer all the time.

The stiffer the mixture, the harder the work. The roll of candy begins to resemble a giant cigar.

This exhausting work is complete when the "bolster" has become a long, thin roll.

The striped sugar roll is now ready to feed into a machine, which cuts it into small sections.

The candies are dried and packaged in colorful assortments – with the exception of the peppermint ones.

THE VELLERON MARKET –
FRESH FROM THE FIELDS INTO YOUR BASKET

Between Carpentras and L'Isle-sur-la-Sorgue is a road which takes you through the picturesque town of Pernes-les-Fontaines to Velleron. Every afternoon, the peace of this flower-filled Comtat village is shattered and traffic begins to build up. It is time for the so-called farmer's market, one of France's hundred best markets.

Except on Sundays and public holidays, a shrill whistle can be heard every evening at precisely six o'clock in summer and half past four in winter signaling the opening of the gates of an open-air market. It is flooded with customers the moment it opens. The stall-holders set up their stalls either side of the single aisle. Totally at the mercy of the vagaries of the weather, baked in glaring sunshine or buffeted by the mistral, the market traders set out their goods for sale including dairy produce, poultry that is fresh from the

Whether it be strawberries or yellow or green zucchini, the vegetables and fruit are picked and sold fresh each day. The fruit juices on sale, such as grape or apricot, are likewise pure and freshly squeezed.

farmyard, cooking herbs, fruit, vegetables, homemade preserves, 100 percent pure fruit juices, flowers, or olive tree saplings.

The crush is so great that it takes considerable effort to make your purchase, often still with some local soil clinging to it, as well as a great deal of patience. It is a matter of inching your way forward and getting pushed and shoved and carried along by sluggishly moving crowds of people, making their way home, heavily laden with crates of peaches or melons. Some of them carry nothing more than a bunch of zucchini flowers which are delicious fried in batter.

And surely it is worth sacrificing a little of your time if, for just a few francs, you can stock up your larder with fresh goat cheese, fresh eggs, garden arugula, and the old-fashioned but still very popular La Ratte variety of waxy potato. It is fun just feasting your eyes on the colorful variety of baskets filled with mange-tout peas and blackcurrants, strawberries, and cherries, all of which have been picked just a few hours earlier.

Now is also the time to grab a bargain among items offered as "seconds" but nevertheless of excellent quality: "Second choice" fruit is ideal for jelly-making, the vegetables perfect for preserving and the tomatoes make a wonderful coulis.

Basil is one of the most popular kitchen herbs: You need only think of *pistou* or tomatoes with mozzarella. It is also good for preserving with olives, however.

Velleron market also has one very special attraction: a cheese-maker, who comes direct from Normandy with his herd of cows! In the Velleron region, which concentrates mainly on goats, fresh Quark, or yoghurt produced earlier the same morning and freshly churned butter from good dairy cows constitute something of a rarity.

L'Isle-sur-la-Sorgue

A few miles farther south is another delightful Vaucluse town. L'Isle-sur-la-Sorgue, with its avenue of plane trees, resembles a miniature Venice and has a particular charm all of its own.

"La Prévôté"

Wherever you go, you will keep encountering the river Sorgue, flowing alongside the street, under the bridges, turning the mill-wheels. At one time, it irrigated the marshes where it was possible to catch up to 10,000 crayfish in a day. Occasionally, its waters rush by in a torrent, but for the most part the deep green river flows peacefully along. Following its course will help you discover one of the most popular towns of the Vaucluse. L'Isle-sur-la-Sorgue is the European center for

As the European center of the antiques trade, the charming, romantic town of L'Isle-sur-la-Sorgue always attracts numerous visitors.

antique shops and second-hand stores. As soon as the days grow warmer, its natural beauty becomes hidden to some extent

---

Canette laquée au miel de lavande

Duck breast fillet in lavender honey

Serves 2

| 2 young ducks |
| Lavender honey |
| 1 carrot |
| 1 onion |
| 1 stick of celery |
| 1 bunch of herbs (thyme, bay leaf, rosemary) |
| 1 tsp butter |
| Salt and freshly milled pepper |

Cut the ducks in half and lift out the breasts. Spread the upper side with honey and set aside. Wash the vegetables and dice. Place in a saucepan together with the carcass and herbs, cover with water, and simmer over a low heat for 90 minutes. Season the resulting stock with salt and pepper and

strain through a sieve. Skim off any excess fat.

Preheat the oven to 375 °F/190 °C. Without adding any fat, sauté the duck breasts, skin side down, in a skillet until the honey caramelizes into a golden brown color. Cook for a further five minutes in the preheated oven, then remove from the oven and allow to stand for ten minutes. Lift the duck breasts from the skillet and keep warm in the oven.

Add the meat juice left in the skillet to the stock and simmer until the liquid is reduced. Add the butter.

Arrange the duck breasts on warm plates, pour over the sauce and serve immediately with potatoes, braised tomatoes, or bell peppers.

Râble de lapin farci à la tapenade

Saddle of rabbit stuffed with tapenade

Serves 2

1 saddle of rabbit

1 carrot

1 onion

1 stick of celery

1 bunch of herbs (thyme, bay leaf, rosemary)

A generous ¾ cup/200 ml of white wine

2 tbsp olive oil

Salt and freshly milled pepper

Tapenade

½ cup/100 g black olives, pitted

Scant 1 oz/25 g of anchovies

1 small clove of garlic

Bone the rabbit, breaking up the bones, and sauté them gently in a saucepan. Wash and dice the carrot, onion, and celery. Add the vegetables and herbs to the bones in a saucepan, pour in the wine, and bring to a boil. Add a little water and simmer for about 20 minutes until the liquid is reduced, then strain the stock through a sieve.

To make the tapenade, pound together the black olives, anchovies, and peeled garlic clove using a mortar and pestle until they form a thick paste with a homogenous texture. Preheat the oven to 350 °F/180 °C.

Remove the fillets from the rabbit (including the thin strips of rib meat), season with salt and pepper on the inside and spread with tapenade. Next, wind the thin strip of meat around the fillet and bind with kitchen string. Sauté the whole on all sides in olive oil and cook in the oven for 15 minutes, basting with meat juices from time to time. Switch the oven off and leave the meat to stand in the oven for a further ten minutes, then set aside. Add the stock to the meat juices. Add a tablespoon of tapenade to the sauce and taste.

Heat up the saddle of rabbit in the oven for a few minutes, carve, pour over the sauce, and serve.

behind a veil of snobbery and it tries hard to emulate Paris. This foible, however, does not detract from its qualities as a historic town, nor does it alter the fact that a culinary stopover here is an absolute must.

The "La Prévôte" restaurant can be found in an old building in the Rue Jean-Jacques Rousseau. Its attractive cuisine is crowned by a comprehensive, quality wine list. The chef, Jean-Marie Alloin, shows the same finesse when preparing ravioli with a lobster filling as he does with his *tatin d'agneau à la tapenade*, a savory tart with lamb and tapenade.

With the assistance of patissier Pierre Guignard, he serves up such delicious desserts as Pear Hélène with its subtle hint of cloves, whiles the coffee at the end is augmented by *financiers*, small almond tarts, *tuiles*, made from wafer thin puff pastry, or homemade pralines.

Apt

Leaving behind the Ventoux hills in the northeast, the Luberon mountain range soon appears on the horizon. The road leads to Apt, a town which Madame de Sévigné described as a gigantic vat of jam. The town is known for its "sweet" reputation which has in no way diminished over the centuries. The "Centre National des Arts Culinaires" has categorized Apt as a "Site remarquable du goût" (a site of special culinary interest).

The "croquants" and bread of "Pierrot Blanc"

Candied fruit has the same significance for Apt as *calissons* do for Aix. Even if its pleasant fragrance is not quite so omnipresent in the streets of Apt as the nougat is in Montélimar, the windows of the town's cake stores are veritable fruit gardens. It is virtually impossible to resist being tempted by the velvety shimmer of a fig or the mother-of-pearl translucence of a candied pear. These delectable fruits have inspired confectioners to create a cake called the *galapian*, which is a substantial, delicious cake, made largely with candied melons and ground almonds.

Seasonal fruit has been harvested, blanched, boiled, and glazed (in other words, candied) on an all-year round basis in Apt since the 14th century.

Apt has more than just one delicacy to tempt the palate, however. The jams produced here

Candied fruits are one of the most delicious sweetmeats that Provence has to offer – they are also one of the traditional "13 desserts" served on Christmas Day.

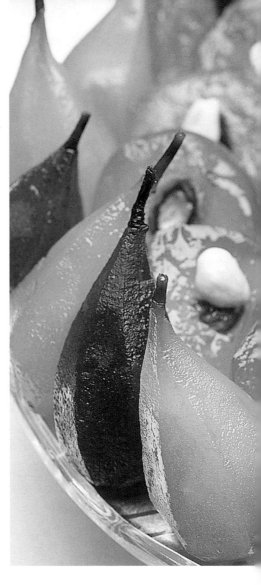

are equally delicious. And there is one other thing – something that is unique to this region but too young to have found its way into the annals of culinary history. It is only on sale in one bakery and confectioner's store, modestly displayed on the shelves but nevertheless a big draw for those in the know. The delicacies in question are "Pierrot Blanc's" *croquants*.

The Biancos in the Rue des Marchands are third-generation bakers and and run their business from the above-mentioned store. Pierre Bianco, the present owner, is the innovative creator of the *croquants aux amandes*, a crisp confection whose main ingredient is almonds.

The epitome of a southern landscape: gentle mountains, vineyards stretching as far as the eye can see, an olive tree and, in its shadow, a simple, traditional little house.

The crisp meringue and the aroma of burnt almonds of "Pierrot Blanc's" *croquants* are so tempting that they are best sampled rather than described. Caution is recommended if you do try one, however, since the *croquant* is so light and delicate that it disintegrates at the first bite.

The list of ingredients is short and sweet: almonds, egg white, sugar and flour. It is "Pierrot Blanc's" magical confectionery skills that turn this into an elegant dainty.

In addition to his *croquants*, Pierre's herb ice cream also merits a mention. This is made

from a mixture of cream and eggs, flavored with herbal teas that are made from infusions of thyme, vervain, savory, or mild, fresh essence of lavender from the region.

As a little digestif following a rich meal, "Pierro Blanc" recommends his melon or pastis sorbets – although the pastis sorbet gets its flavor more from an aniseed-based syrup than from pastis otherwise it might go too much to your head! Pierre has also invented a type of bread made from chestnut flour, ideal for weekend breakfasts: Its natural, slightly sweet flavor makes it perfect with butter and jelly. Nor should you miss sampling his fine rustic bread and rye bread. Or his *tarte du Luberon*, a kind of flying-saucer-shaped pastry filled with bilberry, raspberry, or apricot jelly. Then there is his almond cake made with plain pastry. The almond cream with which it is layered makes it soft, while the sliced almonds on top give a delectable contrast by making it crunchy.

Coffee time with a *croquant*: the temptation is far too great to resist.

The *tarte du Luberon*, another creation by "Pierrot Blanc," which poses a serious threat to one's figure.

Bernard Mathys' kitchen

Just a few miles on from Apt is Gargas. At the end of a rough track stands a splendid mansion from the 18th-century, surrounded by 300-year-old plane trees. If you climb a few steps, you will suddenly find yourself in an elegant restaurant with a terra-cotta-tiled floor. The owner admits to hating the town and is bored with

The restaurant of this splendid manor house offers very sophisticated cuisine to tempt the visitors.

cooking. A joke? For ten years, he looked after a large and loyal clientele in his Paris restaurant, which was considered one of the capital's top eating places.

Bernard Mathys once had dreams of becoming an actor, but his grand gestures have instead been channeled into cooking. In order to learn some sort of "proper" job, he studied as a chef. No sooner did he get his diploma from catering college than he was drawn back to his first love, the theater. Then, one day he suddenly saw a bistro for sale on the street where he lived in Montmartre. On an impulse, he decided to buy it and had soon turned it into a first-class restaurant, acclaimed by the critics. Eventually, the theater drew him back to Avignon and introduced him to the sunnier and less hectic life of the south. Bernard Mathys enjoys being in his restaurant: He likes the contact with his guests and loves making enthusiastic recommendations as to what dishes to choose. He himself is not involved

with the cooking any longer – he has hung up his apron and, instead, employs qualified staff who will live up to his standards. He does, however, always draw up the menu himself. The warm Munster cheese on potatoes with caraway salad that features on the menu is an indication of Mathys' Lorrainese roots.

Although he uses regional products, Mathys is loath to offer purely Provençal cuisine. As he maintains, his guests' childhood memories of this will always be better than the reality. No *bourride* then, and no bouillabaisse, instead a fresh, truffled duck liver pâté, together with mild garlic and eggplants.

Just listing the vegetable accompaniments is enough to make anyone's mouth water: caramelized cauliflower purée with mustard grains, creamed potatoes, tomato balls with Provençal herbs, chicorée fondue with filberts, mini-ratatouille with Tandoori sauce, fried vegetables with small violet artichokes. The Marseilles and Roscoff fishermen provide daily supplies of fresh fish. Bernard Mathys loves lobster, sea bass, and pilgrim scallops from the Atlantic, anglerfish, and small Mediterranean rock fish. Popular side-dishes to these are *gâteau de courgettes à la fleur de thym* (zucchini cake with thyme blossom), or *papeton d'aubergines frites à la tomate* (fried eggplant with tomatoes).

Ragoût de homards bretons aux artichauts violets

Ragout of Breton lobster and purple artichokes

Serves 4

20 purple artichokes
Juice of two lemons
4 x 1 lb/500 g lobsters
2 ½ tbsp/40 ml olive oil
2 ½ tbsp/40 ml cognac
4 tbsp concentrated tomato paste
8 cups/2 liters vegetable or fish stock
1 cup/225 g butter
2 tbsp parsley, roughly chopped
3 cloves of garlic, finely chopped

Remove the artichoke stalks, cut off the outer leaves and clip the tips off the remaining leaves. Press apart the leaves in the center, scrape out the heart and cut the artichoke into eight pieces. Place in lemon water and set aside. Cook the lobsters in boiling water for five to ten minutes until they turn red, then drain and run under ice-cold water. Extract the meat from the shell, and put the claws and tail in a cool place. Break open the rest of the shell and sauté in a generous tablespoon of hot olive oil. Flambé in cognac, add the tomato paste, then pour in the stock, simmer until it is reduced to three quarters of its original amount, then strain through a sieve.

Sauté the artichokes in a generous tablespoon of olive oil and 4 tablespoons of butter, then pat dry.

Cut through the lobster tails and claws lengthwise, sauté lightly, then set aside. Add parsley and garlic to the skillet and pour in the sauce. Mix in the rest of the butter. Simmer until it reaches a syrupy consistency.

Arrange the artichokes, lobster tails and claws on plates, pour over the sauce, cut the lobster meat into pieces and serve along with the rest.

The proprietor of the restaurant is also a wine connoisseur. Mathys chooses his wines with great care. They include many Côtes du Rhônes as well as Côtes du Luberon. The *Château La Canorgue*, a Côtes du Luberon wine, is his favorite and he offers various vintages of it.

If you wish to end the meal in a manner appropriate to this sophisticated atmosphere, you have to contend once more with the dilemma imposed by the dessert menu compiled by René Solnon, Bernard's kitchen companion of 20 years: *gratin de pamplemousse de Champagne* (grapefruit gratin with champagne sauce), *Saint-Honoré aux apricots* (Saint Honoré cake with apricots), *ganache au chocolat noir* (Ganache with dark chocolate), *mille feuilles aux citrons de Menton* (puff pastry with Menton lemons), to name just a few delights which might provide the exquisite finale to an excellent meal.

En Route to Bonnieux

The village of Bonnieux clings to the slopes of the Petit Luberon like a beautiful blossom on a climbing plant. It is a pretty village with its old stone houses, two church towers, and the plentiful remains of the old town walls. From the village, there is a wonderful view to the Calavon valley and Vaucluse plains with its delightful villages of Gordes and Roussillon – a view that eventually leads to the silhouette of Mont Ventoux.

The alleyways of Bonnieux are like a labyrinth. One minute, they are winding upward, next they pass under an archway and start leading downhill, as if they are trying to find a way to the old church, surrounded by its wonderful hundred-year-old cedars. The white stone of its Gothic silhouette towers above the village roofs. It is pleasant to rest in the shade of the trees here before continuing your exploration of this typical Luberon village.

The fascination and charm of Bonnieux, like neighboring villages blessed by sun and good light, have captivated numerous artists and writers through the years. Perhaps even today there is still one or another of them concealed

A wonderful view over the Calavon valley. The huge, yet elegant *bastides* are mainly farms, devoted to vegetable, fruit, and wine growing.

behind the walls of one of the splendid 18th-century houses or behind one of the many flower-bedecked façades.

A visit to the picturesque and interesting bakers' museum is enough to whet the appetite. The garden of the "Hostellerie du Prieuré" inn in the heart of Bonnieux offers the perfect natural surroundings in which to enjoy the typical Provençal cuisine: The menu includes the dishes *pissaladière croustillante de rougets* (crisp pissaladière with sea bass), *caviar d'aubergines* (aubergine caviar), with *tapenade*-vinaigrette, *bottillon d'asperges au beurre d'orange et aux amandes grillées* (asparagus with orange butter and toasted almonds) as seasonal specialties. And the desserts? They lend an

Little Bonnieux looks out almost majestically over the valley. It is a typical Luberon village which tries to preserve its intimate atmosphere behind the ruins of its circular walls

exotic touch to the meal: for example, *macaronade de mangue* with *coulis de pruneaux* (mango macaroons with plum purée).

Aiguebrun is part of Bonnieux despite the fact that it lies a few miles away. Not only is the beauty of the place captivating, but the sophisticated cuisine to be found there is likewise a big draw: Zucchini flowers from the village's own vegetable plot, watered by the river Aiguebrun running through it, are stuffed with herbs and mild goat cheese and made into *beignets* (fritters). *Pieds et paquets à la marseillaise* (Marseille-style stuffed sheep's feet)

simmer away for hours on end in a cast-iron pot over a fire in the old fireplace until they are ready to melt like butter in your mouth. The dessert finale will often incorporate the taste of vanilla, which is imported direct from the former colony of Tahiti – there is no better way of enhancing the flavor of chestnut cake, ice cream, or other desserts.

The roads leading out of Aiguebrun are named after the many chateaux and wine growing estates that are spread throughout the region. They too are well worth visiting for a wine-tasting session.

123

The wines of the Luberon

This ancient winegrowing area stretches more than 9,100 acres (3,700 ha) across the slopes of the Luberon, a region exposed both to the heat of the sun as well as to frequent buffeting by the tramontane and mistral. The soil is stony, the climate Mediterranean, sometimes even temperamentally continental. It is cooler here than in the Rhône valley. Spring frosts can occur quite unexpectedly and there are dramatic variations between daytime and nighttime temperatures. There are 42 private cellars and cooperatives in the Luberon producing over 4,750,000 gallons (180,000 hl) of wine each year. The vintners prefer small yields – about 450 gallons per acre (42 hl per ha) – in order to ensure that their wines are of fine quality and have a distinct character.

Everyday life in Provence: At the first sign of spring, the outdoor cafés begin to fill up. The regulars meet to discuss the day's events over a pastis.

Winegrowing in the region can be traced back to ancient times – a Roman bas relief from Cabrières d'Aigues is thought to be the oldest evidence of wine cultivation in the Durance valley. The Court of Versailles is also known to have favored wines from this region, which exude the scent of raspberry, blackcurrant, and liquorice and have an unforgettable bouquet. It would seem that the soil, which produces truffles, olives, lavender, and thyme, blesses all the plants it nurtures with a distinctive character of their own. It is a soil which flavors its white wines with the subtle hint of wild peaches, apricots, dog roses, and linden blossom.

Thanks to the exceptionally intense sunshine, the Côtes du Luberon wines – which, in 1988, were granted their own Appellation d'Origine Contrôlée – have a big and long-lasting flavor and are extremely full-bodied. The blending of different varieties of grape can produce sophisticated wines.

The Appellation includes red, white, and rosé wines. Although the reds are dominant, the white wines nevertheless make up 20 percent of the production. The red wines consist predominantly of the blue (*noirs*) Syrah, Grenache, Cinsault, Carignan, and Mourvèdre grapes. The Grenache grape, which does well in dry soil, is

The variety of an excellent Appellation. The Luberon produces wonderful red wines, as well as rosés and whites.

responsible for the fruit flavors that are dominant; the more refined Cinsault modifies these a little; the Syrah grape gives the wine its ruby red color and smooth flavor. These wines are full-bodied and vigorous and are a perfect accompaniment to dishes of red meat and game.

The white wines are mainly comprised of Grenache and Ugni Blanc grapes; less than 50 percent of the entire vinestock is made up of Clairette, Vermentino, and white Bourboulenc grapes. The delicate flavors of the Grenache, blended with the elegant and fruity Clairette and Bourboulenc, produce a delightful combination of full-bodied, vigorous, and smooth wines which are perfect with broiled fish and goat cheese.

The rosé wines are a blend of equal proportions of the same grape varieties which go to make the reds and the whites. Like the whites, straight after being pressed and filtered, they are left to ferment at a low temperature. The prevailing aromas of rosé wines come from red fruits, such as raspberries and wild strawberries. They go extremely well with fish and white meat.

The tannins contained in the grape skins and stalks used in rosé wines have a natural preservative effect. This means that rosé wines keep well without any deterioration in quality.

Château wines

As Bonnieux recedes very slowly into the distance, the vineyards imperceptibly encroach upon the road until it eventually dwindles into nothing more than a track. It ends at the point where pleasure begins, in the first instance, as a feast for the eye.

A sense of nostalgia is evoked by the sight of an old country house, fronted by a majestic terrace with its stone fountain. The place is redolent with atmosphere.

Experiencing the wines of the Château La Canorgue for the first time can be the kind of discovery that makes a special meal unforgettable. *La Canorgue – Côtes du Luberon* has been awarded several gold medals at the Concours Générale Agricole de Paris, and the Concours

The Château La Canorgue estate produces fine quality wines of the Appellation Côtes du Luberon.

des Grands Vins in Mâcon, Blayais, Avignon, and Orange. Jean-Pierre Margan, the vintner of La Canorgue, is himself the recipient of an award: In 1995, a well-known wine magazine awarded him the prestigious title of Vintner of the Year for the entire Rhône region.

The château has increasingly gained in importance since Margan, a winegrowing expert by trade, devoted himself to reviving this abandoned vineyard 20 years ago. Getting this family estate back on its feet took several years; the harvests were very modest to begin with but gradually improved until the yields reached their present-day figures of 150,000 bottles of organically produced wine per year. Sixty percent of these are red wines, produced mainly from Grenache and Syrah grapes – "vines that grow well in this terrain"; 20 percent are whites – "which I enjoy pressing and drinking" and the rest are rosés "which are so difficult to produce." Jean-Pierre Margan loves his wines and everything to do with growing and producing them.

The track leads to a romantic country estate, the Château La Canorgue.

The grapes are picked by hand and carefully sorted on the spot, then pressed in accordance with château tradition. This is a small estate with a small yield – just over 300 gallons per acre (30 hl per ha) – all château-bottled. Of such decisions are great wines made.

The red wines mature for six to twelve months in oak barrels and can easily be left for eight to ten years. The *Cuvée La Canorque* is also very attractive. This high-quality vin de pays matures for one and a half years in special 600 liter barrique barrels. The whites should be drunk within three years and the rosés are best drunk while they are still young. Some of the other local wines of the region are also worth sampling. Even though their Chardonnay and Viognier grapes do not

The wine maturing in the massive oak barrels in this cellar, under the strict supervision of the vintners, fills 150,000 bottles a year.

count as Appellation Côtes du Luberon, they have still enjoyed the luxury of maturing in barrique barrels.

The Côtes du Luberon wines include other big names such as the Château Val Joanis in Pertuis, which has also managed to recover after falling into a bad state of neglect. The 420 acres (170 ha) of vines, cultivated in the best château traditions, consist mainly of Syrah and Grenache and produce wines which, over the past ten years, have won several awards. The white *Château Val Joanis*, a dry, lively, racy wine, is a popular aperitif and is also excellent with goat cheese.

The château's young, full-bodied, and very fruity red wine can be served with red meat and cheese even within its first year; a fully matured 1994 vintage comes into its own as an accompaniment to broiled meat whereas the purplish red 1995 has to be left to mature for three years in the cellar. The 2003 vintage is well regarded by wine experts, and promises much enjoyment for patient wine lovers.

The extremely aromatic *Val Joanis Rosé* is highly regarded as an aperitif since its crisp, long-lasting flavor goes very well with shellfish of all kinds.

Val Joanis also produces two further wines: *Les Griottes*, produced from the château's best vineyards, are pressed separately, stored in oak barrels, bottled and finally sold after having matured for at least a year at the château. They are full-bodied wines, elegant and powerful. *Les Merises*, one of a limited number of great rosé wines, makes an excellent accompaniment to game and fish dishes. These wines, made from the best red grapes, are produced

Not only the wines but also the architecture of Château de l'Isolette merit the visitor's attention.

in very limited quantities and bottled in half-liter numbered bottles.

A walk through the delightful grounds of the château is the perfect way to recuperate from a wine-tasting session. They are laid out in three terraces in imitation of some of the beautiful 18th-century garden designs.

"The management may change, the label or origin may alter, but the quality remains the same." This statement refers to the Château de Milles, which, over the past 80 years, thanks to the vagaries of bureaucracy, has numbered among each of the neighboring Appellations, such as the Rhône, Provence, Ventoux, and finally Luberon. It is the Luberon's oldest winegrowing château and its amazing 12th-century building is set amidst vineyards and woodland. Reds, rosés, and whites are produced here. The Château reds are left to mature in oak barrels.

The 1996 whites were another exceptionally good vintage and the young whites have turned out to be very pleasant and drinkable even now. The winegrowing owner of the château has proclaimed 1999 to be an exceptionally good year for white wine, the unique

A gently curving flight of steps leads the wine enthusiast up toward the Château de l'Isolette, an estate that has collected over 200 gold and silver medals for its wines.

character of which will be a tribute to the old millennium.

Not very far from the Château De Milles is the renowned Château de l'Isolette. This almost 250-acre (100 ha) estate has won more than 200 gold and silver medals over the past 20 years for its predominantly Syrah-based red wines, and its white wines that are made mainly from Roussane grapes.

The *Cuvée rouge Sélection 1998 Prestige* is ready to be savored as a perfect accompaniment to meat dishes and broiled meat, whereas the full-bodied and powerful *Cuvée Prestige 1997* can continue to mature in peace.

The *Blanc de Blancs 1998*, which should be drunk well chilled, has a strong bouquet and is excellent with fish, truffle omelet, and strongly flavored cheeses.

The Château's rosé wines are crisp, well-rounded wines with a lively, smooth character. The *Cristal,* which is made predominantly from Grenache grapes (70 percent), has already developed its full aroma and its full-bodied flavor is an ideal accompaniment to classic summer dishes, such as mussels, pizza, and hors d'oeuvres.

A visit to the "Auberge des Seguins" is a pleasant start or finish to a walk.

"L'Auberge des Seguins"

A twisting road winds its way from Bonnieux to Buoux, like a snake looking for refuge in the cool green shade. This simple settlement off the tourist track has its own charm – as well as evidence of a historical past: a citadel, whose ruins dominate present-day Buoux, and a secret flight of steps which entice the visitor for a brief visit. The journey then continues for almost another three miles through the Aiguebrun valley to where a small road leads off through a rocky landscape, dotted with imposing trees.

The "Auberge des Seguins" suddenly appears in the midst of this rocky terrain. It is the starting and finishing point for all kinds of climbing tours and emanates the sort of intimate atmosphere that you might expect of the French Logis Hotel-Restaurants.

If all you want is a simple sandwich, you can enjoy this at the bar, then plunge into the pool for a refreshing swim. Or else, you can enjoy a more substantial meal on the shady terrace.

Whichever menu you choose, the meal always begins with the famous Provençal crudités platter consisting of sticks of celery, anchoïade, chickpeas (garbanzo beans) with cumin, mushrooms with local herbs, tomatoes with basil, olives, mussels with tarragon, and tiny game patties – all washed down with a well chilled rosé wine.

The cuisine is in keeping with the outside of the building. It is inviting, with its simple Provençal style fully reflected in an extensive menu: *magret de canard aux cèpes* (duck breast fillet with cep mushrooms), *brouffade* or *daube de boeuf aux câpres et anchois* (braised beef with

Sometimes, tasty home-produced trout feature on the menu. They are particularly delicious when they are freshly caught and cooked.

capers and anchovies), *estouffade* or *épaule d'agneau dégraissé avec sa sauce à la purée d'olives noires et oignons* (shoulder of lamb in sauce with black olives and onions), *cailles farcies* (stuffed quail), or *côtelettes d'agneau grillées à point et parfumées d'herbes* (medium rare broiled lamb cutlets with herbs), *truites du vivier* (local trout) or *écrevisses fraîches à la vauclusienne* (fresh Vaucluse-style crayfish).

Also worth a mention are the zucchini gratins and leek gratins as well as the oven-baked potatoes, which must compete with the salad of the day, liberally sprinkled with olive oil and lots of garlic.

The meal finishes with the inevitable cheese – made from goat's milk or, if you prefer, cow's milk.

If all you want is a light snack, you can just have a sandwich, then jump into the pool afterwards.

LOURMARIN

A colorful, bustling market is held every Thursday in Lourmarin. Albert Camus, author of *The Plague* and *The Stranger*, also happens to be buried in the cemetery here.

Lourmarin, a town of narrow, twisting little streets, is situated in the heart of the Luberon with its streams, cherry trees, and vineyards. Perched on a hillside overlooking the village is a relic of the Middle Ages, the 15th-century Château Vieux, to which elaborate fireplaces and staircases were added during the subsequent Renaissance period.

However, this peaceful village of the 21st century is very well aware of the ephemeral nature of pleasure: Indulging in a meal at the "Moulin de Lourmarin" is a wonderful, albeit fleeting, experience.

The chef de cuisine

When a sea urchin is offered unadorned and unaccompanied as a titbit to nibble on before the main course, when locally grown vegetables are enlivened by the wild herbs of the *garrigue*, when the leaves of nettles no longer sting and pine cones are found, not on the trees but on your plate, then you may be forgiven for wondering if the kitchen has been affected by a hint of creative madness.

Edouard Loubet, young, handsome, and gifted, whose establishment has twice been awarded stars by the *Guide Michelin*, performs daring experiments in his kitchen. Everything that can be said has already been said and written about his culinary art; namely that it

is impulsive, "delightful," incredibly "delicious," explosive, subtle, and magical.

His life story is told again and again. The pages of cooking magazines are full of stories about his happy and turbulent childhood and how he vacillated between the attractions of alpine skiing and the kitchen.

Edouard, an *enfant terrible*, left the mountains not realizing that he was going to swap his skis for a chef's hat, and his golden chamois emblem for Michelin stars. He went first to the United States, then to France's top chefs, Alain Chapel and Marc Veyrat.

Eventually, he acquired a magnificent mill dating from the 18th century, and located in the heart of the Luberon. Edouard has a pronounced weakness for the fragrances of this region and he enjoys trying to enhance them even more.

It is an extremely pleasant experience to sample Edouard Loubet's culinary expertise in the light, elegant dining room of the "Moulin de Lourmarin."

"Le Moulin de Lourmarin" not only symbolizes a joint enterprise between Edouard, as chef, his mother Claude Loubet as decorator and advisor, his grandparents, and the gardener, Adrien, but it also represents over 12 acres (5 ha) of cultivated land, including a five-acre (2 ha) vegetable garden. This is home to 60 different varieties of kitchen herbs, 50 fruit trees, 60 olive trees for the oil as well as old-fashioned types of vegetable. These often have unfamiliar or long-forgotten names but have a flavor worth investigating, such as *topinambour* (Jerusalem artichoke), *crosne* (Chinese artichoke), and *tétragone* (New Zealand spinach).

Edouard loves nature and feels at one with it. Perhaps that is why he enjoys creating aromatic, herb-based dishes, sunny and unpredictable in character and served in a casual, unfussy manner.

He uses a minimum of cream and no butter in his dishes, favoring instead cedar bark, grapes, burnet saxifrage, deadnettle leaves, and wild thyme. His is a very unusual cuisine featuring intriguing dishes such as goose liver sautéed in the caramelized juice of pine ratafia or poultry served with almond milk and fruits of the forest.

Eating in Edouard's restaurant means embracing mother earth, surrounding yourself with her fine aromas and eating all her fruits. It also means paying tribute to her and indulging in an unforgettable experience.

Each day, Edouard Loubet and his gardener proudly harvest vegetables from the restaurant's own garden.

Pommes de terre rôties au lard maigre et aux herbes relevées d'un gaspacho d'herbes, salade à l'huile de truffe

Potatoes with lean bacon and herbs, with herb gazpacho, salad, and truffle oil.

Serves 4

8 yellow, waxy potatoes (about the size of an egg)
8 slices of lean bacon
20 tender celery leaves
4 tbsp/50 g butter
1 tsp sugar
Salt and pepper

Gazpacho

About ¼ lb/130 g of ice cubes
Scant half cup/100 ml water
5 tbsp/70 g olive oil
1 tbsp/10 g fresh bread crumbs
1 tbsp/12 g celery leaves, finely chopped
About 4 oz/270 g Swiss chard leaves

Salad

3 tbsp oil
2 tbsp vinegar
8 lettuce hearts
2 truffles
Salt and pepper

Boil the potatoes with their skins on. Meanwhile, dice the bacon and mince the celery leaves. Heat the butter in a skillet, season with salt, and then add the sugar.

Allow this to caramelize, diluting with a little water. Sauté the pieces of bacon in this and add the celery leaves.

Cut the cooked potatoes in half, and remove the middles, filling the hole with the bacon mixture. Keep warm.

Mix together all the ingredients for the gazpacho.

Make the salad dressing by combining the oil, vinegar, salt, and pepper. Brush the truffles clean and carefully shave into thin slices.

Arrange four halves of potato, a small amount of gazpacho, and a little salad on each plate and sprinkle a few slices of truffle over the potatoes and round the plate.

Edouard Loubet's cuisine is uniquely sophisticated: Poultry and almond milk, which is seasoned with aromatic Provençal herbs.

Chateaubriand bien rassis et son jus fou d'herbes

Chateaubriand with herb sauce

Serves 4

½ lb/250 g puff pastry

1 bunch of marjoram

1 bunch of mint

1 bunch of savory

1 bunch of rosemary

4 filet mignon steaks (each weighing about 5 oz/150 g)

1 egg yolk, beaten

Salt and freshly milled pepper

Sauce

2 cups/½ liter vegetable stock

2 cups/½ liter beef stock

2 cups/½ liter red wine

2 tbsp/20 g cilantro

½ tsp cornstarch

Roll out the puff pastry into a very thin sheet. Cut out four circles large enough to accommodate a steak. Chop half the herbs very finely and divide between each of the pastry circles. Season the meat with salt and pepper and lay on the bed of herbs.

Pour the stock and the wine into a saucepan; finely chop the cilantro, add to the pan and bring to a boil, then leave to simmer over a low heat.

When the sauce has thickened, add the rest of the herbs and allow to stand with the lid on for seven minutes. Taste and thicken with a little cornstarch.

Fold the pastry over the steaks and seal edges firmly (the shape should resemble an old style purse, an *aumônière*). Brush the pockets with beaten egg yolk and cook for five minutes in a preheated oven at 480 °F/250 °C.

This dish is delicious served with gratin potatoes, seasoned perhaps with thyme, rosemary, and bay leaf and with a layer of melted cheese baked over the top.

A bakery and grocery store down memory lane

Both sides of the Rue Henri de Savourin are lined with shops. There is one shop in particular with the unusual name of "Super Taf Firmin" that is impossible to pass by. Here you find a veritable profusion of goods. It is unsurprising, therefore, that this little shop, instead of conforming to modern traditions, is more evocative of a bygone age. It simply cries out for closer inspection.

It is by no means unusual on a cold, wet November day to find delicious strawberries among the goods on display at "Super Taf." It sells everything conceivable to tempt the appetite and satisfy the most discerning palate. Even the owner can be seen indulging himself. Around breakfast time, when the croissants are still being crumbled at bistro tables, he cuts himself a fat slice of black blood sausage, which he eats with a hunk of baguette from the counter. As with any grocery store worth its salt, the freshly baked bread from the nearby bakery is also on sale here. The fridges are filled to capacity with different sausages – some of them homemade – and various drinks, including Lourmarin wines. You can find everything you need here either for a simple snack or an elaborate

"Super Taf": a store so filled to the brim with Provençal specialties that it defies any visitor to the area to pass by without stopping.

picnic. There is a delightful mingling of aromas: preserved olives, ripe fruit, and cheese that is sometimes meltingly ripe. Inside the store, customers jostle for space in a limited area, primarily reserved for the goods on sale.

A metal ladder outside the store looks as if it is doing the splits, but it is actually a good means of displaying the packaged hams hanging from its rungs.

Olive oils from nearby mills and baked goods from traditional local bakeries are all that is required to attract the customers: *fougasses* (flat rounds of bread) filled with bits of bacon, walnuts, olives, pizzas, cakes, the very fragrance of which tells you that they are not industrially manufactured,

"Super Taf" also sells pure, fresh pear juice which comes virtually straight from the tree.

golden brown croissants with almonds or pine kernels, *pains au chocolat* (a breakfast snack, made from croissant-type pastry and filled with chocolate), as well as the famous *gibassiers de Lourmarin* (yeast cake).

"Super Taf" is just like Ali Baba's cave, offering every conceivable means of satisfying the appetite, be it small or hearty. From a simple, delicious-smelling slice of ham to an entire haunch of Alpilles mutton, it will be selected and prepared for you by the owner himself adding the personal touch.

The smells are absolutely delicious. Fresh croissants with pine nuts, another sweet Provençal specialty to be found at "Super Taf."

You are spoilt for choice: Alongside golden brown *pains au chocolat* are tempting *chaussons* (similar to apple turnovers) filled with apple purée.

Aix-en-Provence

The Luberon recedes into the distance, giving way to the large towns of Salon, home of Nostradamus, and Aix-en-Provence.

Aix-en-Provence was once the capital of Provence. The impressionist painter Paul Cézanne (1839–1906) died and was buried here.

The elegant streets of Aix with its magnificent buildings and their imposing façades bear testimony to the wealth of the 17th and 18th centuries. The sun-filled squares, picturesque fountains, and shady

It is a long climb to the summit of Mont Sainte-Victoire, but the view is well worth the effort.

alleyways, on the other hand, are entirely typical of Provence.

Aix is a sophisticated town with an aristocratic background. It keeps its courtyards, its discreet stairways, and secret gardens hidden from prying eyes. It is a lively town with a host of cultural opportunities and numerous markets. Its café terraces draw hordes of visitors, especially in summer when it is very difficult even to find a seat. On public holidays, the cake and confectionery stores are simply not big enough to accommodate all the customers wanting to

The streets of Aix-en-Provence throng with people, especially in the high summer months.

sample the region's sweet specialties, such as *calissons* and other dainties made from almonds and honey. The residents of Aix-en-Provence stand in line along with visitors outside the delicatessen, which produces *pieds et pacquets,* small stuffed sheeps' feet that are unequalled.

Everyone has his own favorite store when it comes to buying *aioli* and *tapenade,* two other Provençal specialties. Aix-en-Provence is a gourmet's paradise and is particularly proud of the fact that it is home to one of the best restaurants in Provence, the "Clos de la Violette," which offers its guests a choice menu.

"Le Clos de la Violette"

Situated higher up the hillside in Aix, in a quiet street, "Le Clos de la Violette" is sheltered from the hectic bustle of the town. Time and time again nowadays you will hear it said that the "Clos" is the best restaurant in Provence.

Jean-Marc Banzo, a native of Vaison-la-Romaine, claims that he never strays far from home without a few twigs of thyme. In this way, the innovative chef of the "Clos de la Violette" never loses touch with his childhood since this herb embodies the fragrances of the *garrigue,* which he manages to impart so very

skillfully to his dishes. However, apart from giving expression to this yearning for home in his *tarte renversée de petits gris* (pasty filled with small snails) in rosemary sauce with garlic and thyme or in his herb vinaigrette with basil, he also possesses a wonderful gift for imbuing his dishes with particular aroma and unique flavor, like a magician standing at the stove and conducting – superbly successful – experiments in alchemy.

His choice of fresh produce, bought from one of the town's numerous markets, before being prepared to perfection is, in itself, evidence of his artistry.

On balmy summer evenings, the "Clos-de-la-Violette" pampers its guests beneath the chestnut trees on the terrace.

Biscuit friable de noisettes, framboises de pays et brousse battue à la vanille

Delicate cookies with hazelnuts, raspberries, and whipped cream cheese with vanilla

Serves 8

For the filling

4 sheets of gelatin (or 1 envelope of powdered)

Scant cup/200 g granulated sugar

4 egg yolks

Generous 1 lb/500 g Brousse (ricotta-type cheese)

Seeds from 4 vanilla pods

2 cups/500 ml of cream, whipped

Generous 1 lb/500 g raspberries

Cookies

³/₄ cups/160 g cup flour

Scant ³/₄ cup/160 g softened butter

¹/₂ cup/100 g roasted filberts, chopped

2 egg yolks

Icing

Generous 1 lb/500 g white chocolate

9 oz/300 g cooking chocolate

The day before: Soak the gelatin in warm water. Boil the sugar in a little water until the resulting syrup forms strands. Beat the egg yolk until frothy and add the syrup. Beat the mixture vigorously until it thickens, then add the gelatin. Mix in the soft cheese, the vanilla seeds and fold in the whipped cream. Shape the mixture into eight rounds (the best way to do this is to fill cookie rings) and refrigerate the rounds of mixture overnight.

Melt the white chocolate, then pour into rounds, ¹/₈-inch (2 mm) thick, using cookie rings as before. Refrigerate.

Mix the cookie ingredients together and knead to form a dough. Using a rolling pin, roll this out to a thickness of about a quarter of an inch (5 mm), then cut out circles to match the cookie rings. Bake these in a preheated oven at 350 °F/180 °C.

Scrape off flakes of cooking chocolate using a sharp knife. Lay the filbert cookies on a platter, place one of the little cheese cakes on top of each one, cover with raspberries, then a circle of white chocolate and finish off by decorating it with chocolate flakes.

Sanguettes de pigeon en éclatée aux herbes fraîches Croûte de blette à l'anchois et aux aromates

*Pigeon in its own juices
with fresh herbs
Swiss chard on a pastry base with
anchovies and herbs*

Serves 8

About ½ lb/200 g plain pastry

1 tsp thyme

Filling

Generous 1 lb/500 g Swiss
chard stalks

Generous ½ lb/250 g Swiss
chard leaves

2 tsp olive oil

1 clove of garlic, finely chopped

1 finely chopped onion

½ cup/100 g chopped anchovies

1 tsp chopped parsley

1 tsp chopped tarragon

½ cup/100 g capers

Salt

8 wild pigeons
(each about 1 lb/400g)

2 tbsp oil

1 clove of garlic, chopped

2 shallots, chopped

Scant ½ cup balsamic vinegar

2 tbsp chopped parsley

Salt and pepper

Roll the pastry and sprinkle with thyme. Cut circles measuring just over three inches (8 cm) across and bake in a pre-heated oven for 30–40 minutes at 350 °F/180 °C. Blanch the Swiss chard stalks and leaves in boiling salted water, drain.

Gently sauté one of the chopped garlic cloves and the onion in olive oil, add the anchovies, then add the vegetables. Cover and simmer for several minutes before draining off any liquid. Add the herbs and capers and season with salt to taste. Arrange in the middle of the pastry circles.

In an ovenproof dish, sauté the pigeons on all sides in hot oil. Cook for another seven to eight minutes in a preheated oven at 400 °F/200 °C. Remove from the oven and allow to stand a while before removing the drumsticks and the breast fillets.

Cut the leftover bloody carcass into pieces and put through a poultry press, if you have one, to extract as much juice as possible from the bird.

Gently sauté the garlic and shallots in a roasting pan, pour in the vinegar, and bring to the boil before adding the pigeon juices. Bring back to the boil to thicken. Add the parsley and season with salt and pepper. Keep the sauce hot. Cook the pigeons in the oven until they are done. Place the drumsticks on the pastry circles, arranging the fillets around them, finally pouring the very hot sauce over the meat.

PAUL CÉZANNE

Cézanne was born in Aix-en-Provence on January 19, 1839. His father, a successful milliner, had great ambitions for his son from an early age. In 1852, Paul entered the Collège Bourbon (today it is called the Lycée Mignet), where, like his friend Émile Zola, he underwent a religious and humanist education. Young Cézanne roamed the countryside around Aix with his friend Zola, climbing up to the summit of Mont Sainte-Victoire. As a native of Provence, he had already fallen under the spell of the landscape, the scents, and the famous "light of the South." He delighted in them and was insatiable for them. At the age of 14, he attended the non-fee-paying drawing school in his home town where he distin-guished himself by winning second prize in a painting competition.

During his younger years, Cézanne spent his life commuting between Paris and Aix-en-Provence. He final-ly returned to the south of France for good in 1881.

His father, who had meanwhile gone into bank-ing, did not think much of his son's artistic abili-ties and put his name down to study law when he was 19. Around this time, his parents' fortune was considerably increased by a substantial legacy; in the form of Le Jas de Bouffan, an estate situated a short distance from Aix. Cézanne, who came to love this country resi-dence, was to paint it again and again in later

years. In 1861, he dared to break free of his father's influ-ence: He fulfilled his dream by moving to Paris, where Zola was awaiting him. When he failed to be accepted at the École des Beaux-Arts, he returned to Aix. From then on he worked in his father's firm although, during the ensuing years, he kept shuttling back and forth between Paris, where he became firm friends with painters who were later to become known as the Impres-sionists, and Aix, which contin-ued to be a steady and strong inspiration to him.

At the start of the Franco-Pruss-ian War in 1870, Cézanne fled to L'Estaque, which proved to be the inspiration for a major series of paintings (27 alto-gether), including *La mer à L'Estaque*, bought by Picasso in 1940. Later on, he left his native Provence yet again to meet Pissarro in Auvers-sur-Oise. From 1881 onward, however, Cézanne remained in the south where he was always hap-piest. He was visited by his friends: Renoir worked with him on the L'Estaque theme, staying at Jas de Bouffan, and Monet came to visit him in Aix.

Obsessed by the untamed power of light in Provence and the contrasts it produced, Cézanne

turned again and again to the subject of Mont Sainte-Victoire. He simply could not leave this theme alone. He would roam the Arc valley, weighting his easel down with a stone when the mistral was at its worst, and paint the majestic mountain range from where he stood. "I paint what I see, what I feel," he said. On an October day in 1906, he was overtaken by an unexpected

Paul Cézanne loved nature and the light of his native Provence. He was almost obsessed with the Mont Sainte-Victoire theme.

thunderstorm, yet remained where he was in the rain to capture the scene he loved so much. He contracted pneumonia which, on October 23, 1906, finally claimed the life of this "mysterious native of Provence."

Vegetables of Provence

Any region that can boast traditional dishes such as ratatouille, pistou soup, salad Niçoise, aïoli, and stuffed small vegetables, must have an abundance of such produce to hand. Provence is a very fertile region which, every spring, produces a profusion of top-quality early vegetables. Provence's markets provide endless evidence of its fertile soil – as well as bearing testimony to the efforts of the people who cultivate it. Each day, the farmers and agricultural workers bring their harvests to town. The squares, streets, and alleyways are alive with the constant coming and going of delivery trucks, the familiar clattering of tables being set up, the same echoing voices calling to each other, and the joyous sound of ringing laughter.

In addition to the herbs, there are flowers and sun-ripened fruits, not to mention the vegetables, still damp with morning dew, mischievously flaunting their tender age. One look at these and there is no need to elaborate on the familiar expression "Good enough to eat."

First the tomatoes: Full and firm though they may be, a few grains of salt do not come amiss in order to allow the full flavor of the fruit to develop.

No summer is complete without fresh, juicy, red tomatoes: They provide the finishing touch to salads, sauces, soups and, of course, the famous ratatouille.

Purple artichokes are the best: Serve with a little olive oil and just a suggestion of lemon juice to bring out their flavor fully.

The tomato is actually a newcomer to Provence: It was introduced during the 17th century – today the region produces 40 percent of domestic production – and quickly became an integral part of Mediterranean cuisine. It has a unique flavor and is second to none when it comes to appearing at table at every possible opportunity. Small cherry tomatoes are good for serving with an aperitif, sliced cherry tomatoes are ideal in a salad. They are good for stuffing and can be made into tomato paste. In days gone by, tomatoes were used in a very basic sort of starter, and were served with just a little chopped parsley. Nowadays, the tomato hardly ever appears without mozzarella and basil. Oh yes, it has some very important qualities indeed, one of them being its ability to ripen on a window sill, quite a long way from the plant that nurtured it.

Beware of its temperamental side though: It can sometimes be very sour in cooked dishes and some diets expressly advise against using it in any form.

Then, there is the purple artichoke: the "I am dressed in nothing" variety, but more discreet. With a few of its outer leaves removed, it can be enjoyed very simply with a little salt. Some lemon juice and the same amount of olive oil turn the small artichoke into one of Provence's starters: A little bigger and the best way to discover the melting delicacy of its heart and leaves is by cooking it in a pressure cooker.

A bit expensive, but nevertheless a delicious side-dish: Zucchini flowers are delicious stuffed or when turned into *beignets*.

Another particularly tasty dish is aubergine caviar, which can be nibbled along with an aperitif and toasted slices of rustic bread.

Bell peppers, green, yellow, and red and sometimes as thick as two hands, are among the main constituents of the dish: ratatouille.

Mange-touts are called *pois gourmands* in France. These peas are very tender and delicious, and are a real delight for the gourmet.

And what about the zucchini? Its true greatness is only revealed after a few drops of hot olive oil in a skillet have turned it into a delectable vegetable with a mild, delicate flavor. It is by no means a boring vegetable even though it may appear so at first glance. There is one particular variety to be found in Provence, and in Nice in particular, the delicious *petite ronde*, which is especially good for stuffing. The delicate zucchini flowers when fried into beignets (fritters) are also really delicious no matter what the variety.

The eggplant with its purple exterior is very adaptable and can be put to a number of different uses. It may be wrapped in light pastry or stuffed, or even turned into eggplant "caviar." The white-fleshed eggplant from the south has surprisingly delicate flesh.

The eggplant, like its companion the bell pepper, be it red, green, or yellow, is not content with merely being a constituent part of ratatouille. It is equally delicious broiled, sprinkled with a little olive oil and seasoned with garlic. Fennel, too, is popular, eaten either uncooked or with *anchoïade* in the typical Provençal manner.

Before the cultivated asparagus season gets underway, it is worth sampling its cousin, wild asparagus. This variety is as thin as macaroni and as long as a knitting needle and is made into delicious soups and flavorsome omelets. Most city dwellers have never heard of it, but people in the south are familiar with it and like to pick themselves a bunch of it in the springtime.

Another Provençal vegetable that is so small, smooth, and delicately green that there hardly seems any need to cook it is the broad bean. It is delicious just as it is, plain, with a few radishes and a little salt as an accompaniment to an aperitif

If you want to be a little bit more adventurous, try scallions or tender onions that are finely chopped, salted, and, it goes without saying, sprinkled with a little olive oil.

Provence's garden of vegetables goes on forever: beans, green, red, or scarlet runner beans

for pistou soup; carrots, cauliflower, beet, and cucumbers with *aïoli*; spinach or Swiss chard in pasties from Nice, sugar beet and ordinary peas, not to mention the numerous kinds of lettuce varieties. The lettuce grown in the Provence and Côte d'Azur region constitutes almost half the national production. And it is rare for southern dining tables not to include a salad with the meal. Hardly any dressing is needed and it is usually left just to develop its natural flavor. A particular favorite is *mesclun*, a salad consisting of mixed leaves and herbs, for example arugula, dandelion leaves, and cress. There are mountains of all these tender, crisp, mild, or bitter types of lettuce available at the market.

Occasionally a little garlic is added to the vinaigrette. Garlic, in white or pink bulbs, bound in thick strands or bunches, comes in many different shapes and sizes. What's more, it really does typify southern cuisine, either as part of the vegetable accompaniment, or as a vegetable in its own right.

It is not only fresh vegetables and food produce that are on sale at Provence's markets. Flower lovers can also make lucky finds: These rose buds have a wonderful scent.

A "calisson" – a sweet tooth's dream

The story goes that *calissons d'Aix* first made their appearance in 1473 for the wedding of King René. The king's chef, troubled by the sad expression of the future queen, apparently created them especially for her.

It is also said that they take their shape from the ships that once sailed the oceans, or perhaps from the weaver's shuttle that fishermen used to repair their nets. Then again, it may have been modeled on the mandorla surrounding the figures of Christ in Cistercian abbeys. Perhaps that is why Pope Pius V was so fond of *calissons*. Alternatively, they could simply be based on the shape of an almond, their main ingredient. However, regardless of whether the inspiration for these oval sweetmeats was earthly or divine, *calissons* are above all else a Provençal specialty produced in Aix from ground almond paste and candied fruits.

It is no simple matter becoming a *calissonier*, and a great deal of skill is required to make a *calisson* which, despite its rather pale exterior, will melt in the mouth, unlocking a delicious flavor. When you bite into a *calisson*, you expect to meet resistance, but surprisingly, encounter softness instead. Beneath the glistening sugar coating is an almond paste that is made from sweet and bitter almonds, combined with the paste is the sweet and sour flavor of candied fruit.

Some people maintain that since the *calisson* contains 99 percent almonds and candied melon, all that the tiny percentage of honey or other ingredients does is to foment arguments between the different confectioners, who believe this one percent makes all the difference. But with or without "that little extra," with or without candied oranges, mandarins, or apricots, depending on the season, it is the confectioner's magician-like skills which turn the *calissons* into a true delight. Melon is crystallized by first blanching it in boiling water and then cooking it in a light sugar syrup. It spends an entire month undergoing repeated boilings and coolings until it is removed to be pounded and mixed with ground almonds. The consistency of the mixture must be perfect. It then has to cook for a further 90 minutes and then be set aside for two to four days.

The *calissons* are nearing the final stages of preparation: The work surface is covered with

There are mountains of candies on display in this store, including *calissons*, crystallized fruits, and chocolate.

rice paper, on which is laid a template of lozenge-shaped molds into which the mixture is poured. A *calisson* should weigh no more than half an ounce (10–14 g). Finally, the lozenges are coated with a thin layer of sugar glaze. The rest of the procedure is done mechanically. The *calissons* go into the drying oven, then, once they are cooled, they are packaged into eye-catching little boxes or cellophane bags for display in shop windows. *Calissons* with the Appellation d'Aix-en-Provence are only genuine if they are made within the town.

So many myths have been woven around *Calissons*, which feature prominently at Christmas. They are one of the 13 traditional desserts that grace a Provençal Christmas table. To describe them simply as marzipan does not do justice to their unique flavor.

Sugar syrup is added to the fruit and almond paste until the consistency is just right.

Candied melons from Apt are the main ingredient of Appellation Aix-en-Provence *calissons*.

Blanched almonds, most of them locally grown, are added next.

The candied fruit and almonds are pulverized together in a processor.

The fruit and almonds remain in the processor until a very stiff mixture has formed.

The sugar syrup is boiled separately before being added. It acts as a natural preservative.

The 13 Christmas desserts

The 13 Christmas desserts are supposed to symbolize Christ and the Twelve Apostles at the Last Supper. They are the culmination of what is still very much a traditional meal. The differences between a Provençal Christmas table and what is customary in the rest of France are immediately apparent in the table decorations. In Provence, three white tablecloths overlap each other, symbolizing the Holy Trinity. Candlesticks complete the arrangement. As far as the food is concerned, it is true to say that Provence is a law unto itself. Some traditional dishes, like vegetable fondue with anchovies or dried salt fish, various Provençal cheeses, followed by cakes and fruit are "obligatory." These are accompanied by sweet dessert wines from Rasteau or a Beaumes-de-Venise Muscat. So, what is the story behind these 13 Christmas desserts which exclude cream and candies from the table?

To start with, there are the four *mendiants* (mendicant monks): raisins, the amber color of which is reminiscent of a Dominican monk's habit, dried figs, almonds, and hazelnuts or filberts, symbolizing the Franciscan, Carmelite and Augustinian monks.

Then come fresh seasonal fruits, usually apples, pears, mandarins, or oranges, occasionally melons or grapes. Depending on local traditions and personal taste, these can be followed by nuts or other dried fruits, such as dates or prunes, or possibly, candied fruits and quince bread.

Next comes the white, softer-type nougat, followed by black nougat with its harder consistency, accompanied by a few *calissons d'Aix*.

A magnificent *gibassier* provides the grand finale to this banquet. This is a yeast cake enriched with eggs, flavored with lemon and orange peel and a little orange blossom water. It is still as soft and sweet as in the days when the baker used to give it to his customers as a seasonal gift. It is traditional to break the *gibassier* into pieces instead of cutting it.

January is the traditional month for honoring the Three Wise Men and, once again, the festivities are accompanied by sinful sweetmeats. The *galette des Rois*, or Epiphany cake, is on sale everywhere and is often served with coffee during a family get-together. Sometimes, it is made of puff pastry and filled with almond cream, or it can take the form of a yeast cake ring filled with candied fruit and sprinkled with sugar crystals. The latter version is the one preferred in the south of France. Traditionally, it is supposed to contain a lucky charm, such as a little porcelain figure depicting a particular trade or a biblical figure.

Candied fruits, white and black nougat, seasonal fruit, all kinds of almonds and nuts – these, together with *calissons* from Aix-en-Provence, are some of Provence's 13 traditional Christmas desserts.

Nougat

Nougat glacé au miel
Iced nougat with chestnut honey

Serves 10

¼ cup/50 g chopped almonds
1 generous cup/250 g sugar
12 egg yolks
5 level tbsp/150 g chestnut honey
3 cups/750 ml of whipping cream
2 tsp/10 ml water
Selection of fresh fruit

First of all, make the brittle. Put a scant ½ cup (100 g) sugar in a pan together with three tablespoons of water and heat until the syrup becomes a golden color and reaches about 320 °F/160 °C. Then add the chopped almonds and mix well, heating for a further minute. Pour the mixture onto a greased baking tray and spread it out in an even layer. Leave until set.

Beat the egg yolks until light and frothy. Heat the honey, the remaining sugar, and water to 250 °F (120 °C) then add to the egg yolks, stirring constantly. Leave to cool.

Break the brittle up into small pieces, whisk the cream until very thick, then carefully mix all the ingredients together using a wooden spoon.

Put the mixture into a freezerproof mold lined with plastic wrap and freeze for twelve hours until the mixture is of solid ice cream consistency (after five hours it should be set). Before serving, tip the block of nougat out of the mold and peel off the plastic wrap.

Cut the nougat ice cream into slices with a knife dipped in hot water and decorate with fresh fruits, such as kiwi fruit, or strawberries, and serve immediately.

First of all, make the brittle, chopping it up very finely once it has hardened.

Honey, sugar, and a little water are thoroughly mixed together in a pan.

Slowly heat this syrupy mixture to 250 °F (120 °C).

Beat the egg yolks until soft and frothy, then add the mixture of honey and sugar.

The ingredients must be thoroughly blended into a homogenous, very creamy consistency.

Now it is time to add the finely chopped brittle, stirring well to ensure even distribution.

The stiffly whipped cream is then folded in and the nougat placed in a freezer mold lined with plastic wrap.

After a few hours in the freezer, the nougat is set and can be tipped out of the mold.

Cut the nougat into slices using a knife that has been heated in hot water.

THE CRIB FIGURES OF THE FOUQUE STUDIO

With his coat undone and his body bent into the wind, the aged shepherd is leaning on his crook, making little headway. He is clinging onto his wide-brimmed hat with one hand. This old man is one of the figures that form part of a typical Provençal nativity scene. A great deal of skill and craftsmanship goes into the making of these figures and each one says something about everyday life. The "Coup de Mistral," as this old man is called, seems to bear the whole burden of human existence on his shoulders and is by far the most poignant of all the crib figures. The "Coup de Mistral" was created by Paul Fouque over 50 years ago.

In the Fouque family, this craft of making crib figures is handed down from generation to generation: The son, like his father, is a *santonnier*. A world of poetry is contained within the family's workshop with its cameos of everyday life captured in clay. Comprising 1,800 figures, it is the world's largest collection of crib figures.

The history of the crib figures begins in 1223, when St Francis of Assisi first introduced a model of a scene depicting the birth of Christ. During the 16th century, crib scenes also began to appear in churches. During the French Revolution, however, churches were closed and these holy figures or *petits saints* (little saints) – in

The clay miniatures are meticulously retouched with a fine brush and liquid clay. They then disappear for some time into drying rooms before being fired and eventually painted, a task which demands skill and precision on the part of the craftsmen.

Provençal, *santouns* – were given refuge in private households. The first crib figure market was held in Marseille in 1803, since which time the city's famous Canebière market of crib figures has become an annual pre-Christmas event.

To fashion a crib figure, you first have to prepare the clay by kneading it with a little water until it is soft and carefully removing any impurities. The resulting clay should be as smooth as possible. It is then stored in a cool cellar for one year before the *santonnier* molds it into a figure, from which he then also makes a plaster cast. The first figure, the "mother figure," is used to make a second identical figure, which can be used to make additional copies.

The little figurines are carefully removed from their molds for the *santonnier* to put the final

The little crib figures represent many different walks of life. Their clothing is accurately depicted down to the smallest detail. They can be bought at a special market on the main Canebière thoroughfare in Marseille.

touches to them. After being retouched and polished, they spend eight weeks in drying rooms. Drying them too quickly would invariably lead to the appearance of cracks.

Firing the figures helps to make them robust as well as durable. The temperature is allowed to climb slowly to 1,760 °F (960 °C) and is then reduced just as slowly until the kiln is completely cold. The fragile figures are then removed with the utmost care.

They must then undergo a further session of treatment. This final, though no less important, step can take hours, or even days, and requires painstaking care: The *santonnier* paints the figures one by one, highlighting a flower on a figure's clothing here, a mustache there or perhaps a hat ribbon.

The little saints are in this way finally transformed into ornaments.

CHÂTEAU SIMONE

The small winegrowing estate of Palette, which has had its own Appellation d'Origine since 1948, is only about 70 acres (30 ha) in size and produces around 19,800 gallons (750 hl) of wine each year. Two thirds of this is red wine, while whites and reds make up the rest. The Appellation only encompasses two districts, Meyreuil and Tholonet, and two vineyards, Château Crémade and Château Simone, but what it lacks in size, it makes up for in quality.

However, without wishing to diminish the significance of the former, it is undoubtedly the latter which deserves to be labeled a great wine. The vineyards are on a north/northeastern slope 650 feet (200 m) above sea level which affords them natural protection against bad weather. The chalky soil boasts established vinestocks, some of them a hundred years old. These factors provide ideal conditions for producing outstanding wines, although credit is due also to the skill of the vintner and his dedication to traditional winegrowing and maintaining an ecological balance.

The three wines of this Appellation are all matured in oak barrels. The reds mature within three years and are then decanted into bottles without filtering. These wines are extremely good for laying down. The 2001 vintage, for example, is now just right for enjoying with game birds, but it could easily be left for another ten years in the wine cellar. The rosé wines, like the reds, of this Appellation, are comprised of ten varieties of grape, the most important of these being Cinsault, Grenache and Mourvèdre. These, too, can easily be stored for some time, like the 1995 vintage, which goes very well with broiled fish dishes.

The shimmering golden white wines, produced mainly from Clairette, as well as Ugni Blanc and Muscat grapes, are outstanding. Their full-bodied and unusual character adds to their potentially complex flavor and they can be laid down for a long period – in the case of the 1996 vintage, for over 20 years. Basically, this Appellation produces very elegant, aromatic wines which are among the best of Provence.

These dusty bottles contain exceptional wines. The reds and whites both age well, becoming more complex as they mature.

You can sample or buy any of the excellent wines of the Palette Appellation d'Origine Contrôlée during a visit to the Château Simone.

THE ALPS OF HAUTE PROVENCE

The Alps of Haute Provence are an absolute paradise for butterflies. One thousand three hundred species, including some extremely rare varieties, live out their brief lives here. In summer, the air is filled with their shimmering colors. There are very few large towns in this region and it derives its main income from agriculture, tourism, and local crafts.

From Manosque to the other side of Barcelonnette in the Ubaye valley, from the Gorges du Verdon to the Gap basin, the Alps are Mediterranean in character, with sun-baked mountains under a dome of clear blue sky, lashed by the mistral which sweeps across them. These are mountains in the proper sense of the word, catering for winter sports during the winter months and providing a habitat for chamois and mountain goats on their rocky crags.

In summer, when the lavender and thyme are in bloom, there is cool shade to be found beneath the larches higher up the mountainside. Storms are a frequent occurrence in

Provence as we imagine it: Waves of fragrant, purple lavender flowers stretching away far toward the distant Provençal mountains.

autumn, although the storms are quickly forgotten when the sun reappears. The countryside looks particularly beautiful once the skies have cleared after a heavy downpour. The quality of light is wonderful as it falls on the forested slopes, tinged with the reddish brown colors of late autumn.

Forcalquier has always profited from the rich abundance of the Lure mountains, a natural habitat for a wide variety of plants. Valerian, belladonna, angelica, gentians, and artemisia grow there in large quantities. It is a natural garden producing all the herbs needed to make pastis. This region of remote villages, surrounded by green mountains, is also home to Jean Giono, the writer.

Farther north are the Sisteron hills, famed for the lambs that graze there and the delicious meat they produce. The local population enjoys it all year round, prepared in a variety of ways. Isolated sheep pens are scattered all over the hills and valleys of the region and the pastures are grazed by long-horned goats whose milk is turned into a delicious fresh cheese. One of these excellent goat cheeses is called *Banon de Banon*.

FORCALQUIER

Built on a hill between the high plateaux of the Luberon, the Lure mountains, and the Durance river, Forcalquier is an appealing little town, steeped in history.

A brief history of pastis

While there is nothing whatsoever wrong with kir in its many forms, one thing is certain: Whether you are on the south coast or in northern France, pastis must surely be the most typical aperitif found in French bistros. And rightly so, if you consider how much the *petit jaune* ("little yellow drink") has had to endure to gain its place at the bar.

Two hundred and fifty years ago, a liqueur called "vinum silatum" was created from fennel and wormwood (absinthe) to quench the thirst of folk in the Mediterranean region. Its more recent history, however, begins in 19th-century France.

In 1805, Henri-Louis Pernod, a distiller, settled in Pontarlier, near the Swiss frontier. Each day, his distilleries produced around four gallons (16 liters) of a herb-based spirit with a very high alcohol content. This drink, which became very popular with the French, was known as *Fée verte* or absinthe.

During the colonial wars in 1830, absinthe was handed out to French soldiers suffering from dysentery. The drink had a medicinal effect, and at the same time satisfied the soldiers' thirst and helped them to endure the rigors of war. It is hardly surprising that the soldiers developed a taste for it and continued to enjoy their absinthe long after they returned home to France. And the people, full of pride for their soldiers, followed suit.

Drinking absinthe entailed a special ritual which further enhanced the experience. Water was poured onto some sugar on a perforated spoon – often a beautiful silver specimen. The water trickled through into a crystal glass containing absinthe, which gradually turned cloudy and lost its greenish tinge.

Countless varieties of herbs and medicinal plants grow in the Forcalquier region.

One part pastis is mixed with four to five parts of ice-cold water. (A real connoisseur would eschew ice cubes.) Adding water to the clear, shimmering greenish-colored pastis releases the aniseed flavor and turns the liquid into a cloudy mixture.

From around 1860 onward, absinthe began to increase in popularity and was a favorite of both workers and artists alike. Its 72 percent alcohol content made it a very potent brew, often with devastating consequences. Alcoholism increased and this legendary tipple, which had inspired no lesser men that Paul Verlaine, Arthur Rimbaud, Vincent van Gogh, and Pablo Picasso, fell into disrepute. In 1915, absinthe-based spirits were banned in France – a decision that embraced all aniseed-flavored alcoholic aperitifs.

Distillers were very reluctant to accept this. They joined forces and, after five years of protests, managed to get the government to revoke its ban on aniseed-flavored aperitifs with the proviso that no absinthe would be produced with an alcohol content exceeding 30 percent.

It was not until 1938, following years of administrative and legal toing and froing, that pastis was again permitted an alcohol content of 45 percent. The producers were content since this was precisely the amount needed for the aniseed flavor to achieve its full potential.

The story does not end there, however. Absinthe was to be banned yet again. A century

after being handed out to French soldiers on account of its fortifying properties, it was blamed during World War II for actually undermining the troops' fighting morale and thereby helping to bring about the country's defeat. This ban did not remain in force for very long, however. By 1951, pastis was once again being served in French bars.

Pastis and its extended family

As its etymological roots suggest – "pastis" means mixture – the individual types of pastis are the result of different and quite distinct combinations. It is no wonder, therefore, that the individual aniseed-flavored aperitifs can vary considerably in taste.

At the beginning of the 20th century, a descendant of Henri-Louis Pernod opened distilleries in the Jura region. This is where *Pontarlier* was

Everyone has their particular favorite brand of pastis. One of the most popular is *Ricard*, made since 1932.

first produced, the father of an entire family of pastis drinks. In 1932, Paul Ricard created his "genuine Marseille pastis" (*vrai Pastis de Marseille*) and in 1951, Paul Pernod entered the arena with his *Pernod 51*. Names like *Berger, Duval, Casanis, Pec, Paulanis, Janot* soon followed suit.

As the number of new varieties grew, so, too, did the terminology surrounding the *petit jaune*, a command of which distinguishes the layman from the connoisseur. You first ask

the barman for your usual brand, in other words, a *Casa* or a *51*. If the bartender already knows your preference, you simply ask for a shot of *jaune* or *pastaga*. Then, you have to refine your request: *flanc* means neat pastis without water, *momie* means just a half measure of the desired label, and *102* signifies a double Pernod 51.

There are no limits to the imagination as far as flavor and color are concerned. You can have a *mauresque*, a *perroquet* (parrot), or a *feuille morte* (dead leaf), depending on whether the pastis is mixed with almond, peppermint, or pomegranate syrup, or with a combination of all three.

Whatever your choice, ice-cold water is added to the pastis in the ratio of four (or five) to one. The water releases the aniseed flavor and causes the milky cloudiness typical of this drink. Ice cubes are not recommended as the temperature shock would be too great and cause the aniseed essence to flocculate and lose its flavor.

The pastis bestsellers' list

Commanding 35 percent of the domestic market is *Ricard*, the leading pastis in France, well ahead of Pernod and *Pastis 51* (9.7 percent), *Duval* (6.5 percent), *Berger* (1.3 percent), *Henri Bardouin* (0.5 percent), and *Janot* (0.3 percent). These sales statistics also reflect the preference of consumers in the south of France for *Ricard* and *Pernod 51* over all other available varieties.

Of all the *petits jaunes* available at French bars, only the *Bardouin*, *Pernod*, *Janot*, and *Cristal* labels are 100 percent Provençal in origin.

How traditional pastis is produced

During the Middle Ages, traveling apothecaries used to visit the Lure mountains around Forcalquier to stock up on their supplies of medicinal plants which they would then generally distill. During the 17th and 18th centuries, their descendants settled in the surrounding towns and opened herb stores. During the 19th century, the original medieval herb vendors had evolved into pharmacists, schnapps distillers, and, by the early 20th century, liqueur and aperitif manufacturers. Today's pastis manufacuture is a legacy of that tradition from the Lure mountains.

The history of "Provence's distilleries and estates" (*Distilleries et Domaines de Provence*) includes the story of one man's affinity for the mountains and plants of his native land: Henri Bardouin, born in Forcalquier in 1908, was fascinated by the medicinal plants that grew in the region. He used to enjoy trying out fresh combinations of herbs and spices. He loved his job as a distiller and put the skills handed down from his forefathers to good use in his work. Today, *Henri Bardouin* pastis is considered one of the best so-called traditional pastis, in other words, one distilled according to traditional methods.

1 Mint – **2** Birch leaves – **3** Corn – **4** Vervain – **5** Sapwood – **6** Licorice – **7** Camomile – **8** Blackcurrant leaves (cassis leaves) – **9** Poppy seeds – **10** Thyme – **11** Coriander – **12** Parsley – **13** Cinnamon – **14** Star anise – **15** Fennel – **16** Savory – **17** Cumin – **18** Aniseed seeds

The mountains around Forcalquier boast 1,700 species of wild plants – a paradise for medicinal herb collectors. Some of the flowers and herbs used in pastis are gathered here, although precisely which ones remains a closely guarded secret. Sometimes native herbs are combined with exotic ones: artemisia, centaury, hyssop, thyme, savory, and sage are mixed with maniguette from Equatorial Africa, star anise from China, cardamon from India, cinnamon from Sri Lanka, tonka beans from South America, nutmeg and cloves from the Moluccas.

The traditional pastis flavor comes from a combination of over 50 plants and spices. The various stages in its manufacture must be followed religiously and meticulous attention paid to the precise quantities of herbs used. It is also essential for certain combinations of herbs to be steeped together.

The plants are left to infuse in alcohol for about two to four weeks. They are then pressed, and the essence is combined with the distilled solid residue.

Petits pains d'anis
Small aniseed rolls

Generous 2 cups/500 g sugar	
Generous 2 cups/500 g flour	
4 egg whites	
1 oz/25 g green aniseed	
1 pinch of salt	

Knead all the ingredients together and roll out the dough with a rolling pin to a thickness of at least ¼ inch (6 mm) thick. Cut out small circles and bake at a low temperature in the oven for 12 to 15 minutes.

The Fortified Village of Banon

About fifteen miles (25 km) northwest of For-calquier, the D 950 winds through the green, forested foothills of the Lure mountains before reaching Banon. This medieval village is situated on the Albion plateau, surrounded by fields of lavender and heathland.

Anyone wanting to visit Banon will have to expend a bit of energy. Its fortified walls, a relic of the village's medieval past, are built in tiers into the side of the mountain. The steep streets are lined with some magnificent buildings, their former grandeur evident in their ancient portals and ornate sculptures.

Banon has one small shopping street where you can

> **Key facts about Banon cheese**
>
> **Surname:** de Banon
> **First name:** Banon
> **Place of birth:** Banon
> **Age:** 5–20 days
> **Size:** about 3 in (7–8 cm) in diameter
> **Weight:** around 4 oz/100 g
> **Distinguishing features:** strong taste, creamy consistency

Medieval Banon, a small village with typical Provençal charm, is very famous for its goat cheese, known as *Tomme de Banon*.

buy everything you need to get you through the winter. In the small village square with its telephone kiosk is a food store, and on the outskirts of the village there is a cheese making establishment.

Banon cheese

Thirty years ago, Romain Ripert started farming goats at the foot of the Lure mountains, using their milk to make cheese. He was the indisputed heir to a centuries-old tradition, whose secrets have been carefully passed from one generation to another. Ripert's cheese became so popular that he was soon obliged to expand his operation and settle in Banon. His *Banon de Banon*, one of the region's typical local products and a registered trademark, is considered one of the best cheeses in France. Meanwhile, the Banon dairy, which Romain Ripert sold in 1995, has tripled its turnover.

The milk for *Banon de Banon* comes from superior breeds of goat, like Roves or Communes, which produce extra rich milk. Goat farmers have been trying to introduce more of these breeds back into the region.

At present, it is mainly the Alpine chamoisées and the

Saanen blanches breeds that provide milk for the cheese. Each day, the dairy collects over 800 US gallons (3,000 liters) of milk from its 18 producers in the region. Three times a month spot checks are carried out on milk samples which are then examined in a reputable laboratory to determine the milk's bacteriological and chemical properties and ascertain its protein and fat content. Nothing is left to chance in Banon. The dairy voluntarily pays over the odds for the milk so that the producers will meet the strict requirements. The producers are not allowed, for example, to feed the goats on grass which has been stored in silos or on genetically modified cereals. Instead, the animals must be allowed to graze freely on pasture land.

Once the milk is collected, it is heated to 84–88 °F/29–31 °C, enriched with rennin and placed in basins to curdle. The cheesemaker then scoops the resulting curds into cheese sieves to drain off the watery whey.

Then comes the next and crucial step: The curds are skillfully turned by hand, once in the cheese sieve and again on a wire mesh sheet. It is then salted by hand. They become increasingly solid in consistency and gradually assume the traditional shape of the cheese. It will then spend four to six weeks ripening in the drying chamber. It is traditionally sprinkled with pepper and savory which promotes the growth of microorganisms. These, in turn, help the cheese to mature properly.

Eventually it is time to put the finishing touches to the cheese and dress it in its final apparel. In the autumn, when the leaves begin to fall, chestnut leaves are collected from the forests of the Corrèze, Ardèche, and Haute Provence. Not just any leaf will do – the leaves should only just have fallen from the tree and be virginal, so-to-speak, untrodden by animal or human foot. Around three million leaves are collected in this way for the cheesemaking industry. They are stored in wire baskets and soaked in vinegar baths to make them smooth and kill off any bacteria. Each little cheese is wrapped by hand in five or six chestnut leaves and tied with a length of Madagascan raffia.

These goats are a feature of Banon, supplying excellent milk for an excellent cheese.

Provençal cheeses

There are numerous superior goat and sheep milk cheeses in Provence in addition to *Banon de Banon*. Some are natural, and some contain herbs; they can be dry or preserved in oil. They include the light and creamy *brousse*, which can be served with scallions or with a spoonful of honey as a dessert, *Tomme* in its fresh or dried form, the famed *Crotins* which are perfect for broiling, as well as *Cabécous*, and *Picodons*, which are smaller and have a sharper taste.

The cheese is removed from the drying chamber and is wrapped in chestnut leaves. The tannic acid contained in these leaves lends it additional flavor.

Originally this coating of leaves was merely intended to preserve the cheese. However, the tannic acid contained in them actually penetrates the cheese and gives it an additional distinctive flavor.

The *Banon de Banon*, of which there are many poor imitations, is a truly delicious cheese. Depending on how ripe it is, it can be creamy with a distinctly milky flavor or sharper, with a slightly sour taste, but still creamy and delicate. Enjoy it on a slice of rustic bread, accompanied by a semidry, white *Châteauneuf* – the perfect way to bring out the complexity of the cheese.

Banon, home of Maurice Melchio's food store

Even from the street outside, Maurice's food store exerts a unique fascination. There is no hint of modern design here, just an old-fashioned charm. Behind the little shop windows, a paradise beckons. No sooner have you slowly pushed open the door than you are drawn into the world that opens up inside. Alerted by the loud, continuous ringing of the door bell that echoes round the entire store, Maurice Melchio suddenly

You just cannot resist stepping inside. The door of "Chez Melchio" opens into a veritable Aladdin's cave of sausages.

appears from behind a curtain of sausages. Yards of sausages, all different lengths, hang above the refrigeration unit, in which more sausages and locally produced cheeses are displayed, awaiting prospective purchasers.

Sausages as thick as your thumb or as slender as your little finger, dusky pink or with a coating of white flour, fill the air with their aroma. Maurice Melchio, who discovered his vocation at the tender age of 13, smiles. It is obvious to all and sundry that he reigns over this tempting diversity with pride and enjoys springing fresh surprises on his customers. The strings of sausages are Maurice's own creation and specialty. He calls them *brindilles*, which means something like "twig" or "straw," and sells them whole, well seasoned with walnuts, pine nuts, savory, juniper berries, goat cheese, or pastis, in other words with the flavors of his native Provence.

Maurice is somewhat reserved, and a little taciturn. He can be economical with his words, in the knowledge that business is good. It is almost impossible to leave without at least buying a few slices of sausage or feeling tempted to sample the pork brawn or the freshly salted pork. Everything is homemade, delicious, and of excellent quality.

A few slices of *brindilles* are enough to invest an aperitif with a breath of Provence, no matter where you are in France or even beyond its borders. Maurice Melchio even accepts orders to send his sausages anywhere in France, at any time, and to any recipient. They are despatched in batches of ten – packed in a poster tube. One telephone call is all it takes.

Maurice Melchio, the innovative butcher, appears proud and smiling from behind a curtain of sausages.

A basket appetizingly filled with tasty sausages: *Brindilles* are flavored with herbs, aniseed, or cheese.

Maurice Melchio accepts orders to send his *brindilles* anywhere in France: an original sort of postcard!

A classical recipe: Raw, air-dried ham goes extremely well with melon.

Maurice's terrines are quite delicious. Sour gherkins are an excellent accompaniment to pork brawn.

Maurice sells everything you might need for a picnic, including Banon's famous goat cheese.

Sisteron, Pearl of Haute Provence

Sisteron, situated at the foot of a deep gash in the rock created by the river Durance, has always been known as the "natural gateway to Provence," even by the Romans. This strategically important town, whose Roman name was Segustero, was fortified even in its early days. During the 13th century, a watch-

tower was constructed, followed by a citadel, later redesigned by Henry IV's military engineer, Jean Erard. Louis XIV's chief fortifications engineer, Sébastien de Vauban, also had great plans.

The old part of Sisteron is characterized by the twisting alleyways and houses with tiled roofs that are so typical of this part of France. There are numerous small squares with fountains, their trees affording pleasant shade.

Another notable feature of the town, albeit a considerably less romantic one, is that Sisteron possesses one of Europe's largest abattoirs for sheep and lambs. In peak season, over 2,000 animals a day are slaughtered here.

Sisteron lamb

In the Hautes-Alpes, the blue of the sky often merges with the green of the pastures. The meadows are studded with white, peaceful looking flecks, resembling little stars. Here and there, you hear the sound of lambs bleating softly, almost hoarsely, and the deeper, answering bleat of the mother ewes.

A flock of around a hundred sheep grazes all day long or

The gateway to Provence: The Roche de Baume on the west bank of the Durance towers like a sentinel over Sisteron and the river.

the thyme-filled grass. The lambs are scarcely more than a few days old when they accompany the flock up to the Alpine pastures. Their spindly legs only just manage to carry them up to the high plateaux. During the first three months of their young lives, they cover this distance on a daily basis, feeding on their mothers' good milk. This milk owes its special quality to the wild herbs contained in the aromatic Alpine grass that the ewes graze on.

The Préalpes breed of sheep has a somewhat elongated head, long, thin legs and produces only a small amount of wool. The quality and the tenderness of the meat produced by the lambs, however, are such that its fame extends far beyond Provence's borders.

An "Agneau de Sisteron" (Sisteron lamb) label does not exist as such, but meat from local animals, which have been bred according to traditional methods, fed naturally, and allowed to graze freely, is given a red badge. The best way fully to appreciate this meat, which is virtually fat-free and tastes slightly of filberts, is to complement it with a red wine, preferably from the south or southwest of France.

For the traditional Easter lamb, a leg of lamb is roasted with rosemary, thyme, garlic purée, or a whole clove. Beans are also a typical Provençal accompaniment. It is hard to imagine a more delicious meal for a special occasion than this one.

Gigot d'agneau
Leg of lamb

Serves 6

1 leg of lamb, about 4 ½ pounds/2 kg
3 cloves of garlic
2 tbsp oil
3 sprigs of rosemary
Salt and freshly milled pepper

Preheat the oven to 480 °F/250 °C. Peel the garlic cloves and slice finely. Make cuts in the lamb in several places and wedge the slices of garlic into the cuts.

Rub the lamb lightly with oil and place in an oiled roasting pan. Add half a glass of water and the sprigs of rosemary. Season the meat with salt and pepper, then cook in the preheated oven for 15 minutes. Reduce the oven temperature to 400 °F/200 °C and cook the lamb for a further 25 minutes or until ready.

Carve into pieces and serve with a traditional accompaniment of fresh green beans garnished with finely chopped parsley.

Sisteron and Marseille both claim to have invented *pieds et paquets*, or *pieds paquets*.

"Feet and parcels" have been a traditional dish since the 19th century. If the effort of preparing them is too great, you can buy them as a preserve.

"Pieds et paquets" – "feet and parcels"

Sisteron is very proud of one of its gastronomic specialties called *pieds et paquets* (lambs' feet and tripe parcels). However, there is some doubt as to where this dish actually originated since Marseille likewise lays claim to have invented it.

Toward the end of the 19th century, this city, founded by the Phoenicians, was beginning to resemble the Eldorado of the Durance valley. Marseille was experiencing an economic boom and, as migration from the land increased, was attracting whole population groups from the high and lower Alps. These people naturally brought their best recipes along with them, a point often raised by the people of Sisteron to lend weight to their argument. They also point out that a dish consisting of such cheap and easily perishable meat could only have originated near a slaughterhouse. This argument is not altogether watertight, however, and by no means conclusive. For one thing, Marseille had a slaughterhouse of its own, and for another, the town had strong trading links with North Africa where mutton is a common part of the diet. To add weight to their claims, the people of Marseille have even formed an association devoted specifically to this moot question.

Sisteron has one further trump up its sleeve: It claims, even though this may not be strictly true, that Napoleon partook of this dish in the "Bras d'Or" inn on the Rue de La Saunerie, when he stopped in Sisteron on March 5, 1815 on his journey back from exile on the Island of Elba.

Anyone wanting to sample this culinary treat is unlikely to be overly concerned with the precise origins of *pieds et paquets*. One way or another, they have become one of the region's culinary traditions.

Pieds et paquets
Lamb's feet and tripe parcels

Serves 6

Parcels and filling

7 oz/200 g freshly pickled pork belly	
7 oz/200 g sheep's stomach fat and skin	
3 cloves of garlic	
1 bunch of parsley, finely chopped	
2 sheep's stomachs, cleaned	

Feet

6 lamb's feet, cleaned and seared
3 lbs/1.5 kg lamb tripe
2 cups/500 ml olive oil
3 cups/750 ml white wine
3 cups/750 ml veal stock
3 large onions
2 fat carrots
1 ½ lb/750 g ripe tomatoes
2 cloves of garlic, finely chopped
Bunch of oregano
Salt and pepper

Place the pickled pork belly in boiling water for a few minutes, then dice. Cut up the skin and fat of the sheep's stomach. Crush the garlic, then add the parsley, diced pork belly, and chopped skin and fat. Season with a little salt and pepper and mix well.

Cut the cleaned stomachs into squares, measuring 3–4 inches (7–10 cm) across. Place a little filling in the center of each one. Roll up each parcel and fold in the sides. Secure the parcels by cutting a slit in each one and pulling a bit of the stomach membrane through it. Peel and slice the onions and carrots. Scald the tomatoes in boiling water, then peel and seed them. Dice the the flesh and set aside.

Sauté the lamb's feet and tripe in a saucepan in a little olive oil. Pour in the white wine and veal stock, then add the onions, carrots, tomatoes, garlic, and herbs. Place the parcels in the liquid and season with salt and pepper. Cover and simmer for at least five hours over a low heat.

Serve very hot with boiled potatoes.

Château-Arnoux: "La Bonne Etape"

Not far from the banks of the Durance is an old 18th-century coaching inn where, in bygone days, the mail coach used to change horses. Nowadays, this hotel and restaurant is a member of the very well known Relais & Châteaux hotel group.

The building is surrounded by gardens and springs, creating the impression of an oasis of tranquillity, other-

"La Bonne Etape," hotel and restaurant in one, offering both elegance and quality. The hotel, a member of the Relais & Châteaux association, can be justifiably proud of its ambitious, yet traditional cuisine.

wise known as "La Bonne Etape," or "Pleasant Repose."

In itself, the name is nothing out of the ordinary: It crops up thousands of times all over France, just like restaurants named "Bon Coin." But "Château-Arnoux," situated on "Napoleon's road" (RN 78), is far more than merely a place of repose.

The menu and facilities that make this such a splendid hotel are the result of years of family tradition. There have been three generations of restaurateurs, all experts in the art of making *aïoli,* preparing *pieds et paquets,* and preserving anchovy fillets. Pierre Gleize, who originally intended becoming a lawyer, changed his mind and became a confectioner, married the daughter of the local landlord – and effectively espoused the kitchen at the same time.

The couple built up "Bonne Etape" as you would whip up a *beurre blanc,* single-mindedly and in no time at all. Pierre has passed on the family spirit and skills to his son, Jany, who has been bold enough to try and liven up family traditions a little. He combines experience with creativity and the result is innovative, yet traditional, cuisine.

This is exemplified by the sparkling house aperitif, which combines *Beaumes de Venise,* pear schnapps, and champagne to produce an excellent accompaniment to the day's hors d'oeuvres: *quenelles de brandade de morue dans sa soupe froide de poissons de rochet* – dumplings made from dried cod in cold rock fish soup.

A historic route

In 1815, Napoleon Bonaparte escaped from exile on the island of Elba and landed in Golfe-Juan near Cannes. Napoleon and his troops made their way from the coast through Grasse, Sisteron, and Grenoble toward Paris aiming to regain power. His venture ended on June 18, 1815, at the Battle of Waterloo. In 1932, what is now known as the RN 78 was designated the *Route de Napoléon* to commemorate Napoleon's campaign.

It is hard not to get carried away by or swept up in the gentle culinary adventure which Pierre and Jany Gleize want to take you on. Their culinary repertoire is rooted in their shared Provençal culture. The deliciously fresh ingredients that enliven their creations come straight from the restaurant's own vegetable garden.

Omelettes froides de légumes à la tapenade
Cold vegetable omelet with tapenade

Serves 6

A generous ½ cup/150 g chopped spinach

A generous ½ cup/150 g finely chopped Swiss chard

½ cup/120 g butter

A little finely chopped garlic

3 ripe tomatoes

1 shallot, chopped

1 pinch of marjoram or oregano

Scant ½ cup/100 ml olive oil

Hearts of 4 purple artichokes

1 scant cup/200 g chopped mushrooms

1 tsp chopped parsley, chervil, and chives

2 tsp chopped truffles

12 eggs

6 tbsp/100 g *tapenade* (see p. 31)

Wine vinegar

Salt and freshly milled pepper

Blanch the spinach and Swiss chard, drain well and sauté with the garlic in one generous tablespoon of butter. Set aside. Peel and slice the tomatoes, then sauté them in one heaped tablespoon of butter with the chopped shallot and marjoram and set aside. Cut the artichoke hearts into pieces and sauté in olive oil, before adding to the spinach.

Finally, sauté the mushrooms and herbs, then set aside.

Gradually beat two eggs at a time, and season with salt and pepper. Melt 1 tablespoon of butter in a skillet, then add the two eggs and the spinach and artichoke mixture and wait until it begins to set. Repeat the procedure with the remaining eggs, using two at a time

mixed with the different vegetables, herbs, and truffles, respectively. Arrange the six omelets on top of each other, contrasting the colors (tomatoes, spinach and artichokes, mushrooms, herbs, Swiss chard, truffles), and cook for 20 minutes in a warm oven. Allow to cool before cutting into segments. Serve with *tapenade* and a good wine vinegar to season.

course, an integral part of the food – "butter and cream are considered exotic by the people round here." Truffles are served fresh with a *mesclun* salad, in puff pastry, or sliced on pilgrim scallops.

The beginning of autumn marks the end of the shellfish and salad season. It is game that now takes pride of place at the "Bonne Etape": *lièvre à la royale* (royal hare), fillet of venison with a rosemary sauce, and duck breast in puff pastry.

"We try to give each of our dishes a personal touch." This applies as much to a *vinaigrette de la garrigue*, as to a herby basil butter or to the homemade *tapenade*, which is served with braised pheasant, or figs in Beaumes-de-Venise Muscat.

The Gleizes try to use regional produce where possible, but are not dogmatic about this. Their aim, above all, is to produce good food and where the ingredients come from is of secondary importance. As far as they are concerned, the Easter lamb is not the be-all and end-all of meats: They prefer the *tardon* which has grazed the pastures for six months longer. It is purely coincidence that it comes from Sisteron and the Gleizes would have liked it just as much no matter where it came from. What counts is quality and taste. Olive oil is, of

There is always someone happy to advise you on your choice of wine. A white *Châteauneuf-du-Pape* is recommended with truffles. Finally, it is impossible to resist a dessert: ice cream with lavender honey! A little beehive with a straw roof made from pale golden caramel, a light praline, and lavender, the scent of Provence.

For those with smaller appetites and a smaller budget, Pierre and Jany Gleize have another restaurant just a few steps away from the "Bonne Etape." This restaurant, called "Le Goût du Jour," has all the flair of a trendy bistro, while incorporating the family spirit and traditions. Here the choice of cuisine is more rustic: mussel soup, dried cod soup with olives, rabbit with mustard sauce and savory, followed by warm chocolate cake.

This terrine is best prepared the day before and served with a well-dressed mesclun salad.

Daube d'agneau en gelée
Vinaigrette de la garrigue
*Lamb stew in aspic
Vinaigrette with herbs from
the garrigue*

Serves 8

Leg of lamb or 2 shoulders of
lamb, weighing 2 ½ lbs/1,2 kg

4 tbsp olive oil

4 carrots, sliced

2 onions, thinly sliced

4 cloves of garlic, finely chopped

A generous cup/250 ml
vegetable stock

4 lamb's feet or 1 calf's foot

3 cups/750 ml dry white wine

1 clove

Bunch of herbs – including celery,
chervil, thyme, savory,
and rosemary)

Salt and pepper

Sauce

2 cloves of garlic

1 tbsp fresh thyme leaves

1 tbsp finely chopped savory

1 tbsp chopped parsley

Olive oil

Salt and pepper

Ask the butcher to remove the bones and fat from the leg or shoulders of lamb. Sear this briefly along with the lamb's feet. Cut the meat into four or five pieces. Season with salt and pepper and sauté on all sides in an earthenware or cast iron cooking pot, or large saucepan. Remove the meat from the pot and add the carrots, onions, and garlic and sauté gently. Meanwhile, bring the stock to the boil. Remove the vegetables from the saucepan and pour off the oil. Place the meat, vegetables, lamb's feet, clove, and the white wine in the pan and pour over the hot stock. Cover and simmer for 90 minutes over a low heat. When the meat and vegetables are tender, remove them both and leave the lamb's feet to continue cooking. Remove the bones from the feet. Pour the cooking juices into a dish, very carefully skimming off

the fat. Taste the sauce and leave to cool. Check that the cooking juices are beginning to set into jelly by putting a few drops on a saucer in the refrigerator. If so, pour a few spoonfuls of the liquid into a bowl and place the meat and vegetables on top of this, finishing with the lamb's feet in order to create an arrangement that is colorful.

Cover with the remaining cooking juices and leave to set in the refrigerator. Just before serving, tip it out of the bowl. If it does not come out easily, dip the bowl briefly in hot water to loosen it.

To make the sauce, blanch the garlic and crush it with a mortar and pestle along with the herbs. Finally, add the olive oil, salt and pepper.

THE SCENTS OF HAUTE PROVENCE

Is it a reflection of the sky, an illusion created by the sun's rays, or perhaps a trick of nature that makes the lavender appear to keep shifting color from blue to mauve? The much vaunted violet color of the flowers not only gives the landscape its special character, but is also echoed on the shutters of the houses.

"Lavender is the soul of Haute Provence," as Jean Giono, the writer, once said. It has grown wild on the southern slopes of Mont Ventoux and the Lure mountains since time immemorial, carpeting vast areas in early summer in various shades of violet and blue. Later, a cultivated variety of lavender was introduced as a crop on the high plateaux and mountain slopes of Provence, much to the satisfaction of the local farmers who needed something to compensate for the decline in cereal production. Today, fields of lavender stretch from the pre-Alps near Gigne to the Valensole plateau.

Flowers and essential oils

True lavender, *Lavandula angustifolia*, or *L. officinalis*, which is by far the most widespread variety, grows best at an altitude of 1,970 to 5,200 feet (600–1,600 m) above sea level. Spike lavender, *Lavandula latifolia*, on the other hand, prefers higher temperatures and lower altitudes between 650 and 1,625 feet (200–500 m). The third type of lavender is a hybrid of the two previous ones and occupies the area in between, growing between 1,300

Visitors to Provence see the region at its best when the lavender is in bloom. The sea of flowers is a paradise of shifting colors of blue and violet and the scent is intoxicating. It is hard work for the lavender pickers, however, toiling beneath a scorching sun using just a simple scythe.

transported to the distillery. Some of these factories still use a traditional distilling flask with a straw-fired boiler which enables the plants to be distilled at a much lower temperature setting.

The sheaves of lavender are tipped into large bowls and pressed down hard so that the steam that is then injected through them meets the greatest possible resistance. This helps to extract the maximum amount of essential oil. Generally speaking, a traditional distillation flask can process one ton of lavender in half an hour. This is equivalent to 11–22 pounds (5–10 kg) of lavender essence or 55–88 pounds (25–40 kg) of essence from the inferior variety. The size of the harvest obviously depends on whether weather conditions have meant a good or bad year for the lavender.

The essence from genuine lavender is used in the perfume industry and in cosmetic manufacture. Spike lavender, which smells of camphor, is used for paint and varnish. The hybrid lavender, which has a less subtle fragrance than that of genuine lavender, is used in detergents and other household products.

and 2,275 feet (400–700 m) above sea level. This favorite of Provençal gardens is the result of cross-pollination by insects of the two varieties *Lavandula angustifolia Mill* and *Lavendula latifolia Vill*. The oil it produces is of inferior quality to that of true lavender. It is, however, very hardy and produces a high yield.

When the harvest begins in July, the intoxicating scent of lavender fills all of Provence. Apart from the tractors moving ceaselessly up and down and harvesting the fields mechanically, you will also occasionally see pickers carrying wide willow baskets and cloth sacks, harvesting the lavender by hand. Equipped with just a sickle, they usually tackle the steeper and less accessible fields. The lavender is left to dry for two or three days before being

The lavender harvest begins in mid-July just after the buds open.

The lavender has to be harvested quickly. This is done by machine.

The sheaves of lavender are loaded by conveyor belt onto the trucks that transport them.

The cut lavender is left to dry for two to three days in vast halls.

It is almost time to start the distilling process. The lavender flowers are

spread out on metal grids and slowly lowered into the vats.

The lavender flowers are then pressed hard together to create as much resistance as possible for the steam to pass

through. The fire beneath the vat is fanned to bring the water to a boil. The steam becomes saturated with the

essential oils which are released by the lavender flowers.

Lavender and lavender essence impart a special aroma to many specialty dishes, whether it be a liqueur, a type of honey, an ingredient in cookies, ice cream, or with a leg of lamb.

Lavender in the kitchen

Lavender is finding an increasing number of uses in the kitchen. It has been used for a long time to flavor honey, candies, sorbets, *crème brûlées*, and herbal teas or spicy cakes. It is now, however, beginning to compete with vanilla, chocolate, and seasonal fruits as an ice cream flavor and just lately has even found its way into main courses, usually the exclusive domain of herbs and spices. *Fougasse*, an oval-shaped yeast bread, flavored with lavender and herbs is just about conceivable: Lavender, thyme, rosemary, and savory do, after all, have a fair amount in common. But it rather stretches the imagination to picture a leg of lamb cooked with lavender. And yet, a few lavender flowers sprinkled over the roast toward the end of its cooking time, so that their aroma blends with the meat juices, will give the dish an absolutely delicious flavor. Lavender is thought to reduce blood pressure, heal wounds, have antiseptic and disinfectant properties, help against parasites, and have a soothing effect. Rubbing fresh lavender flowers over your arms and legs is supposed to afford protection against insect bites. This may well work since the beekeepers, who collect the lavender honey, apparently rarely get stung by bees. Lavender honey also has a reputation for providing relief to migraine sufferers.

Lavender is an essential feature of Provence. Festivals are held in its honor all over the country from Vaucluse to the Alps of Haute Provence. In July, there is a festival in Valensole,

Sweet things are often flavored with lavender. Provence is famous for its lavender-flavored specialties, such as nougat, candies, and cookies.

Herbal tea to relieve a cough
Add 1 teaspoonful (5 g) of lavender flowers (*Lavandula officinalis*) to 1¾ pints (one liter) of boiling water. Leave to infuse for ten minutes, then strain and drink hot.

Mousse de fleurs de lavande fine

Lavender flower mousse

Serves 4

3 sheets of gelatin or 1 packet of powdered
1 tsp lavender
½ cup/ 100 g soft brown sugar
2 cups/ 500 ml sweetened cream

Soften the gelatin, lavender flowers, and sugar in a scant ½ cup of water for 15 minutes. Bring to a boil, then leave to cool until the mixture begins to set. Whip the cream and carefully fold into the lavender mixture. Divide the mixture into small bowls and leave to set in the refrigerator.
Serve with lavender honey or an orange fruit sauce, which can be made by simmering the juice from two pressed oranges along with a little honey, until a smooth sauce is then obtained.

while in Digne-les-Bains and Sault, there are similar festivals in August.

The lavender museum in Coustellet has an interesting exhibition of the various types of lavenders. Its fine collection of distillation flasks illustrates the development of distillation techniques from the 16th century to the present time. You will find lavender distilleries, lavender cooperatives, and lavender farms that are open to the public all over Provence. Here, you can buy small bags or bunches of blue or mauve dried lavender flowers, which retain their fragrance exceptionally well.

THE HERBS OF PROVENCE

The gardens of Salagon priory near Forcalquier are a veritable Aladdin's cave of herbs.

Testimony to this is Salagon, situated not far from Forcalquier, one of the loveliest monasteries in Haute Provence. Visitors can stroll through three specially laid out gardens, comprising more than 600 varieties of herbs and medicinal plants.

Mediterranean cuisine is unthinkable without the herbs of Provence and their diversity of taste and flavor. Traditional *herbes de Provence* combine thyme, rosemary, bay leaves, savory, or marjoram. *Fines herbes*, on the other hand, consist of finely chopped parsley, tarragon, chervil, and chives. A *bouquet garni* (small bunch of herbs) is usually a small bunch of parsley, thyme, and a bay leaf. Incidentally, thyme used to have a special significance in Provence in days gone by. A little bunch of thyme sprigs left hanging on a young maiden's door was a token of love from the person that hung it there, in the same way as a red rose today is a universal symbol of love.

The right herb for every taste

Sometimes, you need do no more than bend down and pick some thyme, rosemary, savory, and other herbs from the roadside in order to give your sauce or salad the appropriate flavor.

The herbs should never be picked once they have begun to flower since their flavor

The herbs of Provence are excellent in quality, yet modest in their requirements. They grow in prolific quantities in some of Provence's most arid soil, as if nature is trying to apologize for having areas that are less fertile than others.

In bygone days, they were used as a bartering commodity, along with gold and silver, and were regarded on a par with the finest and most sought after spices. They were also used as medicinal remedies on account of their soothing and healing qualities. During the 18th century, they were actually condemned for a while as "witches' herbs," but by the start of the 19th century, Provençal herbs were once again being used for medicinal purposes. The currently rising star of phytotherapy has added greatly to their importance and popularity.

Pistou
Basil paste

On the other side of the Alps, this is known as *pesto*. In Provence it is used as an accompaniment to fish or lamb and is an important ingredient of a white bean stew, known as *soupe en pistou* (pictured right).

6 cloves of garlic
Sea salt
1 bunch of fresh basil
½ cup/100 g Parmesan cheese
Scant ¼ cup/50 ml olive oil
Black pepper, freshly milled

Peel and crush the garlic with a mortar and pestle, adding a pinch of salt. Finely chop the basil and add to the garlic, mixing to form a homogenous paste. Add the grated Parmesan and season with a little pepper. Add the oil, initially a drop at a time, then in a steady stream, stirring continuously, until a smooth paste is formed.

becomes less intense and their leaves have a high concentration of essential oils. It is best to dry the young herbs in a dark room and then preserve them in small, airtight containers in a dark place.

Basil (*basilic*): Without this herb, there would be no *pistou*, since this is the main ingredient of this basil paste. It also forms an incomparable accompaniment to tomatoes with mozzarella, to pasta, and sauces. Basil is available as a pot plant, or sold in bunches at the market, with small or large leaves. It is a delicate herb and should always be used when it is as fresh as possible.

Thyme (*thym*): This is perhaps the most characteristic herb of Provence, and is essential to a *bouquet garni*. Thyme grows almost everywhere from gardens to sunny hillsides. The distinctive aroma of its tiny leaves is best preserved if it is dried in small bunches in a shady spot in the kitchen and then rubbed over broiled dishes or stirred into marinades. It is also used to make a herbal tea to relieve stomach upsets.

Rosemary (*romarin*): This herb owes its name to the Romans who compared it to the *rosée marine*. It grows in bush form, radiating long side shoots, densely covered with green needles. Its intense aroma is rather reminiscent of resin and it should be used with caution. Rosemary tea drunk on an empty stomach after a long night can work wonders.

Bay (*laurier-sauce*): another vital ingredient of *bouquet garni*. One bay leaf is all you need in a marinade, in braised dishes or in a sauce. A sore throat can be soothed by gargling with a solution made from bay leaf in boiling water. Bay leaves should never be confused with oleander leaves which are highly poisonous.

Sage (*sauge*): This is an excellent herb with pork. The small velvety leaves should only be used separately and not mixed with other Provençal herbs. Sage is believed to be a very beneficial herb. Its healing properties have been common knowledge since ancient times as its name suggests, being derived from the Latin word "salvare," meaning "to save."

Fennel (*fenouil*): Cultivated fennel is used in the manufacture of the popular drink pastis.

Bay leaves   Thyme   Lavender   Marjoram

It is a very undemanding plant and in its wild state will thrive where almost nothing else grows. Its seeds are often used as a seasoning for olives or fish.

Savory (*sarriette*): Fresh goat cheese and savory, accompanied by a small glass of semidry white wine – an unpretentious, but pleasant hors d'ocuvre. Olive oil readily absorbs the flavor of savory. Bean-based dishes and ragouts benefit from its peppery overtones. As with all Provençal herbs, it also has a medicinal value, in this case for alleviating flatulence problems.

Marjoram (*marjolaine*): It is from marjoram that oregano is descended. It is used as a remedy for migraine and insomnia. Its fragrance is very evocative of its native country, of Greek dishes, small keftedes, or broiled fish.

Tarragon (*estragon*): This is a crucial ingredient of Béarnaise sauce and, consequently, an ideal accompaniment to fish. Another less classical but no less delicious dish using tarragon is cucumber salad with light cream and tarragon tips.

Garlic (*ail*): Although garlic is not a herb but a member of the lily family, it is impossible to discuss specialties from Provence without mentioning this most common ingredient of Mediterranean cuisine. Using garlic in cooking requires some experience. As the saying goes, "Use, mais n'abuse pas," which is roughly the equivalent of "Easy does it." Eaten raw, garlic is not very pleasant for those who have not partaken of it, but cooked, it merely leaves a delicious aroma. It is also believed to be valuable in combating arterial sclerosis and raised blood pressure.

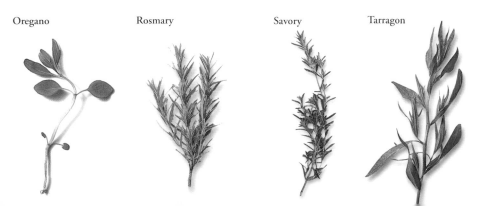

Oregano   **Rosmary**   **Savory**   **Tarragon**

THE UBAYE VALLEY

The Ubaye river flows along the edge of the Haute Provence Alps, within sight of Piedmont. In days gone by, the Ubaye valley, which is surrounded by mountains, some of them 9,750 feet (3,000 m) high, was largely cut off during the winter months. The only way to free the valley's inhabitants from their isolation was by the radical solution of boring a tunnel through the 7,280 feet (2,240 m) high Mount Alos and constructing the Bonette pass, 9,100 feet (2,802 m) in length.

What makes the Ubaye valley so fascinating is its geological diversity and its wealth of flora and fauna. It provides a natural habitat for capercaillies, golden eagles, chamois, mouflons, wild boar, and even wolves. The flora includes arnica, edelweiss, gentian, campion, Alpine forget-me-not, and wormwood, as well as wild lavender. Shepherds use the meadows

Barcelonnette: This village in the Ubaye valley owes its name to the Spanish count of Barcelona.

and the high Alpine pastures as grazing for their flocks of sheep and have done so since time immemorial.

Barcelonnette, a village with an unusual history

Barcelonnette, surrounded by meadows and sun-drenched orchards, is a village with an exotic history, as its unusual name might indicate. During the 13th century, a count from Barcelona built a country house, a *bastide*, on the banks of the Ubaye river, which he named Barcelone. During the 18th century, this evolved into Barcelonnette.

Strolling around the village today, you could easily think you had stepped back 200 years into history. It is as if the houses could talk. They speak volumes about the valley's inhabitants who made their fortune in Mexico and bear testimony to a century of wandering that saw both joy and tragedy. The result is a fairly colorful diversity. The region's cuisine is a mixture of French, Italian, and even Mexican influences. Barcelonnette is home to a type of ravioli (*raïoles*) and smoked mutton and on long winter evenings, the inhabitants drink *Génépy* to warm themselves up.

"Génépy Grand Rubren"

Génépy is a warming drink when the weather gets cold.

Le Grand Rubren both warms and stimulates the senses.

It is a liqueur of the mountains, as you might deduce from the label, depicting a chamois on a rocky outcrop with snow-covered peaks in the background.

Génépy is made from a variety of mugwort which grows at an altitude of over 11,300 feet (3,500 m). The plant is called artemisia, an absinthe, which makes *Génépy* a distant cousin of pastis.

The inhabitants of the Ubaye valley have been picking this special type of mugwort since the Middle Ages and using it to make a range of liqueurs and herbal teas that act as stimulants and aid digestion.

The manufacture of *Génépy* is based on a simple basic procedure which the mountain farmers of the Ubaye valley still follow to make their liqueur: 40 sprigs of artemisia are left in alcohol for 40 days. At this point, a syrup made from water and 40 cubes of sugar is added. After one further month of patience, the liquid is filtered, leaving the liqueur ready to drink.

Le Grand Rubren has been a registered trademark since 1947. It is based on a traditional recipe which uses a specific type of artemisia, *Artemisia mutellina*, and contains 40 percent alcohol. *Génépy vert* not only owes its green color to the chlorophyll in artemisia, but also owes to the plant its exceptional aroma. The organic cultivation of artemisia at 5,200 feet

Old and new bottles side by side. Génépy has been drunk for decades. The shapes might change, but the quality remains the same.

(1,600 m) is hard work. The plants have to be tended regularly. Weeds that might inhibit or suffocate them have to be removed.

The liqueur has a surprisingly smooth and pure flavor and is untainted by any artificial coloring or other additives. Thanks to its traditional production methods and the strict rules regarding which plants may be used in its manufacture, *Génépy du Grand Rubren* carries a "Provenance Montagne" label of quality.

Other specialties of the Ubaye valley

Before allowing yourself a glass of *Génépy* as a digestif, you should first indulge in some of the numerous sausage products or other specialties that the region has to offer.

Start at breakfast by sampling one of the delicious jams, or jellies, perhaps rosehip jam

"Le Grand Rubren," where you can buy traditional *Génépy*. Its manufacture follows a precise procedure and has earned it the "Provenance Montagne" label of quality.

(*confiture d'eglantine*), or plum jam (*confiture d'affatous*) made from small, yellow, tart plums gathered in the forest.

Later on, you might feel like a small snack. How about *pâté de porc au genièvre* or *saucisson de mouton* (pork paté with juniper berries or mutton sausage). Neither of these will leave any doubts as to their main ingredient since the delicate aroma of the respective meat is unmistakable. Another alternative is *fumeton* (smoked mutton). Its aroma is similar to smoked goose breast or dried grison – air-dried beef/lamb/mutton etc. It goes well with raclette and can be used as an – albeit somewhat costly – alternative to diced bacon in quiche or other savory flans.

Perhaps *raïoles* (ravioli) might follow next. Their shape and name are reminiscent of Italy, but that is where all similarity ends. *Raïoles* in this part of the world are stuffed with dried walnuts and eaten with spinach or pumpkin, or perhaps a meat dish, for example, a typical local dish called *fritots de pieds d'agneau de Barcelonnette* (fried feet of

Barcelonette lamb). The lamb's feet are tossed in breadcrumbs and fried in oil, then served with lemon and parsley. Or else a *tourte de veau* (veal pie), whereby a tender shoulder of veal is diced and marinated in onions and garlic, wrapped in pastry and baked in the oven. It can be eaten either hot or cold.

What would a French meal be without cheese – even if it is nearly on the Italian border? People of the Ubaye valley enjoy a *Tomme* made from cow's milk, mild, delicately flavored, and sometimes enhanced with *Génépy*, or, perhaps, some *fromage de chèvre et de brebis* (goat and sheep's milk cheese). This is often flavored with savory or thyme and sometimes preserved in olive oil.

A favorite dessert is *carline*, a soft cheese made from cow's milk, covered with honey – after all, you are in the land of milk and honey – or perhaps a *tarte aux fruits* (fruit flan). The delicious fruit flans made throughout this area are generally called *tourtes*. And the crowning glory to have with the coffee: *chocolats* (pralines) – filled with *Génépy*!

From Marseille to Hyères

Highways and heavy traffic conspire to make one town much like another, yet Marseille maintains a character all its own. It presents a bright, cheerful, blue and white face to the world. Leaving behind the Étang de Berre, and proffering a distant glimpse of the Fos shoreline, the motorway speeds toward the city. The industry of its citizens marks the outskirts, where signs of activity and enterprise are strikingly evident. Refineries pour out their pollution into the air, steelworks gash the landscape, and the roar of aircraft banishes silence. Despite all this, Marseille has a seductive beauty, bordered on one side by the sea, the picture framed on the other side by the Byzantine basilica.

The city can trace back its history for over 2,600 years. It possesses an ancient harbor, and a magnificent cathedral. The various quarters of the town are set out like villages, and its streets are heavy with the odors of its fishing activities and the scent of spices. Marseille is a city of cultural diversity, where communities live side by side, and – not to be forgotten – a place of culinary delights. The number of its devotees is many; they love it for the charm of its small and rugged coves, for its refreshing pastis that quenches the thirst of summer's heat, and for its bouillabaisse.

As the traveler moves on eastward, the parting views are all sweetness: The enchantment of the coastline begins with the vineyards of Cassis and Bandol, and their hint of vinous pleasures. The bays of Cassis and the dizzy cliffs of Cap Canaille are breathtaking in their beauty. Tempting the traveler to pause awhile, the sights remind us that Raoul Dufy, André Derain, and Henri Matisse all set up their easels here. The route leads on along the Départementale 559 toward Sanary-sur-Mer. Here, the German writers Thomas Mann and Franz Werfel, with Alma Mahler-Werfel, found refuge. A short ride takes the traveler to the port of Toulon, unmistakably naval in character. The bay here is the most beautiful in Europe while the town's old quarters and picturesque market would steal any heart. The road now plunges down to Hyères, with its pretty, narrow streets, and fruit and vegetable stalls.

Marseille is 2,600 years old. The view from the basilica of Notre-Dame-de-la-Garde is magnificent.

Marseille

All streets lead to the harbor, the heart of Marseille.

morning; fishermen still wearing their rubber boots, and woolen caps on their heads, transfer the catch into boxes as blue as the sea. The iodine tang of the deep still clings to the fish, many still alive, the shellfish and other seafood so freshly landed. The troughs contain an entire universe of the denizens of the sea, the astonishing sight of huge, gaping mouths, slender bodies with a satin gleam, jaws lined with steely, sharp teeth, tiny shellfish, spiny urchins, and the shimmer of silver, blue, and red, as well as flecks of gold and rust-brown.

Now and again, a couple of sea-horses lie amid the catch, in all their fragile beauty, minute miracles. Here and there are starfish, and abalone shells, the small, pink, mother-of-pearl *œils de Saint-Lucie*, like little, round eyes, that can be bought for a few francs as good luck charms.

As the morning wears on, the fish is sold off cheaply, with price reductions of a few dozen francs for the porgy, conger eel, gurnard, and the whole host of scaly creatures. If buyers hesitate for a few seconds, the saleswomen

The harbor

Sailing boats sway at their moorings along the jetty, their colorful hulls rising and falling with the rhythm of the waves that lap the shoreline of the bay of Marseille, and their tall, bare masts reaching for the sky.

Suddenly, the quayside is alive with noise. Sunbathers stir from their lazy rest as the hubbub approaches. It is the returning fishermen, landing their catch.

Every day the fishing smacks head out to sea to fish the deeper waters, while the *pointus*, the small, traditional craft, and the larger *tartanes* cast their nets nearer the shore.

A bustle of activity engulfs the fishmarket near the ancient harbor of Marseille each

The freshly landed catch from the night before is sold at the harbor every morning.

Sea-blue wooden crates and a set of simple weighing scales are the main tools of the trade for the fish merchants.

call out the high quality of their wares in a torrent of hyperbole: "A splendid fish, fine and firm, look at its fat belly." Every last fish must be sold. There is a saying in Provence: "Fish live in water and die in oil!" and they are hurried from sea to skillet with the shortest possible delay. Tips for their preparation are often given along with the deal. Surveying the remaining fish, people exchange ideas on recipes for stews, curries, and fish soup with enthusiasm.

There is much to see and hear around the old harbor, and much can be learned about fish. The listener discovers the meanings of their sonorous names, the *favouilles*, the *bious*, and the *siouclet* that defeat the dictionary but enrich the cuisine.

The rich harvest of the Mediterranean

A great variety of fish is found in the warm waters of the Mediterranean. Stocks are unfortunately diminishing, and threatened both by overfishing and by the ferry traffic that plies across the spawning grounds, inhibiting the breeding cycle.

Any threat to the sea is at the same time a threat to our culture. The ecological catastrophe also has negative effects for our traditions. However ridiculous our attempts to preserve these traditions may appear, their preservation is important, in the simple, everyday forms in which they find expression. The incomparable complexity of tastes in a true bouillabaisse, the

delicate flavor of sea bass, the pronounced aroma of the local porgy type, gilt head bream, and the conviviality of the *sardinade*, the communal feast, are all treasures to be maintained.

Let us hope that, in the Golfe du Lion, there may still in future be an abundance of its excellent rock fish, and that it will prove possible to maintain the Mediterranean with its fishing ports and its over 600 species of fish, and all who continue to fish there in the traditional way.

Fish is not only a fine delicacy, offering a varied range of flavors, but plays an extremely useful role in a balanced, healthy diet. Mackerel contains almost no cholesterol – no more than 80 milligrams per 100 grams – and is low in calories. Yet it is rich in mineral salts, and an especially good source of phosphorus. So a little indulgence here and there may be permitted.

A Selection of Typical Mediterranean Fish

Anchois (anchovy): Could it be the anchovy's love of congregating in dense shoals that suits it so to its eventual appearance tightly packed in a can or glass jar? Anchovies are delicious fresh, in a marinade, or fried, and are not very expensive.

Chapon or *Rascasse rouge* (brown sea scorpion): This predator lives on other fish, as well as shellfish, octopus, and cuttlefish. Its tender, tasty flesh makes it an indispensable ingredient of bouillabaisse.

Anguille (eel): This comes from the Étang de Berre in the Camargue. It is a traditional fishermen's dish.

Congre or *Fielas* (conger eel): The conger eel's diet of spiny lobster and squid might be forgiven it; less forgivable is the profusion of bony spikes along its slender body, which can reach 10 feet (3 meters) in length. Despite this very unappealing characteristic, it is another indispensable ingredient of bouillabaisse.

Dorade royale (gilt head bream): This excellent porgy fish has jaws powerful enough to crack open a mussel. It is the freely acknowledged star of Mediterranean fish, whether filleted, baked whole, or broiled.

Galinette or *Rouget grondin* (gurnard): An essential part of any bouillabaisse. The gurnard has a powerful head that it uses to feed on crustaceans. This diet may be the reason for its intensely flavorsome flesh. Care should be taken in view of the many bones, and the flesh can become dry.

Merlan (whiting): This fish is the sworn enemy of sardines, on which it feeds greedily. It is delicious to eat, with delicate flesh, but deteriorates rapidly if not eaten freshly caught.

Saint-Pierre (John Dory): This is another bouillabaisse fish. It has a large head and many bones, but firm, delicate, aromatic flesh. It can also be poached, fried as a fillet, or broiled.

Freshness is the key

One of the joys and advantages of coastal regions and their fishing ports is that fish reaches the point of sale within a few hours at most of being landed. It can be cooked and eaten still fresh.

Freshness is high on the list of importance when cooking fish. So buyers should always check that the fish is the same day's catch, or at most from the day before. There are certain signs to look out for – according to variety – to tell whether fish is old.

- The orange spots on a plaice become duller. Mackerel loses its bright shimmer.
- The skin of cod and pollock becomes sticky to the touch, and there is a reddish or yellowish discoloration visible on the fillets.
- Red and striped mullet lose their bright color.
- Sardines and herring lose their firmness and sheen.
- The white skin of sole, which has a pinkish tinge when fresh, begins to yellow.
- Whiting collapses.
- The eyes of all fish become dull and hollow.

Sardine (sardine): This forms the major part of the Mediterranean catch, somewhat to the misfortune of the fish itself. A smaller relative of the herring, it is rich in protein. Once caught, it should be used as quickly as possible to enjoy it at its best. It can be grilled over a fire of pine twigs, prepared in oil to be eaten cold in a marinade sauce, or canned.

Loup de mer or *Bar* (sea bass): An excellent fish with delicate flesh of high quality, and sometimes a price to match. It is delicious prepared simply, broiled or fried. A popular method is to bake it in a salt crust.

Fish for making stock

When making fish stock, it tends to be the inexpensive types of fish that are best suited. They are usually very scaly, with large heads and many bones. The heads and bones alone make excellent stock. Whenever fish is prepared before cooking, instead of being served whole, the bones and trimmings can be boiled down into stock with vegetables, herbs, and seasonings.

Fish bought specifically for the purpose of making stock are generally those with a lot of waste, which are troublesome to prepare for the small amount of flesh they yield. But these apparent disadvantages make them ideal for producing flavorsome stocks and sauces. The types often chosen are: *gobi* (goby), *labre* (wrasse), *sparaillon* (annular seabream), *alose* (shad), *blenni* (blenny), *bogue*, (bogue), *castagnole*, (pomfret), and *serran* (rock bass).

Rouget barbet (red mullet): No fish more typifies the Mediterranean. It lives mainly on small crustaceans. Its delicate aroma makes it an ideal fish for frying, to eat in salads, and for all fine culinary specialties except fish soup.

Baudroie or *Lotte* (monkfish, angler fish): This fish has such an enormous appetite that it even consumes its own spawn. Its flavor is as good as its appearance is ugly. There are no bones. The monkfish is an essential ingredient of bouillabaisse.

Thon (tuna): This tireless traveler can make its escape at speeds of up to 50 m.p.h. (80 km/h), and deserves a better fate than to end up in a can. A broiled tuna steak with local herbs is a pleasure indeed – enough to make one forget the sad fact that dolphins can be injured or killed through tuna fishing.

Mulet, muge (mullet): In Provence, the fish itself is less valued than its roe, called *poutargue*. In Martigues, this is salted. Otherwise, preparation methods for this fish are similar to those used for sea bass.

Mulet doré (golden mullet): This species does not like polluted, offensive-smelling estuary waters, so it can be cooked with confidence.

Slipper lobsters taste delicious, though their appearance is a little fearsome.

Tourteaux (edible crabs) are another culinary pleasure to be sampled in the summer, the time of year when their flavor is best.

Octopus and its various cousins retain none of their gracefulness out of water, slumped amid the catch in the crates when once they had been imposing in their fluidity of movement. The smaller the *poulpe* (octopus), the better it is to eat. The larger ones should be marinated in a little wine to tenderize them. *Calamars* (squid) and *encornets* (little squid) belong to the same family. The small ones are often stuffed or served with small artichokes in a salad. *Supions* (very small, young squid) are a decorative feature on many seafood platters. They have a tender, almost powdery texture when tossed in flour and fried.

It is not uncommon along the coast of Provence to find the *épineux oursin* (sea urchin) on the menu, since these are often caught here. The local name for them is *roi de Cassis* (king of Cassis). Usually, just the roe is eaten, though some aficionados also enjoy the flavorsome juice. Each weekend from February to March there are *Oursinades de la Côte Bleue* held in various of the area's ports, especially around Cassis. One such port is Carry-le-Rouet. At these events, it is possible to sample sea urchins. They are served with fingers of bread to dip into the juice.

Seafood: shellfish, crustaceans, octopus, and squid

The *cigale* (slipper lobster) is related to the spiny lobster and true lobster. Its popularity has been its undoing, since its fine flavor and delicate flesh have led to overfishing, and it is dying out. The smaller ones are generally used for fish soup.

The *langoustine* (langoustine or Dublin Bay prawn) generally prefers colder waters, but can be found in the Mediterranean. It is often lightly fried or broiled, and served on a bed of fresh salad.

Favouilles (shore crabs) can often be found on beaches in the area. The aromatic flesh makes this crab extremely popular in Mediterranean cuisine.

Araignée de mer
(spider crab, sea spider)

Favouille (shore crab)

Tourteau (edible crab)

Poulpe (octopus)

Encornet (little squid)

Langoustine
(langoustine, Dublin Bay prawn)

Épineux oursin (sea urchin)

The seafood platter

Seafood is attraction enough to draw the visitor down to the harbor of an evening. Will it be a small serving to tempt the palate, or a huge platter for the serious devotee? Shellfish in profusion, piled upon a bed of ice, and accompanied by rye bread, butter, lemon wedges, vinegar flavored with shallots, engulf the table, surrounded by the ever-present finger bowls. The selection is all a matter of taste: oysters, perhaps, encircled with shrimps, whelks, mussels of all types, a crab, and a few tasty langoustines.

Oysters are very much part of a seafood platter in Provence, even if their origins seem to lie in Brittany, and despite the fact that oyster beds are so much part of the scenery of Languedoc (Agde, Sète, and the Étang de Thau). There are oysters to please everyone – rounded, flat, small, and pale or large and luscious – some Pacific varieties are as much as a foot (30 cm) across.

There is no need to feel limited by the old adage that oysters should be eaten in the winter months (from September to April) – oysters are good to eat at any time. What has happened is simply that transport is now better, so that the oysters can be taken quickly to every corner of the land. They are wonderful served on a large platter in summer, accompanied by a very dry white wine. Their full delicacy can be appreciated if they are eaten raw, just as they are, or with a few drops of shallot vinegar or lemon juice. They seem to be full of the flavor of the sea.

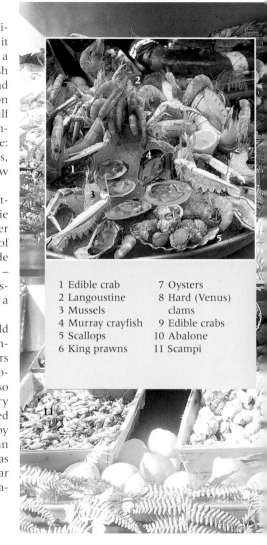

1 Edible crab	7 Oysters
2 Langoustine	8 Hard (Venus)
3 Mussels	clams
4 Murray crayfish	9 Edible crabs
5 Scallops	10 Abalone
6 King prawns	11 Scampi

The art of preparing and eating lobster

Lobsters are kept in the crates for a few days after being caught, to recover from the stress of their capture. They are sold live. Once in the kitchen, they can be kept briefly, by wrapping them in a kitchen cloth and putting them in the refrigerator. They should be cooked for a maximum of 15 minutes. Any longer, and they become tough and the flavor is impaired. Lobster is low in fat and aromatic in flavor. It needs no more accompaniment than mayonnaise, though it may be served *à l'armoricaine* on gala occasions. This is a Breton recipe. The lobster is jointed and flambéed in brandy with tomatoes.

An excellent and very simple way to serve lobster is to halve it lengthways, drizzle it with olive oil, season with salt and pepper, and then broil it.

The way to serve and eat it is to cut it open so that there is one claw attached to each half. The point of a knife can be used to remove the intestine from the top of the abdominal cavity. Then loosen the meat from the tail.

Wrench off the claws with a quick twist, and break the shell with a small hammer, nutcrackers, or specially designed lobster crackers. Use a lobster pick to lift out the meat. The roe should be taken out of the abdominal cavity, placed in a fine sieve, and rinsed. It can then be mixed with a tablespoon or so (20 g) of softened butter. Lobster butter can be kept in the refrigerator and used as a spread on toast to eat with an aperitif or in sauces.

The enjoyment of eating lobster takes time and trouble. Skill and patience are needed to reach the delicious meat.

To serve lobster, cut it in half lengthways with one claw on each portion. Remove the intestine that lies on the top of the rear section of the body.

The delicious tail meat is almost completely exposed, and can be taken out with a knife and fork. The liver is greenish and lies at the head end.

To access the claw, begin with the lower section. Use the lobster crackers. It can be a little difficult to grasp the claw with the crackers.

The pleasure of eating lobster has to be earned. The claw consists of two sections of different size, linked by a joint.

Proceed section by section. It takes a little skill, but is well worth the effort – lobster claw meat is a particular delicacy.

When the claw is finally open, the delicious meat is readily accessible.

Open the thin legs in the same way – break them open with the crackers and take out the meat.

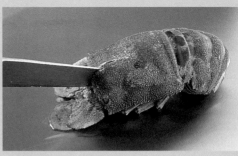

The slipper lobster from the Mediterranean, is related to lobster and spiny lobster. Overfishing has damaged stocks.

Cut the spiny lobster in half with a knife once cooked. Use a spoon to lift out the roe. It makes a delicious sauce.

As with many crustaceans, the tail contains most of the meat. Lift it out with a knife.

It is possible with care and a little patience to lift the meat out in one piece.

The slipper lobster too, the *grande cigale de mer*, has excellent, flavorsome meat.

How to serve and eat spiny lobster

As with lobster, serve with mayonnaise or simply broiled for a delicious feast.

Cooking with alcohol is an alternative method that brings out its fine qualities. To do this, halve the spiny lobster and brush with melted butter. Season with salt and pepper and broil for ten minutes. Then pour over some pastis, and either flambé or broil in the oven for a further five minutes. Stand well clear if using an eye level broiler.

Cut open lengthways to serve, as for lobster, ensuring that there is one claw on each half.

If the lobster is to be served already portioned, the intestine should still be present. Then, using a knife, loosen the meat and lift it out carefully in one piece. Remove the intestine. This looks like a black thread on the white surface of the meat.

Spoon out the eggs of the spiny lobster. These make an excellent flavoring for sauces.

213

Araignée de mer, the spider crab or sea spider, has very aromatic meat. It definitely deserves a place on a seafood platter.

To open, press down the underside of the cooked spider crab. Take care when handling the spiny shell.

The underside breaks away under the pressure. This makes it possible to access the inner cavity.

It is best to prize the meat away from the inside of the shell with a fork.

The meat can then be removed piece by piece more easily.

Another important ingredient in a generous seafood platter is the edible crab (*tourteau*). The illustration shows a perfectly jointed cooked crab.

Crab salad

Serves 2

2 edible crabs
4 cups/1 liter stock
1 cup/200 g fresh soft-curd cheese (quark), beaten until creamy (alternatively, use fromage blanc or drained yogurt)
1 tsp finely chopped chives
1 tsp finely chopped tarragon
1 tbsp vinegar
Salt and freshly ground pepper
1 hard boiled egg
1 tomato
1 tsp finely chopped parsley

Crabs and sea spiders

The meat of the edible crab is flavorsome and aromatic, with a lean and fibrous texture. This type is a true crab, distinguished by having four pairs of legs behind its claws instead of three. To joint a crab, first remove the legs with a twisting movement. Break them open with crackers and use a long, sharp fork to draw out the meat. This meat can alternatively be sucked out. The claw meat is easier to access. In the *tourteau*, as in many other crustaceans, this is also the best meat. Open the main shell on the underside. This gives access to the liver, which is considered a delicacy.

The meat of the spider crab is quite unique. Its fine, aromatic flavor makes it an essential ingredient on a seafood platter. The shell can be broken open by pressing the underside. But beware the spiny shell! The meat can then be lifted out piece by piece with a fork.

Boil the crabs in the stock, calculating cooking time according to weight (about 10 minutes per pound/per 500 g). Lift out the meat from the body, legs, and claws, including the roe. Chop. Clean the shells. Stir the herbs (apart from the parsley) into the curd cheese, and season with vinegar, salt, and pepper. Add to the crab meat and mix well. Fill the shells with the mixture, and decorate with sliced eggs and tomatoes. Sprinkle with parsley to serve.

Dinner is served!

Looking like a venerable *brasserie*, the "Miramar" stands overlooking the harbor, with which it has been so closely connected for over 30 years. Today, the restaurant is still linked by the harbor to the sea beyond, for every day that the fishermen return to moor their boats, they replenish both the harbor and the restaurant with fresh fish and with shellfish.

The "Miramar" is one of the best restaurants on the coast, and is especially famous for its

In the *Vieux Port*, old harbor, stands the unpretentious "Miramar." It looks like a typical old-fashioned French *brasserie*, but is one of the best fish resturants on the coast.

bouillabaisse, its sea bass in salt crust, and the desserts of its talented and creative pastry cook. It is an unrivaled delight to round off a meal with a symphony, sweetly blended with the aroma of olive oil, such as the confit of green olives, ice, and beignets, or with the more traditional classic *pavé de la Canebière au chocolat au lait et réglisse noir* – which translates into English as "paving stone from the prestigious Marseille thoroughfare, the Canebière, with milk chocolate and black licorice."

How to make bouillabaisse

Wash and prepare the fish and seafood. Separate those with firm flesh, such as scorpion fish, greater weaver fish, monkfish, gurnard, edible crab, and spiny lobster, from delicate ones like whiting, sea bass, and John Dory.

Bouillabaisse

In times past, the fishermen would land their catch, and immediately begin to mend their nets. Their wives would meanwhile take all the damaged fish that were unsuitable for sale, and set them on the fire to boil in seawater, sometimes on the beach itself. The fire had to be burning well as the soup began to cook, to bring it to a boil and give it a faint smoky flavor. The heat then needed to reduce while the fish completed its cooking. The family came together around the food, a little fennel, tomatoes, and the bouillabaisse, when the men finished their work.

Potatoes were added to the recipe in the 18th century by Parmentier, the pharmacist and plant explorer whose name is familiar to all French children. The middle classes purchased fine fish for it, and it ceased to be a poor man's dish. Today, it is made from certain particular and expensive fish, flavored with saffron, and cooked in fish stock. It not only provides a good, healthy meal, but fosters a companionable atmosphere – and is typical of Marseille. The "Charter for Marseille Bouillabaisse" watches over the dish in a supervisory capacity to ensure that the original recipe is adhered to as handed down through the generations.

Peel and finely chop the onions. Fry them lightly in eight tablespoons of olive oil until translucent.

Peel and quarter the potatoes, and add to the onions. Skin and core the tomatoes, chop them and add to the mixture. Then add the herbs, orange zest, garlic, and saffron. Season with salt and pepper. Place the crab and spiny lobster (if being used) on top of the vegetables, followed by the firm textured fish. Pour on the remaining olive oil. Cook gently for ten minutes, then carefully add boiling water.

Adjust the seasoning, bring back to a boil, and cook for another five minutes. Now add the remaining fish, and cook all for another five to seven minutes. A good bouillabaisse needs to boil vigorously for at least ten to fifteen minutes so that the oil combines smoothly with the cooking liquid.

While this is cooking, prepare the *rouille*. Soak the pieces of white bread in the chicken stock. Peel the garlic, and crush it with a pestle, together with the chilis. Add the pepper and saffron. Squeeze out the soaked bread, and mix with the spices. Add the olive oil

drop by drop, stirring to create a mayonnaise.

Place a slice of rustic bread in each soup plate, and pour over the fish soup. Serve the fish, crab, and spiny lobster, the vegetables, and the *rouille* separately, with more bread.

The correct way to present bouillabaisse is to serve the fish off the bone in front of the guests.

A refined yet comfortable atmosphere characterizes the dining room of the elegant "Miramar."

From left to right:
To make bouillabaisse, first fry the vegetables lightly in olive oil. Then add the crabs and spiny lobster, followed by the firm-textured fish. Boil these for ten minutes. The more delicate fish are added last, and the whole cooked for another five to seven minutes. The recipe originated as a way of using whatever fish remained, thus many variations are possible. Potatoes have featured among the optional ingredients since the 18th century.

Prepare the *rouille* while the soup is cooking. One or more pieces of rustic bread are placed in each plate of soup. Serve the fish separately from the soup, and the *rouille* likewise separately, to be spread onto the slices of bread.

Serves 6

17 ½ lbs/8 kg Mediterranean fish
(scorpion fish and at least six
other types, such as: greater
weaver fish, conger eel, monkfish,
red gurnard, whiting, sea bass,
John Dory, and, optionally, crab
and spiny lobster)
2 large onions
12 tbsp olive oil
4 tomatoes
1 bouquet garni
Zest of 1 unwaxed orange
4 cloves of garlic, crushed
1 ½ tsp/1 g saffron threads
Freshly milled salt and pepper
½ in/1 5 cm thick slices of rustic
bread (rye and wheat bread)
About 1 ½ lbs/750 g potatoes,
or more

Rouille
Piquant sauce

2 tbsp small pieces of white bread
Scant ½ cup/100 ml chicken stock
2 cloves of garlic
2 small chilis
Cayenne pepper
A pinch of saffron
⅔ cup/150 ml olive oil

Loup de mer en croûte de sel

Sea bass in a salt crust

Serve 2

1 sea bass, about 1 ¼ lbs/600 g
Fresh herbs according to taste

Salt crust

Generous 3 lbs/1.5 kg coarse
sea salt
2 egg whites
¼–½ cup/75–100 ml water

Clean and gut the fish, but do not scale. Mix the salt with the egg white, and gradually add the water. Stir for 2 minutes, then leave to rest.

Preheat the oven to 430 °F/220 °C. Line a baking sheet with aluminum foil, and cover with a thick layer of salt crust in the shape of the fish. Place the fish on this. Stuff the inner cavity of the fish with herbs according to taste, then cover with salt crust to encase the fish completely. Bake in the preheated oven for about 15 minutes, until the crust is a light golden-brown color.

This fish has a fairly rich flesh. It is best accompanied by a white wine. Suggested choices are *Cassis*, a wine from the Pays d'Aude, or a white Burgundy.

Provençal fish dishes

Fish prepared in a host of different ways is extremely popular in Provence and along the rest of the Mediterranean coast. These dishes are a homage to the beneficence of the sea. The best examples of this joyous, simple cuisine are sea bass and scorpion fish, cooked with other local produce.

Chapon farci vieille Provence
Traditional Provençal stuffed scorpion fish

Serves 6

1 scorpion fish, 3 lbs/1.5 kg
2 ½ lbs/1.2 kg potatoes
3 tomatoes
1 red bell pepper
1 green bell pepper
2 zucchini
1 eggplant
Freshly milled salt and pepper
Fennel seeds
3 bay leaves
1 bulb of garlic

Ratatouille for the filling

1 red bell pepper
1 green bell pepper
1 onion
8 tomatoes
1 eggplant
1 zucchini
1 cloves of garlic, crushed
4 tbsp olive oil
Freshly milled salt and pepper
3 ½ cups/200 g fresh white breadcrumbs
Scant ½ cup/100 ml white wine

Clean the fish, slitting it open along the back and removing the major bones while keeping it whole. Rinse under running water. Peel the potatoes, cut into chunks, and boil in salted water. Wash and dice the other vegetables to accompany the fish, and peel the garlic.

Fry the bell peppers lightly in the oil, adding the zucchini and finally the eggplant. They should still be firm to the bite. Preheat the oven to 430 °F /220 °C.

To make the ratatouille, wash the bell peppers and cut into strips. Peel and slice the onion. Skin, core, and dice the tomatoes, and then dice the eggplant and zucchini.

Fry the vegetables and garlic for the filling lightly in the oil. Season with salt and pepper, cover, and simmer for about 20 minutes over a low heat. Gently stir in the breadcrumbs.

Stuff the fish with the ratatouille. Spread the vegetables on an ovenproof dish and lay the fish on top.

Bake for about 15 minutes. Then pour on the white wine and cook for a further 5 minutes.

The "Poutargue de Martigues"

Martigues was once a typical small Provençal fishing port. Artists like Camille Corot and Ziem were fascinated by its charms. Today the oil refineries by the Étang de Berre choke the air, though some nostalgic and delightful spots remain. A local tradition has also been retained: the *poutargue*.

The mullet is a very ordinary fish, and thrives in the warm coastal waters. The people of the Mediterranean have loved its roe since classical times – so much so that Egypt, Greece, Italy, and France still argue over the origin of the famous *boutargue* or *poutargue*. The name comes from the Arabic *boutarkha* and came by way of the Italian *bottarga* into the language of Provence, where it is called *boutargo* or *oeufs de poissons salés* (salted fish eggs).

It used to be part of the everyday diet of the fishermen, who wanted to waste nothing of their catch. Now it can be found gracing the shelves of fine food establishments.

When the mullet return to sea from the Étang de Berre between July and September, the females are heavy with eggs. The fishermen spread out huge horizontal nets 315 feet by 39 feet (96 m by 12 m) called *calen* or carrelets in the water. These are winched up and down, sometimes as often as every quarter of an hour. The catch is too valuable for a single shoal to be missed.

The females are carefully slit open to retrieve the valuable eggs. The roe is difficult to remove, since this must be done in one piece, without damaging the surrounding membrane. The roes are then washed, well salted, and pressed for several hours. This causes them to shed moisture and absorb salt. They are washed, tossed in salt, and pressed again, until they are less than ½ in (1 cm) thick. Then they are rinsed, patted dry with a sponge, and put in a dry, airy place (or alternatively into the smokehouse).

The roe can be various sizes, and may be darker or lighter in color. But whether their weight is measured in ounces or pounds (from a few dozen

In the days when Martigues was a tiny fishing port, the painter Camille Corot was attracted by its charm, and lived here for several years.

Pissaladière
Anchovy bake
(from pissalà, "anchovy paste")

Serves 8

7 ¾ lbs/3.5 kg onions
2 tbsp/30 ml olive oil
2 cloves of garlic
1 bouquet garni (thyme, bay, parsley)
Freshly milled salt and pepper
1 lb 10 oz/750 g bread dough
⅓ cup/50 g black olives (niçoise)
10–12 anchovy fillets
Pepper

Set the dough to rise. Preheat the oven to 350–400 °F/180–200 °C.

Peel the onions and slice them thinly. Fry lightly on a low heat until translucent, together with the garlic and bouquet garni. Season with salt and pepper.

Three quarters cover the pot, and continue cooking gently until soft. Do not allow the onions to brown. Then remove the garlic and bouquet garni.

Grease a large baking pan or sheet. When the bread dough has risen, roll it out to just under ¼ in/0.5 cm thick, to fit the baking pan. Spread the onions on top and decorate with the olives and anchovies. Drizzle with olive oil if wished. Bake for about 15 minutes. Finally, season with pepper and serve lukewarm with green salad.

Pissaludière is also delicious eaten cold with an aperitif.
An alternative method is to spread the base with spicy anchovy paste before adding the onions.

grams to a few hundred), whether they are golden or deep amber in color, the *poutargues de Martigues* well deserve their reputation as the "caviar of Provence." They cost around several hundred Euros per Kilo. Their appearance is deceptive; they melt in the mouth, and even the tiniest portion on the tip of a knife yields the iodine tang of the sea. Genuine *poutargue* from Martigues, the main port for sardine fishing in France today, has no wax coating like other types, and still retains the natural tag of real dried fish at one end, a remnant of the mullet from which it came.

The "sardinade"

Inconspicuous as it tries to remain with its dark hue and silvery gleam – like other fish that feed near the surface, and need to stay

Eating *poutargue*: some serving suggestions

- Sliced, on thin, buttered rustic bread (mixed grain rye bread) or toast. Sprinkle with a little lemon juice, and serve with a dry white wine.
- Blend with butter, leave in the refrigerator to harden, then place on top of broiled mullet or John Dory just before serving. Accompany with a white wine from Cassis.
- Grate generously over noodles in the style of Provence – with garlic, parsley, and olive oil.
- Grate finely, and stir into crème fraîche (or whipping cream with a little buttermilk; mixture should be left at room temperature for 8–24 hours) to make a tasty sauce.
- Just on its own.

Fishermen's *mélet* from Martigues

Mélet, much rarer and more piquant than *poutargue*, is another Martigues specialty. It is a paste made from sprats, and was once a favored dish or a welcome gift; today it lives on in the childhood memories of local inhabitants. Fish merchants no longer stock *mélet* as often as they did, though it can still be found. It takes the form of a brownish, creamed paste, sold in glass jars. Used as flavoring, it is prepared from young sprats, sardines, or anchovies, and resembles *poutine* or *nonnat*, which come from Nice. The small fish are layered in an earthenware pot for preference, covered completely with sea salt, coarsely ground pepper, bay, and branches of fennel. A weight is placed on top, and they are pressed for 14–20 days. At the end of this time, most of the salt has dissolved and been taken up by the fish. The *mélet* is drained and passed through a sieve. The resulting paste is piquant and contains no bones. It is spread thinly onto rustic bread, which is then toasted and sprinkled with a little olive oil. It can be used like *pissalat* from Nice to spread thinly on the bottom of a richly flavored tart such as *pissaladière* or homemade pizza.

undetected by seabirds – the sardine cannot escape from fishing by lantern light. Most sardines caught are sent for canning, but there are more sociable ways to enjoy this fish. The owners of the seaside *cabanons* like to gather on a Sunday for a tasty, good-natured *sardinade*. Sardines are nutritious, fairly oily fish, and stand up well to a sojourn on the grill. They are also quick and easy to prepare. Scaling, gutting, and de-boning are simply not necessary. They just need to be tossed or rubbed in olive oil and coarse salt. The moderate red glow of a fire, often scented with pine needles, does the rest.

Grilled, the fish parts easily from the bone, and melts in the mouth. The flavor is enough to put its dull, canned cousin in the shade.

The Martigues specialty *mélet* is a richly flavored paste that tastes wonderful spread thinly onto freshly baked rustic bread or toast.

Sardines à l'escabèche
Marinated sardines

Serves 10

40 fresh sardines
Salt and pepper
3 tbsp all purpose flour
2 cups/500 ml olive oil
1 cup/250 ml red wine vinegar
1 glass of water
1 bulb of garlic, finely sliced
3 onions, thinly sliced
6 sprigs each of thyme and parsley
1 bay leaf

Scale the sardines, remove the heads, and gut and clean the fish. Rinse in fresh water and pat dry with paper towels. Season and dust lightly with flour. Heat half the oil, and fry the sardines for five minutes each side until golden. Drain on paper towels, then place in a dish. Add the remaining oil to the pan, with the vinegar, water, and flavorings. Bring to a boil and cook for five minutes. Pour over the sardines to cover them completely. Leave them in a cool place for at least 24 hours for the flavors to develop.

225

THE CABANONS

In times past, fishermen forced to return to land quickly to shelter from bad weather took refuge in huts that they had either built themselves or inherited from their forefathers, for the most part Italian immigrants in the 19th century. They then waited in these makeshift buildings for the storm to pass, and ate a meal.

A change has come upon this paradise today. There are now barely a dozen fishermen living in Vallon des Auffes, a small suburb of Marseille. They nostalgically recall the days when they spent their time following their return from sea playing *pétanque* or cards, and when the pastis flowed. The village-like character of Vallon itself has to some extent remained, but up on the hills and promontories between the little bays, the number of *cabanons* has multiplied. The former huts have changed their use and lost their original style. The buildings have been extended or replaced with specially designed second homes. During the season, whole families stay here, friends from town, or vacationers in search of relaxation and a quota of sunshine. Even townsfolk like to take the opportunity to fish. Out come the fishing rods, nets are cast or fish traps set, the hunt is on for octopus or young squid, sea urchins will be sampled, and the barbecue prepared. Sardines and small red mullet are grilled, soup bubbles in the pot, and there is homemade *aïoli* to give a tang to the vegetables. Then, when the chilled rosé has done its work, what could be nicer than a siesta in the shade of the *cabanon*?

Each day, the fishermen's first task on returning from sea is, importantly, to attend to their nets.

The small boats in the harbor serve as a reminder that Vallon was once a fishing village. Now only around a dozen fishermen live here.

Good Old-Fashioned Candies and Cookies

On the farther outskirts of Marseille, at the end of a steep road, and set on the slopes that become the first foothills of the Chaîne de l'Étoile, lies Allauch. The attraction of this place is the "Moulin Bleu," which sells the produce of the firm Maison Brémond, a temptation if ever there was one.

The company has specialized in the production of nougat since the 19th century. There have been several changes of ownership since that time, but that does not prevent its present owners from regarding themselves as heirs in a long line of tradition, remnants of an older age and guardians of things remembered. As confectioners, they continue to manufacture nougat, candies, and cookies following old family recipes. They pack them in the old style, and call them by the time-honored names: *suce-miel, chique, croquet,* and *sucre d'orge*.

Entering the "Moulin Bleu" is taking a trip back in time. *Sucre d'orge*, malt sugar, sounds like a simple enough treat. The reality is enough to make any child's eyes light up: a striped sugar stick of elegant proportions, fruit-flavored, and gleaming in every color imaginable. It is the longer cousin of the round *berlingot* candies. There are older candies still, the ancestors of *sucre d'orge*, as it were. *Suce-miel* is a "honey-lolly" with the same slender shape as *sucre d'orge*, but made with lashings of lavender honey, sugar, and glucose. The finished candy is wrapped in a sheet of paper. Unwrapping it calls for patience, though the maker has a tip: The trick is to warm the end of the stick in one's hand. This loosens the edge of the paper.

The beginning of the 20th century saw a new development. Everyone loves something

"Moulin Bleu" sells delightful, old-fashioned candies.

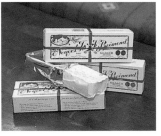

One of their specialties is nougat. They make tender, white nougat, and a hard, dark variety.

One-for-the-road honey: Suce-miel candy made by "Moulin Bleu."

sweet to eat, yet candies had long been a privilege of the middle classes. The big change came when manufacturers chopped up the *suce-miel* into small pieces and sold them separately. Called *chiques*, these candies were inexpensive enough to be affordable by many more people.

Another old-fashioned specialty made here is the *cacho-dent*, which is intended to break between the teeth (not vice-versa, as sweet-eaters might fear!). It has to be sucked in the mouth or softened in a hot drink for a while before it is bitten, whereupon it tastes delicious. There is a story behind these. Buckwheat grew well on certain ground where almond trees were cultivated. The freshly harvested almonds were preserved by encasing them in a buckwheat crust, which was twice-baked to prevent it from crumbling. The finished product, even today, looks a

The products on offer at the candy store "Moulin Bleu" in Allauch are a taste of olden times.

very unremarkable cookie, with a dull surface and topped with an almond, simply loose in a plastic bag. This Cinderella among cookies makes the sweet-toothed go weak at the knees. It is a heart-breaker after all, not a breaker of teeth.

The Testa brothers also preserve the tradition of Provençal cookies such as *navettes*, *oreillettes*, and others. Their main product is nougat, and they make both the black and the white kinds. It is still made by hand, sawn into portions, and wrapped. It is tempting enough to be placed on the list of deadly sins, but for one saving feature: the wafer surrounding the nougat. "Moulin Bleu" is also an official supplier of communion wafers to the Vatican.

CASSIS

As the traveler leaves Marseille along the D 559 toward Cassis, a last look back at the city shows it nestling against its surrounding mountains, and running down to the blue of the Mediterranean. Not even the harsh whiteness of its modern tower blocks can deaden the timeless beauty of these lovely surroundings.

The road to Cassis winds upward in gentle coils to the parched heights of the Massif du Puget, before descending once more through pines, mimosas, and vineyards to the delightful little inlets of the coast, and the harbor of Cassis. Once a Roman fishing port, Cassis today is a lively, popular resort. The inhabitants of Marseille like to retreat here from the hubbub of the city when their work is done. This little town with its narrow streets and harbor has an original and unique charm of its own. It is also famous for its wines.

The harbor

The fishermen sell their wares from crates bearing the names of their boats. They are selling sea urchins, and the purchaser can sample them straight away at the quayside, with a glass of the local white wine from one of the many cafés by the harbor. A conversation starts up with the fishermen, perhaps the visitor inquiring how they ply their trade. They will reply with an account of how they catch the sea urchins from the fishing boats. There are many regulations, each *département* having its own. The urchins are usually picked up with a long, split cane, sometimes, the fishermen dive for them. Around Marseille, they wear complete diving equipment for this. They will tell their listeners how best to open and eat the *violets de la mer*, the "sea violets," so as to lose none of their delicate aroma. And they will report on the *oursinades* held in

Carry-le-Rouet, a small harbor a short distance from Marseille, where people with a taste for sea urchins gather on the jetty to sample them every February.

Spawning time occurs at the end of March, and sea urchins disappear from the fishermen's catch. The harbor itself is active all year round, however, bringing in fish, shellfish, and other seafood renowned for its high quality, and attracting a large clientèle to the quay.

The charm of Cassis lies in its tiny harbor with its colorful boats, the numerous bistros with their promise of many a pleasant hour passed over coffee, an aperitif, or a glass of wine, and the cliff behind, crowned by the Château des Baux that towers over the village. Despite the throngs of visitors that crowd the streets in the summer months, the provincial charm of Cassis endures.

A little preparatory effort is required to arrive at the delicious inside of a sea urchin. First, hold it in the palm of the hand, top side down. Cut into the slightly concave underside with strong scissors or cutters.

Cut carefully and steadily around the mouth opening, removing a sufficiently large circle to provide access. Remove the mouth parts and the inedible part of the innards.

The ovaries, "gonads," or "tongues" now lie uncovered. These are spooned out, and are the only part that is eaten. The liquid inside the urchin is valued as a flavoring.

THE WHITE WINE OF CASSIS

The vineyards at Cassis are spectacular. They rise in terraces right up to the cliffs that descend abruptly toward the Mediterranean.

(equivalent to 666,700 bottles) of white wine and 1,000 hectoliters (roughly 133,300 bottles) of red and rosé. The vineyards lie in terraces stretching to the edge of the dizzy cliffs of Cap Canaille, facing the sea. Wine has been cultivated here since ancient times. This sunny location is now shared by 12 winegrowers, and enjoys an average of 2,800 hours of sunshine a year. The winegrowers all expend great care on developing the characteristic, full-bodied style of Cassis wines, a care that earned them the award of Appellation (AOC) status in 1936.

There is no connection between the wines of this area and the typically French specialty of *Blanc-Cassis* the name given here to kir, the drink made of white wine and the blackcurrant liqueur, cassis. One feature they do share, however, is their reddish tinge.

The area's vineyards are all concentrated within 494 acres (200 hectares) of vineyards, on the low hills by the harbor. Of these, 445 acres (180 hectares) are designated Appellation d'Origine Contrôlée. Cassis produces an annual 5,000 hectoliters

The grape varieties that are grown on this meager calcareous soil, in the warm, dry climate of Cassis, are Marsanne, Clairette, Ugni Blanc, Grenache, Cinsault, and Mourvèdre. Exposure to the sea protects the vineyards

A stop at Domaine de la Ferme Blanche is not to be missed by lovers of good wine.

The valuable wines of Domaine de la Ferme Blanche are sealed and packed with the greatest care and correctness. No harm must come to them during transport.

Domaine de la Ferme Blanche does not specialize in wine of any one particular color. White, red, and rosé wines are part of the repertoire and all are of high quality.

from the harshness of inland winters; even the extremely cold winter of 1956, which severely damaged many vines, did not affect the ones here. In the summer, meanwhile, the sea breezes waft over the vines and diminish the heat to which they are exposed. Too much heat interferes with the long ripening process which the grapes need.

The wines of Cassis have certain surprising features. The yields are remarkably high for Provence, and they are among the few Appellations of the region capable of keeping. The wines are fine, full-bodied, heavy, and robust. They have a fruitiness and astonishing freshness and

softness that harmonize wonderfully with fish and bouillabaisse. If served at not too cold a temperature, they demonstrate a still richer character. They should emphatically be tried to accompany sea urchins.

The Domaine de la Ferme Blanche has behind it a family history going back 300

La Ferme Blanche makes no secret of its trade. The painting on the walls proclaims that everything here revolves around wine.

A good wine must be stored well. If it is to be matured in wooden barrels in the traditional manner, much depends on the choice of wood.

years. It produces one of the typical Cassis wines. Ugni Blanc, Clairette, Marsanne, and Bourboulenc grape varieties produce a wine with a flowery note, followed by a faintly woody finish. It has a rounded character, and should be enjoyed well chilled. It is an excellent accompaniment to fish and shell-fish.

To encounter a Cassis white capable of being stored for 10–15 years without decline in quality, a visit to the estate Clos d'Albizzi is an absolute must. Such wines account for 90 percent of the estate's production, and are

The Clos d'Albizzi estate produces a unique wine, created in a dry style, and capable of being stored for at least 10–15 years.

made from equal quantities of Clairette, Ugni Blanc, and Marsanne. These are dry, powerful wines, the ideal accompaniment for a good bouillabaisse. They are also a good partner for broiled sardines, whose strong iodine tang harmonizes magnificently with the aromatic wine, creating a truly memorable gastronomic experience.

Clos Sainte-Madeleine covers just a few hectares of steep and stony ground, but its panoramic marine views alone would make it remarkable. The estate produces aromatic, fruity white wines blended from Clairette, Ugni Blanc, and Marsanne. These are generous wines that keep well, and are a wonderful accompaniment for fish. They have an alcohol content of 12–13 percent, yet they are not heavy wines. The rosé, made from Cinsault, Mourvèdre, and Grenache, also makes an excellent partner to Mediterranean cuisine. This has a powerful, flowery, fine character that is quite distinct.

The estate of Clos Sainte-Madeleine lies at the foot of the vineyards, surrounded by vines.

BANDOL

The glorious Route des Crêtes runs along the hillcrest to Cap Canaille with its views down to the wharves of La Ciotat, then on to the harbor of Bandol, a popular, pleasant resort.

The Château Pibernon estate makes remarkable wines in its 119 acres (48 hectares) of vineyards. Its red and white wines excite the connoisseur, and it also produces a very appealing rosé.

The fields of the little harbor village of Bandol are laid out in terraces, with stony, calcareous, silicic acid-containing soils where vines are cultivated, and the demanding Mourvèdre variety does well. The coastal situation provides it with a welcome degree of humidity, and the sun-kissed climate suits it. Bandol has made this sensitive southern French grape its trademark. Mourvèdre is high in tannins, and so the wines are best kept in the cellar to mature for a couple of years.

The other varieties used together with Mourvèdre, which must make up at least 50 percent of a Bandol red wine, are mainly Grenache, Cinsault, Syrah, and Carignan. The alcohol content of Bandol has to be at least 11 percent. The wines are matured in oak casks before they are ready to be sold; for red wines, the period of maturation is 18 months, for whites and rosés, 8 months.

The Appellation was awarded to Bandol in 1941, and it is above all the remarkable quality of its reds that justify this status. Consumed young, these wines are powerful and full of tannins; after maturing for 10–15 years, they exhibit a powerful vanilla note on the nose, making them a magnificent partner for red meat, game, or for poultry dishes à la provençale.

The white wines are full and characteristically Mediterranean, mainly made from Ugni Blanc, Clairette, and Bourboulenc, and with a pronounced flowery and fruity character.

A Bandol rosé is striking for the paleness of its color, and its bouquet has a finesse that is a major part of its charm.

A number of great names provide the promise of exceptional pleasure to the wine-drinker. Among these is the domaine of Château Pradeaux. The estate is owned by a family, and has a long, turbulent history. It comprises 44 acres (18 hectares) of vineyards, and produces a great red wine that stores well.

Mourvèdre is of course the main grape used. Demanding as this variety is to grow, it was the owner of this estate who, together with two other local winegrowers, was responsible for its reintroduction following a phylloxera epidemic that all but completely destroyed the Mourvèdre grape in this region. A Château Pradeaux wine will already have been grown and harvested with immense care, and may sometimes spend up to five years maturing in the barrel. It is then bottled without filtering, and can easily be kept for another 20 years or more. The long storage improves it, for only then does it fully develop its complex aroma and full-bodied character. A Château Pradeaux is an outstanding accompaniment for game. The 1986 vintage is practically unrivaled for its a long finish, and has an astounding longevity – it is expected to remain drinkable until 2009. Both the 1986 and 1991 vintages demonstrate the first class quality of Château Pradeaux wines.

The stony, calcareous and silicic acid-containing soil is entirely characteristic of vineyards in the area around Cassis and Bandol.

Work and pleasure go together. It is part of a winemaker's job to taste the wine and check its quality, or to be able to advise customers on each wine's particular merits.

Château Pibarnon lies in Cadière d'Azur, overlooking the sea. The wine made here, in this area of 119 acres (48 hectares), is highly typical of Appellation Bandol. This fine wine, too, calls for patience. The 1996 white, however, is ready for drinking at the time of writing. It has a complex aroma that will complement such dishes as *foie gras* or shellfish. The 2003 vintage, made from Cinsault and Mourvèdre grapes, can already be drunk. Château Pibarnon certainly produces outstanding red and white wines, its red wine consisting of 90 percent Mourvèdre.

However, its rosés are also very pleasing. These are composed of Mourvèdre and Cinsault and their bouquet seems to encompass the entire character of Provence.

Domaine de Souviou has some very good, not too expensive surprises to offer the lover of white wines – well chilled, they are an excellent accompaniement broiled fish. The delicate, refined flavor of red mullet is brought out by a more flowery vintage, which should also be drunk soon. The fruity aromas of the 2001 red are very seductive. The white wines of La Laidière cost a little more. The vineyard lies on the meager, sandy soil of Sainte-Anned'Evenos. These wines account for only five percent of total production, but are often considered the best of the Appellation. The 2003 vintage has proved to be an especially fruity and flowery wine. The lovers of Rosé wines will appreciate the wines of this vintage.

The red wines produced by this estate are made in stainless steel fermentation tanks before being transferred to oak barrels to mature for another 18 months. They benefit from a couple of years' cellar storage.

Château Pradeaux. It is the owner of this estate who is to be thanked for the reintroduction of the Mourvèdre grape to wine production.

AOC wines and wine quality

There are 12 Appellations d'Origine Contrôllée (meaning "Designated Area of Origin") in the Provence-Côte d'Azur region. These define wines or specific vineyard areas in the French administrative *départements* of Alpes-Maritimes, Alpes-de-Haute-Provence, Bouches-du-Rhône, Var, and Vaucluse. An area may also carry the quality designation Appelation Vin Délimitée de Qualité Supérieure. The award of AOC has been made since 1935 by the Institut National des Appellations d'Origine des vins et eaux-de-vie (National Institute of Designated Area of Origin for wines and eaux de vie), as a guarantee of quality and consumer protection. It prescribes the choice of grape variety, based on quality and locality, and the maintenance of local traditions of cultivation and winemaking. It specifies the vine pruning methods and the minimum alcoholic strength naturally achievable from the must. The AOC also lays down the vineyard area of each Appellation. Checks are carried out, normally annually, to confirm that the wines do indeed deserve their Appellation.

The Vins Délimités de Qualité Supérieure are often candidates in waiting for the award of AOC status, and every effort is made to fulfill the requirements for AOC.

Vins de Pays are "country wines" whose origin is often less precisely determined. Their alcoholic strength is on average less than ten percent, and they are often produced by cooperatives.

Vins de table are "table wines." The origin is not precisely stated, and they are industrially produced.

"L'Île Rousse"

The restaurant "L'Île Rousse" in Var, on the western shore of the Bay of Bandol, was regarded as a palace in the 1970s. The building belonged to the variety artist La Mistinguett, star of the Paris variety stage in the 1920s and 1930s, who was even for a time owner of the city's famous "Moulin Rouge."

Today the renovated "L'Île Rousse" has rooms overlooking the Bay of Renécros, a pool, a thalassotherapy area, and a hammam – in short, everything necessary to compensate for the culinary excesses resulting from giving in to the greatly tempting culinary artistry of the chef. Jean-Paul Lanyou is the master of all the glories the menu has to offer, without revealing too much. What, for example,

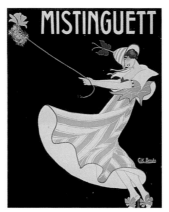

A poster advertising a performance by Mistinguett. Her name was in itself sufficient to announce the program, and drew the public to the variety theaters.

might be the reality behind a *biscuit d'araignée de mer* (spider crab cookie)?

The chef likes painstakingly prepared creations, innovatively conceived and put through their trial preparation every day, a process that combines improvization and experience. On an early morning visit to the harbor of Sanary, he will fill his basket with tiny pink shrimps, which, after a few moments' contemplation, he will fry with olive oil and basil as an *amuse-bouche*, an appetizer.

Jean-Paul Lanyou loves fish, always preferring it to meat. He serves delicate sea bass with a white wine from Cassis or a chilled Bandol rosé – to him it is a matter of his duty to ensure that the wines and dishes harmonize.

Among his delicious creations are *rougets en escabèche* (fried red mullet, served cold in marinade), *Saint-Pierre sur arêtes* (John Dory, served whole, on the bone), and young Provence pigeon stuffed with *foie gras*.

The terrace of "L'Île Rousse" offers a lovely view of the Bay of Cassis, inviting the visitor to recline in the sun.

Lanyou also knows how to prepare meat and delights his guests with braised calf's knuckle with pickled shallots. In the other restaurants that Lanyou manages with equal success, restaurants that are only slightly simpler than "L'Île Rousse," the cuisine is more traditional and Mediterranean – oyster gratin with wine from Bandol at the "Auberge du Vieux," and broiled meat specialties at "La Goélette."

The dining room of "L'Île Rousse" is at the same time elegant and cozy. Visitors place themselves utterly in the capable hands of the *chef de cuisine*, Jean-Paul Lanyou, who conjures the most delicious masterpieces from his kitchen The menu features mainly fish and shellfish dishes.

Langoustines du Guilvinec rôties, coussin de pommes de terre au caviar d'Iran et beurre coraillé

Fried Guilvinec langoustines on potato medallions with Iranian caviar, served with roe butter

Serves 4

Generous 1 lb/500 g potatoes
4 fine langoustines
3 eggs
½ cup/60 g all-purpose flour
Generous 1 cup/250 ml crème fraîche
Scant ½ cup/100 g butter
4 tsp Iranian caviar
Salt, cayenne pepper
A few leaves of basil

Cook the unpeeled potatoes, in salted water. Meanwhile, remove the langoustines from their shells leaving their tails intact. Cut the langoustines open carefully along the back, and remove the intestine. Briefly sauté the langoustines in a pan. Take off the heads and reserve. Take out the roe, and blend with half the butter. Boil the shells in about 1 cup of water to make a stock.

Peel the potatoes when cooked, and dry them in the oven. Then pass them through a sieve. Warm the crème fraîche, but do not allow it to boil. Add this to the sieved potatoes, together with the flour and eggs. Shape the mixture into four cakes, and fry them in melted, clarified butter. Keep hot. Boil the stock until reduced by a third, and beat together with the roe butter. Season.

Place the potato medallions onto plates, place a spoonful of caviar on each, and drizzle some langoustine sauce over the plate. Place a langoustine on top of each, and decorate with the head and a few fried leaves of basil.

A very suitable accompaniment to this gourmet feast is a white wine from La Laidière.

VAR'S "HOSTELLERIE BÉRARD"

The small village of La Cadière d'Azur in Var overlooks the green slopes of the Bandol vineyards. Formerly a medieval market town, it is now the neglected neighbor of the famous Formula 1 racing circuit at Castellet.

In the 11th century, the monastery of La Cadière housed the monks of St. Victor; today, a welcome change has come over the building. The bareness of the monastic cells and the modest fare of the monks have given way to the comfort, charm, and fine cuisine of the "Hostellerie Bérard," where it is easy to forget that stern asceticism was once the rule of the day, rather than more indulgent fleshly delights.

Petits farcis de tomates, courgettes et poivrons
Stuffed tomatoes, zucchini, and bell peppers

Serves 4

5 cups/200 g white bread (torn into pieces)
2 glasses of milk
4 firm but ripe tomatoes
4 bell peppers
4 zucchini
4 small eggplants
1 1/2 cups/150 g grated Parmesan
2 eggs
A pinch of nutmeg
1 cup/150 g diced ham
Scant 1/2 lb/200 g ground meat (pork, beef, and veal)
1 bunch of mixed herbs (*fines herbes*) finely chopped
2 cloves of garlic, chopped
Olive oil

Soak the bread in the milk. Cut the lid off the tomatoes, and hollow out the insides, reserving the flesh. Cut the tops off the bell peppers, and remove the ribs and seeds. Cut the zucchini in half lengthways, and hollow out. Reserve the flesh of the zucchini, adding it to that from the tomatoes.

Preheat the oven to 350 °F/180 °C. Squeeze out the soaked bread. In a large bowl, mix it with the Parmesan, eggs, nutmeg, ham, ground meat, herbs, and garlic. Stir in the tomato and zucchini flesh until thoroughly mixed.

Stuff the shells with this mixture, and replace the lids. Place on a greased baking sheet and bake for 30–40 minutes.

The "Hostellerie Restaurant Bérard" is a place with a great deal of charm. Its owner and cook has outstanding abilities. The building is a former monastery, dating back to the 11th century. It has a comfortable atmosphere.

"Nouvelle cuisine? – I do not even know what it is. The only cuisine in my book is the sort I enjoy." The acknowledged chef René Bérard – to give him his full title, *Maître Cuisinier de France René Bérard* – rehearses a story that is recreated every day as it has been for 30 years. It is a tale of provençal cooking, generous and inventive, a cuisine that values the products of soil and sea, and uses the best local produce – everything from the olive oil of Souviou to the fish and seafood bought fresh that morning from the market at Sanary-sur-Mer. The menu includes truffles from Aups, provençal asparagus, mixed garden-grown salad, and desserts made with lemons from Menton among many other flavorsome dishes.

Here, the customer can enjoy the typical hospitality and cuisine of Provence in all its time-honored perfection.

The countryside and the cuisine are not the only provençal features of the "Hostellerie Bérard," the huge fireplace and stone sink in the kitchen also have a rustic air that appeals to guests.

Cookery, viticulture, and watercolors à la carte

The guests of the hotel wave farewell with the jars of jelly from breakfast carefully secreted in their luggage – and the management smiles its benevolent approval! Danièle and René Bérard not only permit this; they are delighted and flattered, because the guests in question have made the jelly themselves in these very kitchens, from the fruit grown right here in the vicinity.

Danièle and René Bérard have been running cookery courses for more than ten years. During the four days that the course lasts, René Bérard introduces his guests not only to the art of cookery in general, but to the

Aïoli is made by crushing the garlic in a mortar, and stirring it together with olive oil to produce the well-known garlic-flavoured mayonnaise.

preparation of certain provençal specialties.

All the skills and dishes that people might think only the professionals can master – making *aïoli* or *tapenade*, preparing a tomato *confit*, or producing a bouillabaisse – the course participants are able to accomplish with ease by the end of their stay.

The amateur cooks, clad in their hats and aprons, day by day file into the kitchen of a homely, atmospheric old cottage likewise belonging to the family. Under the direction of the friendly and attentive chef, they prepare lunch. Then, as the sun outside begins to tempt them to thoughts of pastis on the covered terrace under the wisteria, the cooks sample the dishes they have created, astonished to have produced it themselves.

The day's tuition includes expeditions to the local markets, collecting herbs in the *garrigue*, selecting fresh fish down at the harbor itself, and visits to local winegrowers, as well as an oil mill. The exploration of the area and its

The rustic kitchen speaks of the long years of experience and countless dishes that have been prepared here

On the terrace outside the *bastide*: When the cookery course is finished for the day, participants enjoy a well-earned rest in the shade of the wisteria and a glance at the newspaper.

glorious bounty is all an essential part of understanding the cuisine of Provence. This is by no means all that Danièle and René Bérard have to offer their guests; Danièle also teaches courses on winegrowing, providing an introduction to winemaking and a tasting of the fine wines of Bandol and Côtes de Provence. The participants on the jelly-making course, meanwhile, she ushers into her orchard, where they fill their baskets with delicious cherries, apricots, peaches, and quinces.

Visitors who want to immerse themselves in the beauties of the Provence countryside can settle down with their easels in a favorite spot, to capture the scene in watercolors.

Freshly picked peaches make a delicious jelly.

A very tasty and refreshing summer treat: cherries.

Home-grown artichokes feature on M. Bérard's menu.

Toulon

Toulon has made its name mainly as a naval port. From time immemorial, this has stamped its character on the town; even in the time of King Louis XIV, the navy was stationed here, and the royal architect, Vauban, built fortifications.

The market

Toulon's market has been world famous for decades past, and will doubtless remain so far into the future. The sunshine colors, scents, and flowers of the Cours Lafayette, with the market stallholders crying their wares, are said to have inspired Gilbert Bécaud to write his song "Les marchés de

The market on the Cours Lafayette is vibrant with color as cheerful shoppers crowd around the great range of produce on offer.

Provence" (The markets of Provence). In his wonderful southern French voice, he tells the listener about the thyme of the *garrigue*.

A leisurely tour of the stalls in this market will send the shopper home with a whole basket full of vegetables – time for *petits farcis*, a dish of stuffed vegetables.

Olives in all their splendor

What but the olive is capable of filling an entire market stall, and still providing a delight to eye and palate alike? The choice is overwhelming! Perhaps the customer's best option is to take home a handful of each to nibble with an aperitif.

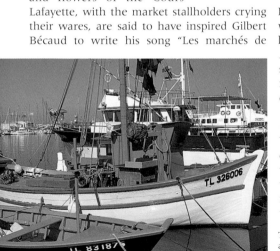

Toulon is not only one of France's main naval ports, but a place that impresses the visitor by its authentic, natural character, as a stroll around town reveals.

Petits farcis de légumes
Stuffed vegetables

Serves 4

4 new potatoes (round, firm when cooked)
4 medium tomatoes
Salt
4 small, purple artichokes
½ cup/50 g grated Parmesan

Filling

Scant 1 lb/400 g cooked beef or ground meat
Scant ½ lb/200 g potatoes
Olive oil
1 large onion
4 cloves of garlic
1 bunch of parsley
1 bunch of basil
2 tbsp freshly grated Parmesan
Salt and freshly milled pepper

Boil the potatoes, unpeeled, in salted water. Cool, and cut off the tops about ⅔ of the way up. Hollow out the potatoes with a spoon. Hollow out the tomatoes in the same way, sprinkle the insides with salt, and then invert them on a rack to drain.

Cut off the tops of the artichokes ⅔ of the way up, and remove the harder outer leaves and the stem. Boil the artichokes in salted water for about ten minutes. They should remain firm. Cool, then remove the chokes with a teaspoon. Preheat the oven to 350 °F/180 °C.

To make the filling, first chop the lids of the tomatoes. Peel and dice the lids of the potatoes, and sauté them lightly in olive oil. Crush them with a fork.

Peel and slice the onion, and fry lightly in a saucepan. Add the ground meat and brown.

Peel the garlic, wash the herbs, and chop them all finely. Add the potatoes, tomatoes, meat, and the 2 tablespoons of Parmesan. Mix well and season. Place the hollowed-out vegetables on a baking sheet, stuff with the filling, and sprinkle with the ½ cup of Parmesan. Bake for 15 minutes in the preheated oven. Serve the stuffed vegetables with the typical local salad, *mesclun*, with a dressing that is made from *pistou* and lemon juice.

Other vegetables can be stuffed in the same way: small red or green bell peppers, eggplants, and onions. The filling can also be varied according to taste. One possibility is to use a mainly vegetable filling; another is to replace the ground meat with diced ham.

The tempting aromas of summer in this typical provençal dish mean that a fresh, light red wine from the region is the ideal accompaniment to *petits farcis*.

With so many delicious varieties of olive, the choice can be daunting. A sample, perhaps?

The olive is full of surprises; like the courtesan companion of light wines and *pastis*, it constantly changes its garb and its fragrance. Now luxuriant with herbs, now madly devoted to an anchovy, next moment to a capsicum, it may be slender or it may be buxom. It simpers with an almond smile one minute, and inflicts the searing heat of chili the next.

Sometimes, the olive is less careful of its natural good looks; crushed, but with the pit intact, it makes its appearance as *cassé-fenouil*, marinated in a light brine flavored with fresh fennel. The marinade used for its forebears

was a paste based on wood ash, but the brine has now replaced it.

The *picholine* olive is smooth, beautifully green, rather slim, crunchy, and versatile in flavor. Some people like to enjoy these soaked in a mixture of grated ginger, caraway, lemon juice, and oil. Others choose to eat them stuffed with a sliver of red pimento, a caper, or an anchovy. Or their preferred accompaniment may be garlic and basil, summer savory, bay, thyme, or coriander.

The olive stall is sure of plenty of customers; no aperitif is complete without olives in Provence.

Black olives in brine

very ripe, smooth, black olives

Fill a pot (ideally earthenware) with the olives and cover them with a ten percent brine solution. Add a bay leaf. Cover the pot, allowing a little air still to reach the brine. Leave for four to five months. Then drain and rinse the olives, and replace them in the pot with a clove of coarsely chopped garlic, a bay leaf, and a little olive oil. Olives prepared in this way will keep for several years.

Olives piquées

fat, black olives, a little wrinkled

Make a "hedgehog" by sticking needles carefully but firmly into a cork. Use this to pierce the olives, then toss them in fine-grained salt on a plate. Transfer them to an airy basket, and hang outside the window where the sun can dry them. If this is not possible, put them near a source of heat. After three or four days, shake the basket of olives to remove as much of the salt as possible. Then sprinkle with herbs as liked, and carefully pour over some oil.

The markets of Provence display olives in overflowing abundance.

Picholines au fenouil
(olives with fennel)

Olives vertes goût piment
(olives stuffed with pimento)

Olives cassées en escabèche
(large marinated olives)

Petites olives façon niçoise
(small olives, Nice style)

Olives farcies à l'anchois
(olives stuffed with anchovies)

Olives niçoises
(large purple Nice olives)

Olives noires provençales
(black Provençal olives)

Panaché d'olives pimentées
(olives with chili)

Olives dénoyautées
(pitted olives)

Olives cassées à la provençale
(crushed piquant olives)

Olives cassées paysanes
(piquant, marinated olives)

Picholines
(traditional variety of Provence)

"Cade de Toulon"

During the winter, hot chestnuts or sugared crêpes, wrapped in a swirl of paper, are on sale everywhere. Lunch might be a hot dog or sandwich, made with butter and ham. In Nice, the local specialty is called *socca*, and in Toulon, it is the *cade*. The difference is in the flour used: for the Nice version it is supposed to be made from corn, and in Toulon, from chickpeas (garbanzo beans). Or perhaps

Cade is not always baked on the market stall; supplies are sometimes rushed in from the kitchen by motorbike.

the other way round – we shall never know. What is not in dispute is the deliciousness of the product. Both *socca* and *cade* have been around for a long time, and used to be the regular breakfast snack for hungry workers.

Cade is an inexpensive, everyday snack that has survived modern competition, but the culinary tradition and regional history behind it make it as precious as the best caviar.

Unassuming as it is, *cade* is delicious, rather like a very thick pancake, which puffs up and turns golden brown in the cooking. After cooking, it is cut into small squares, sometimes flavored with *pistou*, and served in a strip of paper, to be eaten by hand on the way down the street.

There is no need to be asked twice if a portion of *cade* is on offer. The stallholder serves it wrapped in paper.

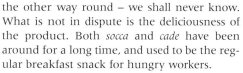

La cade
Pancakes made with chickpea flour

2 cups/500 ml water
1 ½ cups/250 g chickpea (garbanzo bean) flour
2 tbsp olive oil
1 tsp fine-grained salt
Oil
Pepper

Preheat the oven to its maximum temperature.

Stir together the water, flour, olive oil, and salt in a bowl, then beat vigorously with a hand blender, ensuring that no lumps are remaining.

Grease a baking sheet (roughly 18 in/50 cm diameter), and pour the batter thinly and evenly onto this. Bake or broil the pancake until golden. From time to time, burst the bubbles that form on the top.

The *cade* is ready when golden brown. It does not matter if there are a few burnt patches. Season it with pepper, cut into roughly 2 in/5 cm squares, and serve immediately.

Friture de mer
Fried fish morsels

A number of very small fish
3 tbsp all-purpose flour
Oil
Salt and pepper
Vinegar

Friture is the savor of the sea, nibbled in crisp, salty, bite-size morsels. The local name for it in Toulon is *la sardagnato*. A mixture of tiny fish is used, usually sardines and anchovies (also called *blanchaille*). They can be bought by the handful from fishermen returning to port, the quantity depending on appetite. The fish are washed and well dried, but not gutted, then tossed in flour. The best way to do this is to put them into a plastic bag of flour and shake it. Then transfer them to a plate and season with salt and pepper.

Heat the oil in a skillet until very hot. Fry the fish, turning them once but without stirring, until golden on both sides. Deglaze the pan with a little vinegar, then pour over the fried fish and serve immediately. The vinegar is frequently dispensed with and the fish simply served on their own or with a little lemon juice.

HYÈRES

Hyères has seen many transitions, from Greek colony to Roman fort, from elegant 19th-century bathing place to the Eldorado for windsurfers that it is today. Hyères nestles between the coast and the foot of the Massif des Maures, and its beautiful villas bear testimony to distant times in the past, when it was the favorite haunt of the English aristocracy.

Kiwi fruit: a tiny cornucopia of vitamins

The market in Hyères takes place every Tuesday and Saturday morning on the Boulevard Gambetta, where 33 growers sell the finest produce of their fields. Hyères has always been an important center for early vegetables, fruit, and flowers. The colorful market stalls overflow

The Lacours' charming villa gives no hint of the fruit gardens that lie behind. Organic kiwi fruit are grown here.

with fresh strawberries and meadow flowers. Among the produce sold here are the kiwi fruit of "Domaine des Fenouillet." These are grown organically by Denise Lacour and her husband, who owns the Domaine. They entrust their carefully selected young plants to the microclimate afforded by the southern slopes of Mont du Fenouillet, and use no artificial fertilizers or weedkillers, or sprays of any

sort. Each growing stage, right through to harvest, is carried out with the utmost care. The fruits are picked when still quite hard, to prevent damage in transit. When ripe, the fruits have a light brown skin that yields slightly to pressure. If the fruit is not quite ripe enough to be eaten, it can soon be ripened by placing it in a plastic bag with two apples for a few days. Kiwi fruit can also be kept very satisfactorily in the bottom of a refrigerator, where they will gradually ripen, without losing any of their exceptional content of precious vitamins.

Caution is the watchword when buying kiwi fruit that is already soft. In most cases, this means that the fruit has begun to ferment slightly.

Denise Lacour tends her fruit lovingly. She is convinced of its flavor and healthgiving

Kiwi fruit are a health cure in themselves. No other fruit contains so many vitamins.

benefits, and with reason: One single kiwi fruit contains a day's recommended intake of vitamin C, as well as generous quantities of vitamins A, E, and B, iron, calcium, and potassium. The kiwi fruit is the sworn enemy

of free radicals, which have been found to hasten the human aging process, and maintains the body's stock of useful minerals – all this without being particularly fattening, as kiwi fruit contain just 57 kilocalories per 100 g (about 16 per ounce). Wickedly delicious they may be, but they are positively virtuous promoting health and long life.

Madame Lacour also sells her homemade kiwi fruit jelly.

Kiwi fruit are the specialty of "Domaine des Fenouillet." They are delicious raw, or used in a tasty chicken recipe.

Poulet aux kiwis et reinettes
Chicken with kiwi fruit and apples

Serves 4

1 tbsp clear honey
1 chicken (3 lb/1.5 kg)
¼ cup/50 g butter
4 Reinette apples (or other dry cooking apple)
2 kiwi fruit
2 pinches of cinnamon
1 small glass/20 ml Calvados
2 tbsp crème fraîche
Salt and pepper

Preheat the oven to 400 °F/200 °C. Season the honey and rub into the chicken evenly all over. Melt just under half the butter in a large, heavy pan on the top of the cooker, and brown the chicken on all sides over a high heat, turning frequently. Meanwhile, peel and slice the kiwi fruit and apples.

Melt the remaining butter in a lidded roasting pan, add the apples, and sprinkle with cinnamon. Brown lightly for five minutes until golden. Lift the chicken out of its pan, leaving behind the cooking juices. Place it on top of the apple, cover, and cook in the preheated oven for 50 minutes.

After 40 minutes, replace the pan with the chicken juices on the heat. When the contents are hot, add the kiwi fruit and fry lightly for about one minute each side. Season lightly with salt and generously with pepper. Add the Calvados and warm. Draw the pan off the heat, and stir in the crème fraîche.

PORQUEROLLES

The islands of Hyères once, during the Renaissance, bore the name "Golden Isles." They are a favored stop for migrating birds on their way to Africa or to Europe. Porquerolles, which is within easy reach of Hyères by boat, is a veritable Garden of Eden – though high season is best avoided.

A special meal on the island
The "Mas du Langoustier" is situated at the western end of Porquerolles, and is a culinary gem. It lies hidden behind pines and eucalyptus

Whoever comes to Porquerolles must be prepared for leisure. It is worth discovering the island on foot or by bike. You can wait for the boat to the mainland in the wooden "station."

trees, planted by François Joseph Fournier at the beginning of the 20th century. Fournier had bought the island at auction, and gave it to his wife, Sylvia, as a wedding present. The provençal charm of the building and its old-world interior is jealously guarded by its present custodians, Richard by name. The kitchen chef of the restaurant, "Le Mas du Langoustier," is Joël Guillet, a highly talented man from Burgundy. He learned to cook from his mother. He was then seized with a passion for cooking, and his profession drew him entirely under its

Porquerolles belongs to the Îles d'Hyères, named the "Marquisat des Îles d'Or" by Henri II. Since then they have also been called the "Golden Isles."

spell, as did Provence. Guillet moved here, leaving Burgundy behind, and draws his culinary inspiration from Porquerolles – from the sea and the fresh garden vegetables. He has developed his own individual and unusual style, which has become his trademark: His cuisine is simple and natural, and has at the

Joël Guillet is respnsible for the cuisine of "Le Mas du Langoustier."

same time a polished elegance – the summit of delicious perfection. One of the restaurant's best-known specialties, is tuna steak wrapped in a parcel of tender vine leaves. Tasting the steak is a great pleasure that leaves little appetite for everyday canned tuna, however convenient that may be.

Velouté de tomates glacé à l'origan
Petites tomates à l'aïoli
Iced tomato velouté with oregano
Small tomatoes with aïoli

Serves 6

Soup

Generous 2 lb/1 kg selected red tomatoes
3 anchovy fillets
Juice of 1 lemon
½ bunch of oregano
2 tsp olive oil

Small tomatoes with *aïoli*

6–8 cloves/25 g finely chopped garlic
2 egg yolks
Salt and pepper
4 tsp olive oil
Juice of ½ lemon
6 vine tomatoes
a little fresh oregano

Skin, core, and quarter the tomatoes the evening before use. Place in a bowl with the anchovies, lemon juice, oregano leaves, and olive oil, and leave to infuse all night in the refrigerator.

Purée with a blender, then pass through a fine-meshed sieve, and season.

Place the garlic and egg yolks in a bowl, and season. Add oil gradually, working it in as for mayonnaise. Finally add the lemon juice. Adjust the seasoning according to taste.

Cut a lid off the top of the vine tomatoes, and hollow them out with a teaspoon. Sprinkle lightly with salt, and invert to drain for about ten minutes.

Fill the shells with the *aïoli*, and replace the lids.

Serve the chilled tomato soup in soup plates, placing a small tomato in each. Pour on a little olive oil, and decorate with fresh oregano.

CÔTES DE PROVENCE

The winegrowing area that stretches from the Massif Sainte-Victoire in the west to Saint-Raphaël in the east is the oldest in France. Wine has been produced around the towns of Aix-en-Provence, Aups, and Draguignan for 2,600 years. The region of Haut-Var is criss-crossed with narrow, winding roads, some of them running straight out of the Grand Canyon of Verdon.

The River Verdon has carved out a steep-sided, impressively beautiful gorge, a succession of dizzy cliffs and rock formations 1,300–2,300 feet (400–700 m) high. Trout and pike in abundance swim in its waters, and thyme-scented paths run along its banks. Provence has its spectacular scenery, too, delightful and less tourist-frequented, as the visitor to its oak and pine woods very soon discovers.

The road leads from Aups, with its medieval character and enticing smell of truffles and honey, past vineyards in the direction of Les-Arcs-sur-Argens. On the way the road passes

through pretty villages with narrow streets and a rich medieval history, past abbeys and castles, to finally finish up in Lourgues.

The distant outline of the Massif des Maures appears as a silhouette against the sky, its flanks darkened with oak forests and chestnut groves. Cork oaks are native to the area. They like acid soil and the proximity of the sea, and these ancient woods are worthy of interest, despite the greater fame enjoyed by viticulture in this part of Provence. Sweet chestnuts are once more regaining the high point of development reached in the 1950s. It is a tree whose origins lie in the Mediterranean region. Chestnuts are once more being cultivated, and the produce from them finding its former place in the local markets. A very flavorsome honey, for example, is made from the nectar of chestnut blossom, lavender, or mountain flowers collected by the bees, and the chestnuts themselves are harvested in autumn, some being made into marrons glacés.

Travelers who seek out wild nature aside from the beaten tourist track discover a different face of Provence.

THE WINES OF CÔTES DE PROVENCE

Eleanor of Aquitaine loved the wines of Provence. Through her marriage to Henry II, the Plantagenet king of England, in the 12th century, she became the country's queen, and introduced the wines of her homeland to the court in London. The kings of France did not taste them until the 17th and 18th centuries. These fine wines have borne the name "Côtes de Provence" since the 19th century, though they did not receive AOC recognition until 1977. The production area of these wines occupies 44,500 acres (about 18,000 ha), and is divided into five regions:

- the coast from Toulon to Saint- Raphaël
- the valley to the north of this, from Toulon to Fréjus
- the adjoining hill country of the Haut Pays to the north, as far as Les-Arcs-sur-Argens and Draguignan
- the basin of Le Beausset between Cassis and Bandol
- the Massif Sainte-Victoire

The Côtes de Provence covers a large area and there is great variety in the type of country surrounding the vineyards.

These areas vary greatly from each other in soil, in climate, and in the winds that blow there, and the wines they produce are different in character. The white wines, depending on the *terroirs* where they are cultivated, are made from Ugni Blanc, Clairette, and Sémillon; the reds and rosés from Syrah, Carignan, Cinsault, Tibouren, Mourvèdre, and Cabernet Sauvignon. The selection of the grape varieties to be used, and the winemaker's skill, which draws its inspiration from the area's long winegrowing tradition, produce wines of remarkable quality and rich aroma. Viticulture spread here, to the area around Marseille, Nice, Antibes, and Saint Tropez from Asia Minor; new varieties were introduced by the Romans, who were expert in winegrowing, from the second century BC. They created large vineyard estates. Winegrowing has been an essential part of Provence ever since. The Appellation includes about 450 producers, whose output fills an average of 100 million bottles a year. Rosé heads the list of Côtes de Provence wine, accounting for 70 percent of production. The quality and volume of the wine made here have earned it top place in the world hit parade of rosé producers. Red wines make up 20 percent of production, leaving only a few barrels to be filled by the fresh, soft, aromatic whites. Both are achieving

The Appellation has its own Maison des Vins. All the wines of the area can be tasted and bought here at the same price as the one charged by the winegrower.

increasing success on account of their quality. Maturation in oak casks has proved its worth for these, and promises to produce sturdy wines with good keeping qualities.

The grapes from which Côtes de Provence wines are made enjoy up to 320 days of sunshine a year, as a result of which chaptalization is forbidden. This applies both to the Provence AOC and for Côtes du Languedoc. The wines are characterized by a natural ripeness and a very powerful aroma.

The path from grape to finished wine is a long one, but the pleasure makes all the effort worthwhile.

Summer Isn't Summer Without Rosé

Rosé is the ancestor of all wines. The custom until the Middle Ages was to separate the skins, which are responsible for the color, from the fruit and juice of the grapes at an early stage. The resulting wine – though it was probably close to being vinegar – was pink or at least pale (*clairet*) in color.

The techniques of producing wine and improving its keeping qualities were further developed, and methods of storing it became more sophisticated. Drinking habits and preferences as to color changed with time, but Provence kept on the rosé tradition.

It is a wine type that has often been derided as neither one thing nor the other, as if its color stemmed from indecision or carelessness. On the contrary, its production demands unending care. Constant attention is needed to achieve the subtle color. It is vinified from red grapes, and since the grape skins give color to the wine, the grape mass (the "must") has to be pressed and the juice run off when the desired depth of color has been reached. The wine has a clear, glowing color, with occasionally a brownish tinge. Certainly it is an inviting color, encouraging the taster to sample its freshness, and truly bringing the savor of summer.

Rosé wine is usually drunk as an aperitif. Its liveliness and aromatic character make it an ideal partner for nibbles and canapés, perhaps toast with *tapenade*, or olives, which it enlivens with its hint of acidity. It is neither too heavy nor too dominating on the palate, and is served to arouse the appetite for the wines to come. This does not do full justice to rosé's many qualities. It can in fact be an entirely appropriate accompaniment to an entire meal of Mediterranean dishes. Neither lobster nor truffles overwhelm it, though they are usually partnered by other wines. It is above all a wine that goes excellently

293.—Wine-Press. (Cotton MS.)

Grapes used to be crushed by treading. Book illustration dating from around 1000 AD.

Tomates à la provençale
Tomatoes in the style of Provence

Serves 6

3 cloves of garlic	
½ bunch of parsley	
12 small, nicely ripe tomatoes	
A pinch of sugar	
3 tbsp olive oil	
Salt	

Peel the garlic, and wash the parsley. Chop together, and set aside. Cut the tomatoes in half horizontally, and sprinkle a little sugar on the cut surface.

Heat a little oil in a large skillet, and put the tomatoes into it, cut side down and closely packed. Sauté briefly over a medium heat until the juice has completely evaporated, and a caramelized coating has formed. Then turn them over carefully, and sauté the other side. Season generously with salt, sprinkle with the parsley mixture, cover, and simmer very gently.

Serve hot or cold, with a young, lively, dry, aromatic Côtes de Provence rosé.

with broiled fish, seafood, shellfish, and cold ratatouille. It best comes into its own when served with other produce of the same region; the fruity, spicy aromas of rosé blend beautifully with the herbs of the *garrigue*, with *petits farcis* (stuffed vegetables), and *tomates à la provençale* (tomatoes in the style of Provence), simple dishes that are very quick to prepare.

Summer is not summer without rosé! The extraordinary hot summer of 2003 left the vineyards prey to extreme conditions. However, no harm seems to have been done to the rosé wine.

Rosé has not lost its link with street cafés and summer. What has happened is that it has ceased to be merely a holiday wine. Its fruity, fresh fragrance corresponds well to the development in consumer taste toward light, aromatic cuisine. Rosé wines should be consumed the same year as they are made, or at the latest within three or four years. They are making huge strides to catch up with the rank of the great reds and whites.

The guidelines for enjoying rose wines are the same as for red or white: The glass should be no more than a third full, to allow room for the bouquet to collect in the top of the glass. The glass should be set down before taking the first sip, and the wine gently agitated to coax from it still more aromas.

WHITE AND RED WINES

The name "Blanc de Blancs" is the clearest statement that we can possibly have of the color of a wine. The Provence white wines use no red grapes, but are made solely from various blends of Clairette, Ugni Blanc, and Sémillon. The red and rosé wines of Provence derive their character from a much wider palette of grape varieties. These varieties are Grenache, Syrah, Cinsault, Mourvèdre, and Cabernet Sauvignon.

Ugni Blanc
The grapes are rich and full of juice, giving the wine clarity and quite a fruity character.

Sémillon
This grape makes up a smaller proportion of the wines than the other varieties. It gives white wines an elegant note.

Clairette
This variety has been grown in Provence for a long time. It has a low yield, but provides strength and an aromatic character.

Grenache
The characteristics of this grape vary with age, lending the aroma of red fruits when young, and a spicy, animal note when older, with fullness and power.

Syrah
This grape comes from Spain, and has a warm note that is reminiscent of vanilla, Havana tobacco, and red candied fruits.

Cinsault
Cinsault is an excellent grape for the table. It has a freshness that moderates the power of other varieties.

Mourvèdre
This is the typical southern French variety. It is temperamental and demanding. It produces wines with good longevity.

Carignan
Perfect to round off the assembling of a wine, Carignan lends strength and color.

Cabernet Sauvignon
A much-cultivated variety with a pronounced tannin content, which helps to produce a well-matured older wine.

There is very little white Côtes de Provence – it accounts for only five percent of production – but the wines exhibit considerable variety of flavor. They are soft and rounded; young, they go well with seafood or an *anchoïade*. To partner cheese and meat, they need to develop more maturity.

1998 was a very good year for Provence reds. Some of these have a nervous, aromatic quality that lends them to a period of cask maturation. They develop spicy notes of licorice and pepper, and aromas of wood and vanilla. Ten years is an ideal length of time to allow their spiciness expression. Game, a Provençal pot roast, or a selection of local cheeses are the perfect partners to these wines.

The wines of Côtes de Provence are a delight, with great variety of flavor.

Fresher, lighter wines with more restrained tannins are enjoyed at their best when consumed in the first three years. They have a long finish, reminiscent of the fragrance of red fruits. They are ideal with grilled dishes with herbes de Provence.

Some Noted Vineyards of the Côtes de Provence

Domaine Ott, founded in 1896 by a wine-maker from Alsace, can justly be considered the ambassador for Côtes de Provence, although its excellent wines are not necessarily representative of the average classified under this Appellation. Only 25 percent of production is exported. The estate produces very powerful red wines, which improve with aging, whites which are capable of storage, and some exceptional rosés. These can be consumed in the year of production or after three or four years, and count among the great wines of France.

The owners of Domaine Ott determined on the goal of quality from the outset, a century ago. This quality drives every level of production: the choice of the soil, the variety, and the method of tending the vines. They use traditional, native southern French varieties for all three types of wines, and practice organic cultivation without pesticides, but do use trace elements and Bordeaux mixture to combat disease. This copper-and-lime preparation is classified here as a natural treatment, and considered very effective. The production of these wines is characterized by the methods employed: the vines organically tended and protected and carefully harvested, the grapes meticulously sorted and pressed, no addition of sulfur, long fermentation, and maturation in oak casks, together with a wealth of enthusiasm. There are three different winegrowing areas, Château de Ramassan at Beausset, Clos Mireille by the sea, and

Wines have been grown at Domaine Ott for 100 years. Experience leads to great quality.

Excellent wines lie maturing in fine oak barrels in these huge cellars.

Château de Sclle on the hills of the Haut-Pays, in which the Otts exercise their expertise. The wines of all three bear the characteristics of their particular *terroir*, and contribute to the good reputation of the Appellation.

The estate also produces a *marc*, called their *Marc de rosé*, and an *eau de vie de Provence*. The production process takes six years, conducted in a strictly regimented manner, with an almost ritual solemnity. Stern legal controls are imposed, affecting each stage of distillation. The still used to produce the spirits of Domaine Ott is sealed, and remains so until a customs official unseals it. The exact date and time of filling the still, the weight of the marc (the pomace) used, and the strength and quantity of the alcohol produced must be precisely noted and adhered to, and the moment when the distillation process is halted has to be declared. Only the spirit produced during the middle period of distillation is kept. This fraction contains the finest alcohols, which make up only five percent of the total volume. The distilled *marc* is then transferred to casks and matured for six months before being licensed by ONIVINS (the *Office National interprofessionel des vins*).

After it has matured for a further three or four years, the *marc* has a pale yellow color that develops to an orange-brown hue over the next four years. The flavor mellows with age, without losing the original strength of its alcoholic content.

Blending is the final stage in the production. It, too, demands all the skill of the winemaker-distiller. Several vintages are mixed, to

Domaine Ott encompasses three Châteaux, all of which produce wines of excellent quality.

achieve a balance of flavor, and the resulting blend allowed to rest for a further four months. Finally, the desired *marc* is ready to be bottled and sold.

Château de Selle has a neighbor, Château Rasque. This vineyard maintains the cultivation of traditional grape varieties by traditional methods. Harvesting, for example, is done by hand, to minimize the damage to the grapes. This in itself is enough to suggest the character of the resulting wines: elegant, fine reds, aromatic, delicate whites, and soft, aromatic rosés. The *Cuvée Alexandra* 2003 is a rosé that is excellent with seafood.

The *Blanc de Blancs* is a choice, aromatic wine that goes well with green asparagus.

In Puyloubier at the foot of Sainte-Victoire is Domaine de Richeaume. The cultivation

Château Rasque lays stress on organic methods of cultivation and winemaking. Wines of all three types are produced here.

practiced here is strictly conducted, combining a concern for quality with modern technology. The vines grow on stony soil, are tended with the utmost care, and increasingly approach organic standards. The winemaker's care is shown both in environmental matters – the diversity of varieties, natural methods of storage, and recycling – and in the choice of grape varieties, careful harvesting, and storage in oak barrels from the *département* of Allier. All these factors are important and contribute to producing wines of high quality.

The rosé is made up of southern France's finest grape varieties, Grenache, Syrah, and

Cinsault. It has a delicate citrus fragrance. The red has a bouquet that is often reminiscent of red fruits and spices. The 1996 vintage in particular, calls for a little patience, and a beautiful carafe into which to decant it, for by 2006 this vintage will develop its full potential in richness.

The *Blanc de Blancs* are matured in oak barrels. They are elegant, lively, and supple, with a very flowery bouquet.

The estates Domaine Réal Martin, Clos Minuty, Domaine Gavoty, Commanderie de Peyrassol, among others, produce wines of very good quality that can serve as advertisements for the Appellation.

It is evident that Côtes de Provence has much more to offer than straightforward rosé table wine. The wine estates of this area prove that a rigorously controlled production method, whether using traditional or modern technology, is the most important factor contributing to the production of fine quality wines.

Château Rasque produces wines composed of traditional varieties. Harvesting is done by hand.

COTEAUX VAROIS

The two mountain chains of La Sainte-Baume and Les Bessillons enclose a winegrowing region of 4,450 acres (1,800 ha), encompassing 28 communities in the area around Brignoles. This area, referred to as Provence calcaire (calcareous Provence) once contained the summer residence of the Counts of Provence.

Here on the gravelly, calcareous soils of the slopes, protected by the mountains, the wine enjoys a climate that is more continental than otherwise, with cold winters and warm, dry summers. The annual production in Coteaux Varois is 85,000 hl per year (equivalent of 11,334,000 bottles), with an average yield of 2.2 tons/acre (38 hl per hectare). Sixty-eight percent of this consists of rosé wines, mainly made from Grenache and Cinsault, as well as Mourvèdre, Carignan, Syrah, and Tibouren. The rosés have a balanced, fresh, rounded character, which they owe to the altitude of the vineyards, between 350 and 500 m (1,150 and 1,650 feet). White wines account for just two percent of production. These are made mainly from the Rolle, Clairette, and Grenache Blanc varieties, along with Ugni Blanc and Sémillon. Both types should be consumed within 18 months of harvesting. Domaine de la Curnière produces exemplary

Surrounded by the mountains, the vines of La Celle enjoy a sun-drenched location. The viticulture museum gives a general insight into the wines of Coteaux Varois.

white wines. These should be tried with poultry or fish. Red *Coteaux Varois* accounts for 30 percent of production. Grenache, Syrah, Mourvèdre, as well as Carignan, Cinsault, and Cabernet Sauvignon produce powerful wines with good longevity. They can be drunk after three to five years of storage; good vintages, such as the 1998 is considered to be, may even be kept longer.

Another good year for wine was 1999, with good yields and quality. The grapes achieved high sugar concentrations and good acidity, which promises to produce balanced wines with a rich bouquet. It should certainly be a vintage to note, and to lay down for a few years. Château Routas and Domaine de Deffends, which lie along the Route des Coteaux Varois, are places where it is well worthwhile making a stop.

A visit to the viticulture museum, Maison des Coteaux Varois, is definitely recommended to anyone looking to gain a general understanding of this wine-producing region, and an idea of the variety covered by this particular Appellation. The museum has a display about the cultivation of vines and the tools of the trade, as well as a "vinothèque" giving an introduction to the various *cuvées* of the production area. The museum is situated in the circular wall of the royal abbey of La Celle, an example of 12th-century Romanesque architecture, the location itself providing a further attraction. It is a wonderful combination of abbey history, architectural interest, and a fascinating introduction to the wonderful wines of the area.

The vineyard within the museum

The museum in the abbey of La Celle displays an authentic collection of 88 grape varieties that have had a strong influence on the history of viticulture in Provence, but are now disappearing. They include:

- *Panse de Solliès*, grown by the scholar Nicolas de Peiresc, who was fascinated by the study of agriculture and botany, in the 12th century.
- *Pascal Muscat*, the result of a cross between *Pascal Blanc*, a variety once highly valued for the wines of Cassis, and *Muscat of Alexandria*, brought from Egypt by sailors of the Napoleonic fleet.
- *Olivette Rose*, whose plump, lilac colored berries, with their typical plum flavor, earned it the enticing name *tétons de Vénus* (Venus's bosom).

Les-Arcs-sur-Argens

The narrow streets of Les-Arc-sur-Argens seem to lead the visitor back into the Middle Ages.

Les-Arcs-sur-Argens, with its picturesque, medieval quarter full of ancient arcades, narrow streets, and walls bedecked with flowers, lies on the D 57.

The "Maison des Vins" and "Vinothèque"

The establishment serves as a huge shop window for the Appellation. Producers who wish to present their wines to trade or individual customers are all represented there.

The "vinothèque" provides the opportunity of gaining an acquaintance with the variety of styles covered by this region of origin. Almost all the vineyards of the Appellation, which extends from the Mediterranean coast to the mountain of Montagne Sainte-Victoire, are represented here. This wine-tasting experience provides an introduction to the wine for beginners, and an opportunity for experienced wine drinkers to follow the development of a vintage. For professionals operating food and drink establishments, it offers the advantage of finding out about the wines of all the estates in this large production area, under a single roof.

Each day, 16 wines are presented for tasting, under the guidance of a fully trained and experienced, attentive, multilingual staff. The character of the wines unfolds sip by sip – the blend of grape varieties, bouquet, taste, and color. The guests' ability to appreciate these is assisted by means of instructional information leaflets, which also suggest suitable accompanying foods. Such tips can prove their worth when planning a meal, and trying to harmonize the wines and dishes. With over 600 different red, white, and rosé wines being produced each year, this wine region has huge reserves in terms of flavors. Should the wine-tasting spur the visitor to purchase a few wines, willing advice is to hand. The range of reds, whites, and rosés is large, and there is something to suit every budget. Prices at the "vinothèque" are the same as at the vineyard.

Wine-tasting sessions are available at the "Maison des Vins," providing a good introduction to the various wines of the Appellation.

The wines are all presented with the same attention and care, from the light, fruity, warm and soft ones that should be consumed young, and reds that can be drunk chilled without impairing them, to heavy wines of high quality.

Introductory courses in wine-tasting in five languages are run at the "Maison des Vins" in parallel to all this. Participants learn, under the direction of wine experts, to hold and observe the glass, to "nose" the bouquet, and taste the wine. They learn to distinguish the wines. Is it a table wine, a country wine, or an AOC? Côtes de Provence wines inform the taster about their individual character – there is a description printed on the *taste-vins*, the wine-tasting glasses. The bouquet of each wine reveals something about the area from

which it comes, seeming to invite the taster to take a journey of discovery there. Perceptive wine-tasters believe they can detect the tang of the sea, or the dryness of inland locations away from the coast.

The "vinothèque" offers not only wine-tastings, but also the opportunity to purchase wines of the Appellation.

"Bacchus Gourmand"

The exploratory tour of the world of wine continues in the pleasant restaurant of the "Maison des Vins." This time, the way is marked out by the creations of the catering manager. Regional specialties and wines feature together on the same menu, each complementing the other.

The role accorded here to the wine waiter is not merely to advise, as his calling dictates, but resembles rather the part played by the conductor of an orchestra, as he recommends the wine to accompany each course. There is always a Côtes de Provence that forms the perfect partner for each, from salmon *carpaccio* to banana parfait, and this without sending the bill into the stratosphere. So it is a pleasure to experience the entire symphony of wines and dishes. The Côtes de Provence served in the "Bacchus gourmand," whether by the glass or by the bottle, provide the best possible context in which to appreciate the cuisine of Philippe Rousselot.

Filet de rascasse cuit au laurier
Petits farcis de pommes de terre aux moules

Sea scorpion with bay leaves
Stuffed potatoes with mussels

Serves 4

16 small potatoes
4 portions of filleted sea scorpion
8 bay leaves
Scant ½ cup/100 g butter
2 shallots, finely chopped
2 cloves of garlic, finely chopped
Generous 2 lb/1 kg mussels, cleaned
Scant ½ cup/100 ml white wine
½ bunch parsley, chopped
Freshly milled pepper
Scant ¼ cup/ 30 ml olive oil
Juice of ½ lemon

Boil the potatoes in salted water for ten minutes. Cool, remove the skins, cut in half lengthways, and hollow out the center. Mash the contents, and set aside.

Make two slits in each fish fillet, and insert a bay leaf. Preheat the oven to 350 °F/180 °C.

Melt half the butter in a large saucepan with a handle. Sauté the shallots and garlic lightly for five minutes, until translucent. Add the mussels, white wine, and the parsley, reserving a little wine and one tablespoonful of parsley for the sauce. Season lightly with pepper. Cover and cook, stirring frequently. The mussels are cooked when they open. Place a colander over a container and drain the mussels, reserving the liquid. Pass this through a sieve and set aside. Discard any mussels that fail to open. Remove the meat from the mussels and keep hot.

Brown the fish on both sides in a little olive oil, then place in the preheated oven for ten minutes. Meanwhile, combine a scant ½ cup/100 ml of the reserved cooking liquid, the remaining butter, some olive oil, the lemon juice, a dash of white wine, and the remaining parsley. Boil for four minutes to reduce. Mix half this liquid with the potatoes and the cooked, opened mussels, purée, and stuff the potato shells.

Pour the rest of the sauce over the fish and stuffed potatoes and serve immediately.

DELICIOUS DESSERTS

Philippe Rousselot loves desserts. That is quite evident from his menu. He loves to crown a meal with an apple tart or – still more characteristic of the region – with a chestnut pudding. Collobrières, the home of chestnut production, is only about 30 miles (50 km) away from Les-Arcs-sur-Argens. The chestnuts produced from its famous groves have an aroma and quality of flavor that account for the reputation accorded the *marrons glacés* and other desserts. The following chestnut cream mold is a delicious example: Beat together 4 egg yolks and ¼ cup/50 g of sugar until frothy. Warm scant ½ cup/100 ml whipping cream with the pulp from the inside of half a vanilla pod, and draw off the heat. Stir ¼ cup/50 g cocoa powder into a smooth paste and add, together with 1 cup/300 g chestnut purée and a tablespoon of whisky or rum. Stir to blend, then fold in the egg mixture. Transfer to ramekins, and bake in an oven preheated to 210 °F/100 °C for 40 minutes. Cool and turn out.

Tartelette feuilletée aux pommes, noix, pignons et raisins de Corinthe
Millefeuille of apples, walnuts, pine nuts, and currants

5 oz/140 g puff pastry
A walnut-sized piece of butter
4 apples
2 cups/500 ml apple juice
Juice of ½ lemon
¼ cup/60 g sugar
2 tbsp/30 g butter
Scant tbsp/20 g honey
Generous 1 tbsp/20 ml whipping cream
⅓ cup/40 g walnuts
¼ cup/40 g currants
½ cup/60 g pine nuts

Preheat the oven to 400 °F/200 °C. Roll out the pastry thinly. Grease four baking pans of 4 in/10 cm diameter, line with pastry, and bake in the preheated oven, until golden (about 20 minutes).

Peel, core, and slice one apple, and boil it to a pulp in the apple juice. Purée until smooth if necessary. Add the lemon juice and chill.

Heat two tablespoons of water with all but 1 tablespoon of the sugar. When it is almost browned, remove it from the heat, stirring constantly. Add a generous tablespoon (20 g) of the butter, together with the honey and cream. Return to the heat, and simmer for three minutes. Gradually and carefully stir in the walnuts, currants, and two thirds of the pine nuts. Cool, then pile on top of the pastry bases. Peel, quarter, and core the remaining apples, and slice thinly and evenly. Caramelize the

remaining sugar in a skillet, and add the remaining butter. Poach the apple slices in this for five minutes, stirring frequently. Add the remaining pine nuts, then remove from the heat and cool.

Place the apple mixture on top of the tartlets, pour over the chilled apple juice with purée, and chill.

Lorgues

The D 57 leads onward from Arcs to the small, fortified village of Flayosc, which commands a beautiful view of the surrounding countryside. A little farther south lies Lourgues, with the charm of a picturesque old town.

"Chez Bruno"

Bruno sets himself high standards. Not only must he work well; he must do that work wholeheartedly. So says the motto hanging in his kitchen: "Le travail bien fait n'est plus à faire, faisons-le avec le coeur." There are more reasons than this for which his cuisine is so highly esteemed. The food on his plates and his company are more important reasons. They are bliss on earth.

The collegiate church of Lorgues towers over the village which holds a magnificent restaurant, "Bruno."

His cuisine has the personal touch, and sends his guests into raptures. The *maître* of this tiny town thoroughly deserves his fame. His cooking appeals to the senses, and satisfies the expectations of the most demanding *gourmet*. Bruno loves his profession, and the people who delight in what he produces. He is an artist, creating his dishes each day as the fancy takes him, rejecting the idea of a predetermined menu. His invention is active at all times. Perhaps he will present the surprise of a dessert he has just prepared, or maybe he will fall under the spell of truffles, a hobby of his, and of *foie gras*. You can always be prepared for a delicious treat.

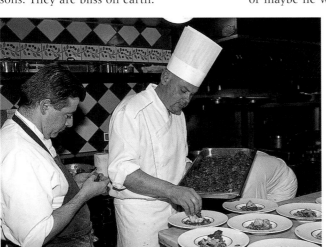

A glance inside the kitchen of a truffle specialist. The noble truffle is prepared according to all the traditional culinary rules.

Comme une bruschetta d'écrevisses aux truffes noires

Like a bruschetta of river crayfish with black truffles

Serves 4

2 cloves of garlic
½ bunch of parsley, chopped
24 fine crayfish
2 ½ tbsp/40 ml olive oil
1 glass of white wine
1 tbsp Cognac
Scant 1 tbsp/10 g butter
2 purple artichokes
4 slices of bread, ¾ in/2 cm thick
2 good handfuls of rocket (rucola, arugula)
3 oz/80 g *foie gras*, in small pieces
2 oz/60 g truffles
8 bottled tomatoes (preserve)
2 ½ cups/120 g grated Parmesan
12 asparagus spears (tops)
Coarse-grained salt

Peel the garlic and chop finely. Heat half the olive oil in a skillet, and sauté the garlic with the parsley and crayfish. Pour on the white wine and Cognac, stir, and add the butter. Set the cooking juices aside, and take apart the crayfish.

Prepare the artichokes. Slice thinly and sauté in half the remaining olive oil.

Toast the bread. Arrange some rocket and *foie gras* on each slice, and pour over the cooking juices. Slice and add half the truffles. Place on top of this two tomatoes, a layer of Parmesan, slices of artichoke, the asparagus, and the crayfish tails. Finish with the remaining truffles, drizzle over it a thin stream of olive oil, and sprinkle with salt.

Massif des Maures

Either side of the Route des Crêtes, the road that leads into the Massif des Maures and on to Saint Tropez, the land is thickly wooded with sweet chestnuts, cork oaks, orange, and lemon trees. The massif takes its name from the Provençal word "mauro," a word that tells of thick, dark groves of trees, as massive as the silhouettes of the mountains themselves. This abundance of vegetation provides bees with nectar in plenty for various types of honey.

Cork oaks are among the most striking and characteristic trees of the Mediterranean. It is an evergreen that grows at altitudes up to 1,600 feet (500 m). The tree develops a resistant bark that is used as cork for all sorts of purposes: bottle stoppers, decoration, and sound insulation material.

For anyone with a sweet tooth and a concern for their health, honey and honey products are an ideal answer. Honey is rich in minerals, trace elements, organic acids, and amino acids. Though its sugar content is 80 percent, this is made up of well nigh 20 different types of sugar, and the main types are glucose and fructose, which are quickly absorbed by the human body. To complete the list of honey's impressive "performance spectrum," it also contains enzymes, hormones, pollen, lysozymes, and natural antibiotics.

The hive

Before bees were domesticated, they used to deposit their valuable store in natural hiding places. Humans, in the attempt to simplify the task of gathering honey, made simple hives, and improved the design most inventively over the centuries. Bees are social insects, living in a clearly defined, hierarchical society under the leadership of a queen. The young bees are initially charged with feeding the queen. They then fly abroad to collect nectar and pollen. Both pass through the bee's honey stomach, being transformed into honey. On their return to the hive, the bees pass the honey on to the workers there. They add an enzyme-containing secretion from their cephalic glands, and store the honey in the waxen comb. The honey continues to develop there, and some of the moisture in it evaporates. The bees speed the process by using their wings to ventilate it. The mature honey consists of only 20 percent water, and 80 percent sugars. The bees finally seal the cell with a small cap of wax.

The beekeeper

Lucien Lamoine has 400 beehives located across almost the entire country from the Jura

Lamoine has sited his hives in various different locations, to produce different types of blossom honey.

A few bees remain on the frame when the beekeeper takes it out of the hive.

Lucien Lamoine simply uses air to drive the bees from off the comb.

This stage of operations demands a great deal of experience to avoid being stung.

First came the pollen, then the bee, and a few months later, all sorts of wonderful honey products.

The wax from the combs is used, too, to make candles.

to Haute-Provence; he has hives in the Massif des Maures, and in the mountains of Sainte-Baume. He has been collecting from them for 15 years. To gather different types of honey, he needs to provide the bees with the right sort of flowers, so he

Pollen has a less interesting flavor, but is rich in vitamins and fiber.

sites the hives where the acacia blooms, chestnut blossom, or lavender may be found. There are only about ten days in the year when the flowers secrete their nectar, and these are dependent on air temperature and humidity, so the beekeeper has to keep a "weather eye" on meteorological changes.

The months for gathering honey are from April to October, and Lucien Lamoine collects nine different types. Many of these are from just one rare type of blossom, collecting tiny quantities – about 22 lb (10 kg) a year – of white heather honey, for example. In spring, he collects thyme and rosemary honey from the *garrigue*, in summer, chestnut and lavender honey, and in the autumn, the usual type of heather honey. Mixed blossom honey is collected throughout the year.

The beekeeper has to drive the bees away from the hive to collect the honey. This Lamoine does by simply blowing air into it. He does not use smoke or chemical means, because these could impair the flavor of the honey. A risk of being stung certainly exists, since some of the bees react nervously, but Lucien Lamoine believes it is possible to get used to that. Once the bees have left the hive, he removes the frame containing the comb full of honey. He uses a warmed knife to remove the caps from the cells, and places the comb in the honey extractor. This uses a shaking movement to release the honey. Once all the honey has been extracted

Honey has an important place in Provence, and small producers often sell their produce by the roadside.

from the comb, it is put into initial storage at 39 °F (4 °C), unless it is to be sold. This preserves the original qualities of the honey.

Sweet temptations, but these products have healthgiving properties: honey as a sweetener for drinks and in foods, honey candies to treat coughs, and mead. There can be no objections to these benefits.

Understanding the label

Honey may come from one single type of flower; this is called *miel monofloral* (single variety honey). Honey from several types is called *miel polyfloral* or *miel toutes fleurs* (mixed variety honey). Single variety honey is rarer and more expensive than mixed, as is honey from a single area (*miel de cru*).

Honey is liquid when it is gathered. It then crystallizes at different rates. The fact that it has become harder and more crunchy in texture does not imply that the quality of the honey is lower, or that it is older. Spreading honey (*miel crémeux*) has a softer consistency achieved by regular stirring. This does not affect the flavor, quality, or nutritional value of the honey.

Honey is subject to legal definitions, and the label may only declare the blossom type, place of origin, and date of production. Labels in France do not normally carry any other wording, so terms such as "natural honey" or "cold extraction" will not be found.

Pain d'épices and other honey products

Honey was an ingredient in every kitchen in ancient times. Fruit was preserved by dipping it in honey. The sugary coating kept out the air, and prevented the fruit from spoiling. The Romans used to enjoy slices of toasted rye bread with honey poured onto it. Then there was mead, the drink of the druids. It has a highly characteristic flavor, and is also distinguished for being the origin of the word "honeymoon" in English and "*lune de miel*" in French. In fact, it was a "honeymonth," the early days of marriage, and the young couple began this time with a drink of mead.

In the 10th century, the silk caravans traveling the trade route from China brought another commodity alongside the silken cloth: a sort of spiced wheaten bread, flavored with honey. This may well be the origin of *pain d'épices* (honey bread).

With all its varieties of flavor and nuances of color, each of which must surely top someone's popularity list, honey itself is delicious. Pale brown chestnut honey has an aroma of tannin, strawberry tree honey has a definite, unpleasant bitterness, then there is the pleasant acidity of golden lavender honey, and white heather honey with its red-brown shimmer develops a distinctive aroma of caramel and cocoa.

It is not only honey that has healthgiving properties; pollen, which the beekeeper can also extract from the hive, is rich in nitrogen, protein, and vitamin B. It is recommended for the treatment of digestive problems, and is generally beneficial to health. So it has more than sweetness to recommend it.

Lavender honey is a very special delight, made from the nectar of lavender flowers.

Caramels au chocolat
Chocolate caramels

Serves 8

3 blocks of bittersweet chocolate
3 tbsp/90 g honey
¼ cup/50 g butter
1 tbsp sugar
Butter for greasing baking sheet.

Grate the chocolate coarsely. Heat the honey, butter, chocolate, and sugar together in a copper saucepan, and simmer for seven to eight minutes, stirring constantly.
Grease a baking sheet (with sides), and pour the mixture onto this. Allow to set until almost firm, then score deeply into conveniently sized pieces with a knife. Cool completely. Separate into pieces along the divisions, using strong kitchen scissors, or by breaking the block.

Pain d'épices
Honey bread

Serves 4

1 ½ cups/200 g chopped candied orange peel
A handful of raisins
1 ½ cups/500 g honey
4 ⅕ cups/500 g all-purpose flour
1 tsp baking powder
1 tsp cinnamon
A little grated nutmeg
Butter for greasing cake pan

Preheat the oven to 300 °F/150 °C. Boil the finely chopped peel and the raisins in a cup of water. Pour onto the honey, and mix well. When the honey has dissolved, add the remaining ingredients and stir carefully to mix. Grease a cake pan, pour in the mixture, then cover the pan with aluminum foil and leave for 30 minutes. Then remove the foil and bake the cake for about 1 hour, until a knife blade inserted into the center comes out clean.

From Saint-Tropez to Antibes

The road now leads along the shoreline. Provence has arrived at the sea. This stretch of coast bears the name d'Azur in recognition of the blueness of the sea, in dazzling competition with the blue of the sky. Here and there, sheep laurel blooms either side of the Corniche des Maures as it runs from Hyères to Saint Tropez, and pursues its way on through pine woods.

From Saint Tropez to Cannes, the road leads along the Côte d'Azur, a beautiful coastline with jagged cliffs, gleaming bays, and delightful footpaths, seemingly conspiring to prevent the traveler from straying inland.

The towns and harbors of the Côte d'Azur reveal their true face in autumn and winter; they have for some decades been the summer stronghold of another lifestyle. These months find them vibrant with the clamor of suntanned vacationers. The Côte d'Azur with its small fishing harbors, now transformed into yachting marinas, is at

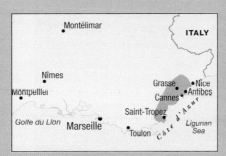

great ease with itself, whether in the quiet months or the money-spinning high season. Nice and Saint-Tropez form the backdrop for the festivals of the international jet set, and once a year, Cannes rolls out the red carpet for its famous international film festival. Islands such as Sainte Marguerite or Saint-Honorat are a destination for luxury yachts, and also offer glorious countryside for a walk or a meal under the shade of the pine trees.

When Picasso was in Antibes, he painted the view down from the heights to the sea. Walking over the ramparts here, a longing is felt for the peace and bright cheer of the country inland. Another artist, the 18th-century painter Jean-Honoré Fragonard, is ever-present there, in Grasse. His name appears everywhere in large letters, a constant reminder that his descendants manufacture perfume. Inland we find a sea of flowers, which serve not only as decorative items, but are in some places, such as Tourrette-sur-Loup, also made into edible delicacies which will delight and tempt any visitor to the region.

Saint-Tropez exudes an indescribable charm. The quality of the light and abundance of colors enchanted painters and writers.

SAINT-TROPEZ

The harbor promenade combines the roles of fishing port and venue for the jet set.

thronged with the extravagant color and style of the many tourists, from the prosperous to the ones of slender means, all, however, basking in the pride and pleasure of being able to make their appearance in Saint-Tropez – above all, on the terrace of the "Brasserie Sennequier." This is a somewhat synthetic world, but with that happy, carefree, holiday spirit – it is, quite simply, "St-Trop," peopled by the pale, tired faces of night revelers, not so lively with their "morning after" headaches.

Once a small fishing village, Saint-Tropez still breathes the aura of Brigitte Bardot. Today it is a yachting harbor and summer meeting place for the international jet set. Yet, to unfold its beauty and its charm, this resort needs some restoration of quiet and anonymity.

The time to seek out this atmosphere of Saint-Tropez, even in the height of summer, is the early morning. Then the visitor can stroll through the streets, and shop the market in the Place des Lices. From midday onward, all hope of a quiet spot is in vain. The streets are

The town empties as the off season begins, and the tourists absent themselves. Saint-Tropez slowly starts to recover from the exhaustion of the summer frenzy. Normal life can resume. It once more becomes possible to listen in on the quayside conversations of fishermen. Restaurants readjust, sane prices reappear on menus, and, from the harbor, one can watch a peaceful sunset. Such is Saint-Tropez out of season. It is possible then to meet with the *tropéziens* for a journey of discovery filled with the aromas of *aïoli* or bouillabaisse. This is the Saint-Tropez that accords with the recollections of the painters Henri

The market is daily full of vegetables, flowers, and fruit, of scents and colors, and of laughter and conversation.

Leather goods are also made and sold in Saint-Tropez, and the typical sandals called *tropéziennes*.

Jeans and shorts are as much in evidence as chic manners and millinery.

The old, narrow streets are full of small boutiques and shops fragrant with olives and herbs.

The Côte d'Azur is crammed with fields of flowers that provide for the whole of France.

Seafood is very much a part of the markets and coastline of Provence.

Matisse and Paul Signac, who lived here and were happy here.

Saint-Tropez now reveals its medieval streets and tiny squares, where culinary specialties are to be found: a fish merchant, a baker, a greengrocer or a little bar in which to take a cup of coffee. The Place aux Herbes is such a place, with its fruit and flower stalls. Its charm

The inhabitants of Saint-Tropez take a midday break with the newspaper, out in the street.

unfolds in the wake of high season. One street leads to another in the tangle of the old town, enticing the curious to wander on, only to arrive in a cul de sac. In recompense, the strolling visitor catches a glimpse of a pretty little flower-filled courtyard, discreetly

screened behind hanging plants. From inside there may waft the delicious and tantalizing smell of squid cooked à la provençale, broiled fish, or tortillas.

The boules players

The Place des Lices is the year-round meeting place of the *boulistes*. For Saint-Tropez, the game of *pétanque*, a variant of *boules*, is as characteristic as the Eiffel Tower is of Paris. In summer, the tourists gather under the plane trees, in groups around the players. The outside tables of the "Bistrot des Lice" are all filled. *Pétanque* is Provence's favorite sport. The rules were set down at the beginning of the 20th century, and they have even been set to music. The song has survived unchanged through all the years.

The game that many consider a leisurely pastime, blissful inactivity hidden behind an illusion of activity, the chance to meet friends and enjoy a glass or two of pastis, turns out in fact to demand alertness, skill, agility, endurance, and loquacity. To play *pétanque* successfully in the south of France calls for a

The abundance of the Mediterranean produces an almost limitless profusion of fish and shellfish.

mastery of the local accent and the necessary vocabulary, and for enough fire to excite the other party. It requires both the capacity for a temperamental outburst and the ability to laugh off a mocking remark. Participants must love to provoke opponents, and love to rejoice with fellow players over a good throw. A player executes a bend of the knee, a skillful swing of the arm, and the ball rolls slowly with a dull rumble toward the smaller ball called the *cochonnet*. The aim is to roll the ball so that it finishes as close as possible to the *cochonnet*. Or the player may hurl the ball instead, so that it lands on one belonging to an opponent, and knocks it out of the way.

Seasoned players select the *triplette* of three balls that they intend to use in the competition with the utmost care. A ball weighs from 650 to 800 g (just under 1 ½ pounds to just over 1 ¼ pounds). It has a diameter between 71 and 80 mm (roughly 2 ¾ inches to just over 3 inches). The heavier ones are rolled, and the lighter ones used to aim at a target. There is also variation in hardness, according to whether the ball is made of Inox, steel, or carbon. Players engaged in competition engrave their initials or a symbol into each ball, so that they can distinguish their own.

Never was distance measured with more jealous interest – *pétanque* is a serious business. The menfolk of Saint-Tropez compete on the Place des Lices.

ROQUEBRUNE-SUR-ARGENS

Inland, midway between Saint-Tropez and Cannes, stands a rock of red sandstone as a landmark to the traveler: Here is the village of Roquebrune, full of historic interest and natural, richly contrasting beauty.

Robert Bedot, master cheesemaker

In France and across the world, the cheeses produced by this man conclude the menus of eminent hotels and restaurants, distinguished by the most stars: the "Carlton" and the "Martinez" in Cannes, the "Negresco" in Nice, the "Jardin des Sens" in Montpellier, the "Mas du Langoustier" on the island of Porquerolles, "La Bonne Étape" in Château-Arnoux, and the "Plaza Athénée" in Paris. They can be found at Harrod's in London,

under the palms of the "Mandarin" in Manila, in São Paulo and Beirut. Menus from all around the world feature a certain peasant goat cheese that is made in the Alps of Haute Provence.

Robert Bedot, *Maître Fromager-Affineur*, acquired his enthusiasm for cheese at an early age. It was his father's profession, and Robert remembers the delivery trips, when the aroma of the Roquefort cheeses rose enticingly from their straw-lined boxes. Almost without his realizing it, the "glory of the nation," this "France of over 400 faces" quietly became his dominating passion.

Viewed from its 1,220 foot (372 m) rock, Roquebrune has different aspects according to the angle of sight: now medieval, now maritime, and now hilly.

The *maître-affineur* is very proud of his cheese.

He has been engaged in his work with raw milk and its delicious products for 30 years. Robert Bedot enjoys an excellent international reputation.

He names and presents his cheeses just as a devoted collector presents the items in a painstakingly assembled collection. He knows each one, with its origin, composition, acidity and fat content, and its flavor. He knows the producer and the animals, the cows and goats, at the very beginning of the production chain. Sometimes, Robert Bedot lets the cheeses go through the maturation process at his

suppliers. An example is the Comté, which he has delivered from the Jura, and buys when the cows are on the high pasture, eating the aromatic herbs and grass – the best time for cheese production, since their milk is full of flavor.

Bedot loves cheese made from the milk of goats *de parcours*, that is, allowed to graze freely. Their milk varies with the time of year, and the herbs of Provence give their milk an incomparable aroma that is quite unmatched by the standardized milk of their sisters housed in sheds. Bedot also prefers cheeses made from milk that is obtained with due regard for the animals' natural rhythms of milk production, and not where their period of fertility has been readjusted by artificial means.

For Bedot, the qualities that distinguish a good cheese are naturalness, authenticity, and careful craftsmanship.

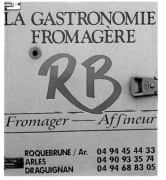

LA GASTRONOMIE
FROMAGÈRE

RB

Fromager —— Affineur

ROQUEBRUNE / Ar. 04 94 45 44 33
ARLES   04 90 93 35 74
DRAGUIGNAN   04 94 68 83 05

French hotels and the best restaurants from around the world order their cheese from Bedot.

CANNES

Cannes is synonymous with international, jetsetting, fashionable society, and not just during the one period of the year when the red carpet is unrolled for the international film festival. This aspect too easily obscures the fact that Cannes has more to offer the visitor: the old houses and picturesque restaurants that still survive in the narrow streets of the hill of Le Suquet, the pleasure of sitting in the shade of the little Cannet squares, and the pine-bordered Avenue de Californie, where Picasso was once resident, and which boasts magnificent villas.

The Boulevard de la Croisette is an old lady now, having taken her first steps in the second half of the 19th century. She has not ceased since then to draw the rich and cosmopolitan under her spell. She shows no sign of running out of face powder yet, and is well skilled at preserving her former beauty. Cannes is a vast shop window of riches. There is not a name in haute couture that is not represented here, nor one that does not adorn the shoulders of VIPs in the luxury hotels. La Croisette is the beach promenade, palm-fringed and adorned with

The road that leads to Cannes is the RN 7, the modern successor to the road constructed by Emperor Marcus Aurelius connecting Rome and Arles.

La Croisette

The impression that first greets the traveler's eyes on arrival in Cannes is one of style, glitz, and luxury. Ferraris make their way down the Boulevard de la Croisette, those, that is, that are not parked for the purpose of delivering guests, in front of one of the luxury hotels. The images of Cannes are its yachts, its palm trees, and the white façades of its buildings – images that represent the town's great past and present.

The two faces of Cannes: in front, the sea and the enchanting scenery, and behind, the palatial hotels and luxury boutiques.

Not just a myth: Cannes really is the haunt of rich and beautiful people with yachts and luxury cars.

flowers. It commands fine views of the Estérel massif and of the islands, the Îles de Lérins. The name "la Croisette" originated from a small cross (*crocetta*) erected on the site of what is now "Palm Beach" by the monks of Saint-Honorat, on the island of that name. Visible from afar, the cross served as a gathering point for pilgrims who were going to the island.

The gardens of Port Canto, near the Palm Beach Casino, have a well-tended charm that expunges from memory the concrete bulk of the Palais des Festivals (the Festival Palace)

that was built at the opposite end of la Croisette in 1982.

The yachting marina brought a great lasting change to the small fishing village of Cannes.

The "Carlton" and the "Martinez"

When it was founded in 1912, the "Carlton" pronounced itself to be the "best hotel for people from the best levels of society." It came into existence with the express intention of competing with another huge hotel intended for the great personages of this world, the "Négresco" in Nice, and with the aim of outdoing it in splendor and luxury.

The fate of the "Carlton" was unusual. It was requisitioned for use as a hospital in World War I, and was taken over by the American General Staff in 1944. They proved to be the first of a long list of famous visitors from overseas. Emirs and crowned heads still make their stay in the "Carlton," and international stars, along with the whole of Hollywood, feel well looked after here. The demands that the famous sometimes seem to make of the world around them do occasionally prove a challenge to the comfortable serenity of the establishment; no one will forget the way Mickey Rourke used to ride his motorcycle

The abode of splendor and luxury: Cannes' most magnificent and palatial hotel welcomes a rich and exclusive international clientèle.

into the foyer in the early morning. The moods of the divas and their exotic lifestyles fill the annals of the hotel. Scandals and delightful moments alike will always be remembered – such as the time Rita Hayworth and Ali Khan greeted the enthusiastic crowds below, thrilled by the wedding, from their balcony.

Built in the style of the Belle Époque, the "Carlton" is like a majestic ship, a luxury liner equipped for a luxury cruise through the pleasures of life. The restaurant on the seventh floor of the hotel always runs at full capacity during the festival or during another large media event, MIDEM.

The hotel "Martinez" also lies on la Croisette. The style and ambience here are art déco. It may not rival the "Carlton" in number of rooms and sheer magnificence, but its awe-inspiring staircases, its plush carpeted floors that give the sensation of walking on cotton wool, and a drawing room in the African style, conjure up exotic reveries. In a bar

Vacation on the Côte d'Azur means sunbathing on the beach at Cannes, gazing out at the Îles de Lérins and across the sea into the distance.

The magnificent lobby of the "Carlton" offers not only opulence but also comfort, where guests can enjoy a coffee or the newspaper.

Columns in the classical style lend the foyer of the "Carlton" a majestic charm. The "Carlton" set out to compete with the "Négresco" in Nice.

where one might easily meet Cathérine Deneuve, jazz melodies serenade the end of the day. The tables of the restaurant, "La Palme d'Or," on the terrace outside the hotel, where Cannes, la Croisette, and the sea can be admired to advantage, hold out the invitation to discover delicious surprises, accompanied by very good regional wines.

Nearby is another grand hotel, again on la Croisette, but a little more modest. The cuisine of the "Majestic," however, receives unlimited and unanimous praise from gastronomic critics.

The cuisine of Bruno Oger

Bruno Oger knows well the very pinnacle of culinary delights. He spent seven years working under Georges

Blanc, one of France's most outstanding chefs. He took his cuisine as far afield as Bangkok, to the "Hotel Oriental," which was the foremost hotel in the gastronomic world for over ten years. He has now set himself the goal of making the "Villa des Lys" in the "Majestic" into one of the best restaurants on the Côte d'Azur. Oger buys his raw materials from the best addresses in Cannes. Fish and fruit are delivered from the Marché Forville. The catch comes from the nearby harbor, La Napoule. Céneri, the *maître-fromager* par excellence, matures only the very best of cheeses for him and the other chefs of la Croisette.

Bruno Oger is young and talented. His cooking is like an ode to Mediterranean gastronomy.

The spiral staircase in the "Hotel Martinez" is quite a miracle of achievement in architecture.

Bruno Oger's menu can often present guests with an extremely difficult choice: *potiron farci aux gambas* (pumpkin stuffed with shrimps), *Saint-Pierre au tian grillé* (John Dory with grilled *tian*), *salade méditerranéenne* (Mediterranean salad), *Saint-Jacques grillés* (broiled scallops), *homard aux fines herbes* (lobster with *fines herbes*), or perhaps *crabe à la coriandre* (crab with coriander).

Bruno Oger shares the management of "Villa des Lys" with a young kitchen chef who was selected as the cook of the year 2000 by what is regarded as the bible of gastronomic criticism, "Gault et Millau."

Saint-Pierre au tian grillé et basilic à l'ail doux
John Dory with grilled tian, basil, and mild garlic

Serves 2

1 eggplant (slim shape)
1 zucchini
1 zucchini flower
Oil for frying
4 canned tomatoes
Salt and freshly ground pepper
2 tbsp/30 ml native olive oil
1 John Dory, about 1½ lb/700 g
1 jar of *pistou*
Scant ¼ cup/50 ml veal stock
2 leaves of basil, shredded

Wash and dry the vegetables. Heat a broiler pan, and preheat the oven to medium. Slice the eggplant into four well-shaped, long pieces, and do the same with the zucchini.
Broil the vegetables briefly on all sides, then transfer to the oven to finish cooking. Cut the zucchini flower in half, and deep fry at 320 °F/160 °C. Drain on paper towels to absorb excess oil. Season with salt and pepper.

Heat the tomatoes. Rinse and descale the fish. Fillet it, but do not remove the skin. Season with salt and pepper. Heat the olive oil in a skillet. Fry the fillets skin side down at first. When ¾ cooked, turn over and finish cooking. Keep hot. Mix the *pistou* with a little veal stock. It should retain a slightly thick consistency. Carefully stir in the basil.
Arrange the zucchini and eggplant slices, the tomatoes, and the zucchini flowers

in a circular pattern on the upper half of the plate. Place the fish below them. Drizzle with a little lukewarm *pistou* before serving. Grilled vegetables taste excellent as a summer accompaniment to many dishes. In general, no sauce is really needed.

Salade variée au homard et fines herbes
Méli-mélo de légumes à l'anchoïade et caviar

Mixed salad with lobster and fines herbes, medley of vegetables with anchoïade and caviar

Serves 2

2 Breton lobsters, generous 1 lb/500 g each
2 small purple artichokes
4 new onions
4 carrots with tops
4 cauliflower florets
4 small champignons
4 green asparagus spears
Generous 1 tbsp/20 ml olive oil
2 cloves of garlic, peeled
1 bouquet garni
1 glass dry white wine
A little balsamic vinegar
Salt and 10 white peppercorns
2 canned tomatoes
1 tsp chopped *fines herbes*
1 oz/20 g *anchoïade*
1 tablespoon/20 g caviar
Freshly milled pepper

Cook the lobsters in boiling water for about 8 minutes. Cool and remove from the shell. Separate the meat into medallions, and also reserve the claws. Prepare the artichokes. Carefully wash and peel the vegetables.

Heat the olive oil in a skillet. Add the vegetables, then the whole cloves of garlic, bouquet garni, wine, vinegar, salt, and peppercorns. Cook gently on a low heat, keeping careful watch. The cooking time will vary between about 20 and 30 minutes, depending on size. The vegetables should retain a crisp "bite."

Add the tomatoes at the end of the cooking time. Then cool and drain the vegetables, reserving the juices. Arrange the vegetables in the middle of the plate. Place the medallions of lobster and the claws on top. Decorate with *fines herbes*, *anchoïade*, and caviar. Check and adjust the seasoning of the vegetable juices, and pour over the vegetables. Season the dish with pepper and serve immediately.

305

VALLAURIS

The small town of Vallauris lies in the south of Provence, and is famous for its pottery. Archeological excavations have uncovered the kilns of the region's first potters, leading to the belief that people were working with clay in Vallauris as long ago as the 2nd century, during what is known as the *époque ligure* (Ligurian period).

It is thought, however, that fixed settlements did not appear in the Val d'Or (the Roman Vallis Aurea) until the 8th century.

The Middle Ages saw 400 years of population decline as a result of wars and plague. At the beginning of the 16th century, the prior of Lérins, to whom

It was the Provençal charm of Vallauris that attracted so many artists of various types to settle here.

Vallauris belonged, arranged for 70 families from the region of Gênes to move to Vallauris to repopulate the area.

These new inhabitants were to rebuild the town and its prosperity. In recompense for their efforts, they received land and the permission to develop it. These people included many craftsmen, in whose hands the clay of Vallauris once more produced a flourishing industry that has continued over the centuries. The town has been associated with its pottery tradition ever since.

Toward the end of the 19th century new materials – aluminum and cast iron – appeared to challenge the preeminence of earthenware for crockery and cooking utensils. Again it was the creativity of the industry that rescued Vallauris. People discovered methods of decorating the simple earthenware products, and this led to

Homme au mouton (man with sheep) a ceramic statue by Picasso, who came to Vallauris in 1946.

Creations from Vallauris. These craftsmen work in traditional clay, stone, and fabric.

the development of enamel ware. Clay vessels were given a metallic sheen, and stood up well to the competition.

The potters of Vallauris received the attention of a famous name in the world of art in 1946, when Picasso took an interest in pottery and settled there. He spent the years from 1948 to 1955 shaping and working the clay; he invented new types of composition, and created over 4,000 artifacts.

Following his example, the film and stage actor Jean Marais opened a studio and gallery in Vallauris. He had become famous especially through his work with Jean Cocteau. He continued to work there until death took him from his wheel and his easel.

Vallauris is often termed the world capital of ceramics. It has given the world a charter of quality, drawn up under the influence of its artists, in which the words of the masters are passed down to succeeding generations.

The art of shaping clay

The sight of a potter working at the wheel is an impressive one: In his hands, the clay loses its formlessness and becomes a unique object. Simple and effortless though it looks, this is a skill that demands years of practice. Countless sunken vases and ill-formed bowls must pass before the art is perfected.

The potter places a lump of clay onto the center of the wheel as it spins. Placing one thumb in the middle of the clay, the potter then hollows

A glimpse inside a potter's studio. Beautiful ceramics have been made in Vallauris since the 16th century.

out the clay to create the base of the vase. The shape is gradually extended until the perfect vessel emerges. Handles, necks, and decorations are made separately and are added to the basic shape at a later stage. The pieces next have to be left to dry before their first firing.

After the vases have been fired and are completely dry, the last stage is implemented. They are decorated with great precision. The finest examples of the potter's art are a result of the artist's experience and knowledge of the material, combined with great skill and talent that comes through years of practice.

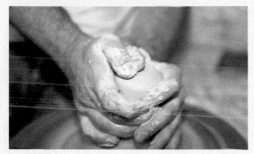

The wheel may be operated by the potter, or may be electrically driven.

Straightforward as it may look, the art of turning demands a great deal of practice, precision, and attention.

The clay pieces have to be handled with the utmost care until they have been fired.

The clay does not attain its final color until after firing.

Another demand on the skills of the craftsman: the last stage is about to begin.

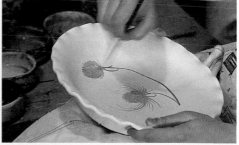

At this stage the earthenware vases, pots, and crockery are decorated. Various techniques are used.

309

ÎLES DE LÉRINS

At Cannes harbor, a stone's throw from the Palais des Festivals, short boat trips to the Îles de Lérins are available every day. The crossing takes little more than half an hour, and the noisy bustle of Cannes is a world away. Filled with the scent of pine and eucalyptus woods, these two small islands, Saint-Honorat and Sainte Marguerite, are an ideal refuge for anyone seeking peace and quiet.

The abbey lies hidden in an idyllic conservation area. The island belongs to monks who grow a wine that shows great promise.

The wines and liqueurs of the monks of Saint-Honorat

It was the hermit Honorat, who founded the first monastery in the western world in 400 AD, who gave his name to the island. When he arrived here, there was no drinking water available. He put his trust in God – and a spring of water gushed forth.

The Cistercian order, which is established here, has always lived from its own agricultural produce: fruit and vegetables, and the cultivation of lavender and vines. Vines began to be cultivated here in the 1920s, on an area of 20

The old fortified abbey was built in 1073 to protect the Cistercian monks from attack.

acres (8 ha). These were later replaced with lavender, which requires fewer workers to tend it. Since the monks lacked young men to work the fields, this crop was much easier for the monks to look after.

Since 1975, the abbey has enjoyed a fresh upturn in its activity, with the arrival of young monks with agricultural training. Vines have again been planted, in keeping with the spirit of Saint Benedict, who said that a true monk is one who lives from the labor of his hands. The winery has been renovated, and the methods of production have been improved. The brothers, whose winegrowing operations are the only such activity in the Cannes region, are convinced that they are cultivating a land blessed by God. Its climate gives it moderate winters and hot, damp summers, favoring the production of great wines. Production today occupies 17 acres (7 ha). The Cistercians have consulted the foremost oenologues in their desire to make best use of this land. They have also studied the basic principles of the art. Their white wines consist of 50 percent Clairette and equal proportions of Ugni Blanc and Chardonnay, and have an average alcohol content of 12.5 percent. They are fruity, very balanced wines. The reds consist of 90 percent Syrah and 10 percent Mourvèdre. They achieve an alcohol content of 13 percent, are very aromatic, and keep extremely well.

Last year's harvest produced a yield of about 25,000 bottles of red wine and 10,000 of white. The future looks promising, since the great chefs of Cannes restaurants and hotels

The rule of Saint Benedict states that a true monk is one who lives by the labor of his hands.

The grapes from 17 acres (7 ha) of vineyards produce 25,000 bottles of red and 10,000 of white wine a year.

The renovated cellars and modernized methods of production, together with God's help, produce fine wines.

Lérina liqueurs are made from 44 plants. These are macerated for several months in barrels.

have decided to include the *vendange des moines* on their wine lists.

Another brother, a former medical student, is responsible for the production of a traditional liqueur, over a hundred years old. Today's method of production was developed 50 years ago by a monk who was a chemist.

If the ways of the Lord are inscrutable, the methods of the monks are unknowable: They guard the secret of producing their liqueur as jealously as a treasure. Brother Marie-Pâques keeps suspicious watch over his copper stills, and betrays only a few merest details of the composition of the mysterious beverage.

The Lérina liqueurs are made from 44 plants. Only one of these is imported, and the others either grow wild on the island or are grown in a hidden corner of the garden.

The brothers conscientiously gather the roots, buds, leaves, flowers, and fruits. They dry and crush them, and store them for several months in barrels to which alcohol is added. This mixture is distilled, and the extract obtained is once more mixed with alcohol, sugar, and water. If the liqueur is emerald

The monks sit down together at the long trestle tables and commemorate Jesus Christ beneath the picture depicting the Last Supper.

The alcohol content must be carefully tested. The color of Lérina liqueur is green or yellow according to its alcohol content.

Brother Marie-Pâques, who is responsible for the production of the liqueurs, tastes one of the spirits.

The special aroma and refreshing flavor of the liqueurs come from the plants of the island.

green in color, its alcohol content is 50 percent, if saffron yellow, 40 percent.

The monks also have the privilege of being allowed to distill brandy. At the monastery, they produce an *eau de vie de marc de Provence*, a Provençal marc, and an *eau de vie de vin de Provence*, a brandy, which is matured for six months in oak casks before it is ready – as a 50 percent spirit – to befuddle the senses.

With their knowledge of traditional methods of liqueur production, the monks also make a whole range of liqueurs apart from the two Lérina types. There is a *liqueur de verveine* (vervain liqueur), a mild *liqueur de mandarine* (mandarin liqueur), and *sénancole*, made from a mixture of thyme, summer savory, orange blossom, and many more, secret, flowers. The monks' latest creation is *mandamarc*, a delicious combination of marc and mandarin liqueur that is drunk ice cold. A dash of this is a wonderful addition to a fruit salad. The wines, spirits, and liqueurs made by the monks of Saint-Honorat all come from organically grown produce.

ANTIBES

Following the coast around, the eye of the traveler is constantly tempted inland; Vallauris, home of the ceramic artists, lies just a little away from the coast, and Biot, with its museum devoted to the famous French graphic artist and painter, Fernand Léger is also nearby. One last diversion over the charming peninsula of Cap d'Antibes, and the traveler arrives in Antibes itself, with its old streets, covered market, and stallholders that sell socca.

Picasso used to love walking along the Promenade Amiral de Grasse, by the town wall of Antibes.

"Les Vieux Murs"

The walls of the town, dating from the 16th century, run like a rampart along the line of the coast, and parallel to it leads the Promenade Amiral de Grasse. The views of the Mediterranean and Cap d'Antibes are enticing enough for the visitor to forget all else, but pleasures of the table await. The experienced kitchen team of "Les Vieux Murs" restaurant in Antibes produces wonderful creations, underlined by the excellent wine recommendations of the sommelier.

Through the windows, the view is of the sea, where the white sails of distant boats perform their graceful arabesques on the horizon. Inside, the journey of discovery of Mediterranean cuisine proceeds.

Choosing from the menu, with all its tempting dishes elegantly composed by chef Thierry Gratarolla, can cause the guest great difficulty. Should one choose the crawfish carpaccio, or the delicate vegetable tart with soured milk? St. Peter's fish cooked in bouillon with beans and squid, or perhaps a pigeon breast with honey and tomato beignets?

The tables and chairs stand outside, as only a climate like this, in southern France, permits. Tempting aromas from the kitchen entice the passing clientèle.

In the covered market at Antibes, all the ingredients of a typical Provençal meal can be found.

All dishes are served with seasonal, fresh produce, such as zucchini blossoms or chanterelles.

Citrus brioches, a choice of pralines, and candied chestnuts round off a delicious menu.

"Les Vieux Murs" is one of the town's best restaurants. The sight of the sea and the aromas of Provence that waft from the kitchen mingle here.

Crème brûlée à la lavande
Crème brûlée with lavender

Serves 4

2 cups/500 ml milk
2 handfuls of lavender flowers
4 cups/1 liter cream
10 egg yolks
Scant ½ cup/100 g sugar
2 tsp superfine cane sugar

The day before, bring the milk to a boil, remove from the heat, and add the lavender. Leave to infuse.

The following day, preheat the oven to 265 °F/130 °C. Pass the milk through a sieve. Add the cream.

Beat together the egg yolks and sugar until blended and pale in color. Add the cream mixture, and mix carefully. Pour into individual molds, and place these in a bain-marie. Bake in the oven for 90 minutes. Sprinkle the tops with superfine sugar, and place under a broiler until caramelized.

Rougets de roche
au parmesan
Red mullet with Parmesan

Serves 4

6 red mullet, 7 oz/200 g each
½ cup/50 g freshly
grated Parmesan
1 tbsp olive oil
1 bunch of basil

Chickpea (garbanzo bean)
purée
2 ⅓ cups/200 g chickpea flour
2 glasses of water
Salt, freshly milled pepper

Descale and fillet the fish, leaving the skin on, and removing any fine bones with tweezers. Shred the basil.

Boil the chickpea flour in the water for four minutes, then season with salt and pepper, and set aside.

Heat a little olive oil in a skillet. Fry the fish on the skin side first, then turn over. Place a little chickpea purée in the middle of each plate. Add the fish, sprinkle with Parmesan cheese, then drizzle with olive oil and scatter over the basil.

GRASSE

Grasse lies to the north of Antibes, 10 ½ miles (17 km) from Cannes, on a spur of the alpine foothills. The town's origins go back to the 7th century, and its name is derived from "terre grasse," the "fat (or fertile) earth" of the area in which flowers grow so well.

The history of perfume

Grasse is the town of perfume and flowers. Each of its many perfumeries receives busloads of visitors every day,

In the 9th century the inhabitants of Grasse fled from the Saracens and took refuge on a massive rock where they founded a new settlement. The town's prosperity began in the 16th century with the manufacture of perfume.

arriving for a short guided tour of its laboratories. The guide explains the essentials only, and the tour participants head outside by the route that leads them through the sales showroom, past the tempting array of bottles and gift packages of scents.

Legend has it that the first perfume came from a drop of Venus' blood, the kiss she gave her son. From it there grew a rose, the first bearer of sweet perfume.

The fascinating and complex history of perfume has its roots in antiquity. It had a very important role for the ancient Egyptians, who used it in their burial rites, and to

embalm their dead. The living, too, loved to rub themselves with sweet-smelling oils and ointments, hoping to augment their attractiveness by so doing. The Egyptian city of Alexandria was like one enormous amphora of perfumes, which were made in the city, and from there spread throughout the Mediterranean region. Athens and Rome were entranced with the perfumes it exported: myrrh, sandalwood, ambergris, and oil of thyme and anise. Such excesses came to an end with the arrival of

Grasse owes the establishment of the perfume industry to the French queen, Catherine of Medici.

Christianity, which limited the use of perfume to the religious sphere. However, the Crusaders, whose expeditions to free the Holy Land had taken them to the Orient since the 11th century, brought back new essential oils and the art of distillation.

During the ensuing centuries, perfume had varied significance: mystical, medicinal, aesthetic, and even maleficent. Its importance was revived in the 16th century, when perfume attained an established place in the magnificence of court life.

Grasse in Provence was able to profit from this renewed interest; its success in doing so is well known. Catherine of Medici, Queen of France, was besotted with oriental perfumes. Hearing that there were flowers growing on the shores of the Mediterranean that smelled more intensely than the oils of the Orient, she ordered one of her men of science to take on the delicate task of creating a lady's perfume from these flowers. At that time, Grasse earned its living from tanning, and the local glovemakers used the essential oils from the flowers of the area to mask the stench of the tanneries. One of these craftsmen was a certain Monsieur Fragonard, father of the painter known for his gallant pastoral scenes. Catherine of Medici's commission was the beginning of perfume manufacture in Grasse. The industry experienced a meteoric rise, and made the town world famous. About two centuries later, the production of leather and the manufacture of gloves had ceased and

disappeared altogether. Grasse had by this time become the undisputed world capital of perfume production.

Perfume is not all the town has to offer; it is also worth taking a stroll through the streets.

How perfume is made

Two processes have long underlain the manufacture of perfume: these being enfleurage and distillation.

Enfleurage was a process in which whole flowers were placed onto a tray spread with neutral, unscented fats. These trays were stacked in piles of up to 40 and left for 48 hours. The flowers were then removed and immediately replaced with freshly gathered ones. This was repeated 30 times in succession, until eventually the fats, now impregnated with essential oils, were melted off into special vessels, to be mixed and stirred with alcohol to extract the oils. The alcohol, now saturated with the scents of the flowers, was distilled to produce a concentrated ointment used in the manufacture of cosmetics.

Distillation was invented in Iran, in the 11th century. This method is based on the fact that the compounds responsible for the fragrance are distilled together with water vapor. The flowers are put into a vessel and covered with one to five times the quantity of water. The vessel is heated. This has the effect of extracting the essential oils from the flowers in the water as it vaporizes. This mixture of essential oils and steam is passed through a tube that is

A perfume laboratory at the beginning of the 20th century. The work of producing the costly perfumes required many workers.

cooled to condense the contents. At the end of the condenser, the liquid collects in a metal or glass container. The oils settle on top of the water when it cools.

Today a method of extraction is used that involves washing the flowers repeatedly in solvents. The solvent becomes saturated with the perfume, and vaporizes at a very low boiling point. As it passes through the apparatus, water and impurities are separated out. Distillation finally isolates the pure essential oil. This flower oil is expensive. It takes ½ ton of jasmine, or 900 pounds of roses, or 300 pounds of broom flowers to produce 1 pound of flower oil (equivalent to 1 tonne of jasmine, or 900 kg of roses, or 300 kg of broom to extract 1 kg of the oil).

Enfleurage is one of the methods of making perfume. The flowers are spread on trays coated with fat.

The trays are piled on top of each other.

For the distillation process, the fresh flowers are put into a vessel with water and heated.

Once distillation is complete, the laboratory work on the perfume begins.

The flowers have yielded up their finest essences. Now these are ready to be blended into a scent.

The essential tool of the trade for a perfumier is a very good nose.

PONT-DU-LOUP

The village of Pont-du-Loup lies half way between Grasse and Tourrettes-sur-Loup, on a rocky promontory. A street lined with palms and plane trees meanders under a railway bridge.

Two old, deserted hotels that doubtless played host to Queen Victoria one summer's day in 1891 now slide inexorably toward decay. Now only their wide balconies and glazed terraces remain as witnesses to the soirées of the elegant society that inhabited them. Pont-du-Loup has the bleached look of a place too much exposed to the sun. The orange and ocher of their façades is overlaid with a patina. Yet this is the land where violets and delicious treats are found. A street name proclaims: chemin de la confiserie (Street of Confectionery).

The confectioner "Florian"

Candied rose petals and delicate crystallized violets, vervain leaves glacé – it is like being Alice in Wonderland. Some people, it is true, might prefer to see flowers in a vase, rather than treated as ordinary food, but when the art of the confectioner is able to transform them into candy while preserving the fine aroma and the delicate arch of the blossoms, there is nothing ordinary here. These are the food of exalted spheres indeed. Roses from Plascassier, vervain from Grasse, violets from Tourrette, and jasmine from Forcalquier are variously made into candies, jellies, and crystallized flowers.

Florian processes about 880 pounds (400 kg) of violets, 880 pounds (400 kg) of jasmine, 1 ½ tons (6 tonnes) of citrus fruits, and 1 1⁄10 tons (1 tonne) of roses a year. Here they exchange their life in the wild for a sweet retirement as sugar candy.

Pont-du-Loup (the wolf's bridge) is the spot where the gorges called Gorges du Loup begin.

The confectioner's business, "Florian," makes delicious candy from flowers.

Turning flowers into candies

The violets are picked fresh with the dew of the early morning, and arrive at "Florian" the confectioner's still moist. First they are sorted to select the best and remove any grass or leaves. The confectioner then mixes them just as they are with gum arabic, and rolls them in confectioners' sugar. They are transferred to a tray, and placed in a drying oven at 175 °F (80 °C). It takes as long as five days for the violets to dry out completely. Then they are immersed in sugar syrup for a further twelve hours. When they are taken out of the sugar, they crystallize when they come

The fresh violets are first coated in gum arabic, then turned in confectioners' sugar. They are then dried out completely in a drying oven.

into contact with the air. They then have to be separated one from another and packed. In their clear cellophane packets that crinkle so invitingly, these violets present a delightful sight to the customer.

Imagine now a crystallized violet, summoned to the dance by the bubbles of champagne in a beautiful drinking glass. The flavor and color of roses and vervain are equal rivals. The only way to decide which is the best is to try both. How delicious is the thought of a

The subtle flavor of violet jelly gives a very special note to a special recipe.

cup of hot herb tea on a cold winter's evening. Beside the cup lies a vervain blossom, conjuring up the distant days of summer, to dissolve blissfully in the mouth between two sips of tea.

These are by no means all the sweet delights made by "Confiserie Florian" in Pont-du-Loup. Jellies, candied fruits, orange sticks, exquisite chocolates, and candied flowers of all sorts also number among the unusual candies to tempt and tantalize the customer here.

Pounds of jelly are boiled and candied fruits prepared in "Confiserie Florian" every day.

The freshly harvested blossoms arrive full of fragrance. They are put in a copper pot.

The flowers have to be handled very carefully to preserve their freshness and shape.

The confectioner mixes the flowers with gum arabic in a copper pot.

The flowers are slowly coated in their new covering.

The flowers are then tossed in confectioners' sugar using light movements.

One by one they are arranged on trays. The flowers are then kept in drying ovens at 175 °F (80 °C) for five days.

The confectioner measures the temperature of the sugar syrup. It must be exactly right.

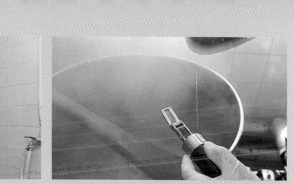

The measuring instruments must be accurate to ensure that the right moment is chosen.

When the sugar reaches the right temperature, it can be ladled out carefully.

With the utmost care, the sugar solution is poured onto the flowers, already dusted in confectioners' sugar.

Coating the flower petals evenly with sugar syrup demands a great deal of experience.

The petals are dried slowly each time, both when coated in confectioners' sugar and after they have been candied.

327

Fondant de foie gras poêlé au confit de fleurs de violette

Fried fondant of foie gras with crystallized violets

Serves 4

14 oz/400 g raw *foie gras*
4 tbsp/120 g lavender honey (or forest/meadow honey)
2 tsp veal stock
½ cup/120 ml water
Juice of ½ lemon
¼ lb/100 g crystallized violets

Slice the goose liver just under ½ in/1 cm thick, and coat the slices in flour. Heat the honey in a saucepan for two minutes over a high heat, taking great care to ensure that it does not stick to the base of the pan and burn .
Mix the veal stock with the water, and add to the honey. Boil for another five minutes over a medium heat. Add the lemon juice and crystallized violets.
In a very hot skillet, fry the liver on both sides. Pour over the sauce to serve. Accompany with corn salad (lamb's lettuce), and boiled potatoes if wished.
Recipe: Jacques Chibois

Fraîcheur aux deux fraises à l'huile d'olive vanillée et confit de fleurs de jasmin
Strawberries with vanilla olive oil and crystallized jasmine

Serves 5

9 ¼ lb/4.2 kg strawberries
Generous 1 cup/230 g sugar
Juice of ½ lemon
Scant ¼ cup/50 ml olive oil
1 ½ vanilla pods
⅓ cup/50 g stoned Moroccan olives
10 oz/300 g wild strawberries
Zest of ¼ lime
1 glass crystallized jasmine flowers
5 olive leaves

Wash, hull, and quarter the strawberries. Mix ½ lb/200 g of them with ⅙ cup sugar and half the lemon juice. Sieve and set aside as the sauce. Warm the olive oil gently, and add 1 tbsp/25 g sugar and the pulp from the vanilla beans. Mix well. Add a generous ½ cup sugar and ½ cup water, and simmer at 175 °F/80 °C for four hours until a thick syrup is formed. Add the olives and candy them. Place the remaining strawberries in the center of the individual serving plates, and add the wild strawberries. Mix the remaining sugar with the lime zest, and sprinkle over the strawberries. Pour over the sauce. Decorate with a few crystallized jasmine flowers. Finally, drizzle with the olive oil. Quarter the candied olives and place on top of the strawberries. Garnish with the olive leaves.

Finally, a refreshing dessert to stimulate the digestion:

Pamplemousse à la fleur de jasmin
Grapefruit with jasmine flowers
Allow half a grapefruit per person. Carefully loosen and lift out the fruit flesh from the skins without damaging them. Chop the fruit and mix it with fresh or candied cherries. Add a spoonful of whisky and a couple of candied jasmine flowers. Refill the fruit mixture into the grapefruit shells. Chill before serving.
Recipes: Jacques Chibois

NICE, MONTE CARLO, AND MENTON

On the drive inland along the D 220, the traveler reaches Vence, a small town in the foothills of the Alps. It is a very different place from the fashionable, cosmopolitan world of the Côte d'Azur, though it does have a number of

attractions to offer, Henri Matisse created the Chapelle du Rosaire, and the Maeght family founded one of the loveliest museums of contemporary art, on the road leading to Saint-Paul de Vence. The extensive collection includes pictures by Joan Miró, Marc Chagall, and Georges Braque, to name but a few. Raoul Dufy, Paul Signac, and all those painters of the past who loved Provence, recorded it on their canvases for posterity as the country used to look, a hinterland with olive groves and broad fields, and villages that have now become tourist haunts with real estate beckoning.

The French Riviera begins in Nice, capital of the Côte d'Azur. Nice, the town of art that gave its name to the new Realist school, is represented by artists such as Arman, Jean

Tinguely, Daniel Spoerri, and Yves Klein. It stages its own famous frivolities presided over by King Carnival. Its cuisine boasts an abundance of specialties, and it is the only town in France to possess a vineyard: A small but renowned AOC is grown on the Bellet.

From the road, the "route nationale" RN98, there is a magnificent view over Eze, a picturesque village that is worth a visit. This is where Nietzsche wrote part of his great philosophical work "Thus Spake Zarathustra."

The principality of Monaco has been less touched by philosophy. Its privileged location high on a rock overlooking the sea meant a history of repeated hostile attack and periods of barbarity. Life in Monaco has become much more peaceful today; people bask in luxury and the pursuit of pleasure.

The Riviera d'Azur continues eastward as far as Italy. Just short of the border lies Menton, wedged between the mountains and the Mediterranean. It has such a mild climate that there is no cold season of the year, and oranges and lemons grow here as nowhere else in France.

Beautiful Nice still bears the signs of its glorious past, when the English aristocracy stayed here.

NICE

In 1388, Amadeus of Savoy caused the citizens of Nice to sign a treaty linking them to what was to become the kingdom of Piedmont-Sardinia. Nice remained Italian for five centuries, and the marks of this association linger on in the colorful house decoration of its old quarter and the transalpine influences in its cuisine.

Candied fruits

Humans have shown much inventiveness in response to nature's abundance. Before our methods of preservation were developed, there was a huge question as to how to stop the delicious harvest of fruit produced by the orchards of Provence from spoiling. The answer was to candy them, a process that has been in use since the 14th century. Pope Benedict XIII, who had his seat in Avignon, was an enthusiast. Within a few decades, candied fruit had become a popular gift in Provence, likely to win the favor of Anne of Austria or Madame de Sévigné. They were then exported to Britain, and candied fruit found its way into cake recipes there. Britain is still the country with the biggest export market for this product.

Candied fruits are made from fresh produce, and retain all the flavor of the original fruit underneath their not-too-thick glaze of sugar. The process of candying demands time and patience. The fruit has to be perfect, and must fulfill all the quality criteria relating to flavor, ripeness, aroma, and size.

The fruit is picked by hand, as even the minutest damage must be avoided. The preparation method applied from then on depends on the particular fruit variety. Pears are peeled; clementines are kept in their skins, but punctured – as are all citrus fruits – to enable the syrup to penetrate inside. Peeling is a painstaking process, as the shape of the fruit has to be maintained, and it is

Here is everyone's picture of France as we know and love it: a small square like any other, where friends meet and enjoy the Mediterranean atmosphere.

important to remove neither too much nor too little of the skin.

The confectioner knows from experience that the flavor of different fruits develops in different ways. The method used to candy them varies accordingly. There are usually three stages. The fruit is first blanched, that is, briefly immersed in boiling water. The length of this immersion depends on the type of fruit: a cherry needs less time than a pineapple. If the fruit is kept in the boiling water too long, it bursts; if not long enough, it will shrivel. Considerable experience and sensitivity are required to see when the fruit has cooked to just the right extent. Following this, the fruit makes its first contact with the sugar. The fruit is placed in a light sugar syrup, which is then heated. This process is repeated once a day for a week, then every other day during the second, week and every third day during the third. The concentration of the sugar syrup is gradually increased.

Each day, with each immersion, the fruit absorbs more and more concentrated sugar solution. The moisture content of the fruit is reduced, and the flesh changes into a soft mass. With their mother-of-pearl sheen and

Enjoying candied fruit

As with cheese, so with candied fruit – though this may seem a rather broad comparison. The various types differ in flavor and consistency, and it aids enjoyment to eat them, as it were, in crescendo fashion. Then the more pronounced flavor of the one will not overshadow the more delicate flavor of the next. It is best to begin with mild flavored fruits such as apricots, plums, strawberries, and figs, then to move on to more intense ones such as kiwi fruit, pineapple, and melon, and finally the most flavorsome, for example clementines, oranges, and kumquats. This way it is possible to appreciate the qualities of each.

new, shiny coating, fruits such as delicate strawberries, juicy pineapples, and tender figs look too precious to touch. This defense tactic on the part of the fruit is quite in vain once the observer has sampled a candied fruit. They are too delicious to be satisfied with just looking.

Confectioner Auer

"I am the last craftsman of my trade" is the instant comment of Thierry Auer, fifth generation member of a family that has been engaged in producing confectionery since the 19th century, 1820 to be precise. There might seem some vanity in a statement like that from Thierry Auer, but sampling his candied fruits is enough to show that he has a right to be proud. His products really do taste of fruit, and make one completely forget the sugar in which they are preserved. Thierry Auer works only with freshly processed fruits. No artificial preservatives are added.

Welcome to the premises of *maître-confisier* Auer! Every one of the products on display is a real temptation, and spells danger to the waistline.

The fresh fruits are blanched in boiling water.

They are carefully stirred with a wooden spoon.

The temperature must be exact. Blanching is precisely timed.

Sugar is added to maintain the syrup at the right concentration.

Samples are removed at intervals.

The candied fruits gleam, saturated with sugar syrup.

The fruits are carefully selected. They should be small, with a thin skin. Consumers like to be able to put a whole candied fruit in their mouths. The strawberries, though they may no longer have the brilliant redness of a freshly picked one, have lost nothing of their flavor. The clementines come from Corsica. They are his best selling line; he sells over a ton a year. Auer has sourced a particularly flavorsome variety on the island, which he finds are just the right size for eating. He obtains lemons from inland Provence, and apricots from Buis-les-Baronies in Drôme. The producer there has reintroduced an old, richly flavored variety.

Candied fruits are not the sole obsession for Thierry Auer, despite his overriding concern with the maintenance of traditional methods. He has made one solitary concession to modernity: He has set up a web address, and is prepared to sell his creations to his customers over the Internet.

A visit to his shop is the best of all. Amid the wonderful fairytale décor, it seems impossible to resist the sweet temptations on display. *Orangettes cristallisées* are candied orange peel with a sugar crystal coating. They combine every virtue: tart, tender, and temptingly sweet. In the chocolate department we find the finest candy of all, which Thierry Auer calls

Thierry Auer's candied fruits are made according to traditional methods.

The clementines come from Corsica, specially selected by the confectioner for their outstanding flavor.

The pears are peeled with great care to ensure that the shape of the fruit is maintained.

Well made candied fruit does not taste of sugar, but retains its natural flavor.

Candied fruits are not the only specialty to be found at the Auer *confiserie*.

The toasted almonds dusted in cocoa are extremely popular with customers.

the "miracle." It consists of a toasted almond, coated in chocolate before being tossed in powdered cocoa. It is sheer bliss as it melts in the mouth.

The *marron glacé* too is no ordinary sweetmeat. Sweet chestnuts used to be made into bread; now they are turned into a delicious, creamy textured indulgence. The process of making them involves a great number of steps, each demanding care, from the first moment of blanching to the final dip in the thin but fortifying syrup, until at last they recline in their wrapping of gold or silver foil in the presentation box. Their natural coating of course provides perfect protection; as confectionery they are very fragile. Broken *marrons* are often sold cheaply as "seconds."

Alongside stuffed fruits and purées, all equally tempting, there stands one more product, regally supreme: the pots of jelly with their nostalgic reminder of grandmother's kitchen.

Lemon jelly

Generous 2 lb/1 kg unwaxed (or organic) lemons
4 cups/1 liter water
5 lb/2.25 kg confectioners' sugar

Place a metal saucer or similar in the refrigerator. Sterilize the jars to be used for the finished jelly. Wash the lemons thoroughly, slice or dice finely, and place in a saucepan with the water. Simmer until the combined weight of the saucepan's contents is 3 ⅓ lb/1.5 kg.

Remove the pan from the heat. Purée the fruit to the desired degree (with larger or smaller pieces as liked). Stir in the sugar, and simmer over a low heat, stirring. When it is fully dissolved, raise the heat and bring to a strong boil. Beware splashes of hot fruit mixture. From time to time, test the mixture by spooning a tiny amount onto the cold saucer. If as it cools it forms a skin that wrinkles when pushed with the fingertip, it is ready to put in the jars.

Thierry Auer's secret: Bring the jelly rapidly to a boil over a high heat, stirring well. Boiling quickly makes for a clearer jelly.

Nice, capital of the carnation, and the Festival of Flowers

The Cours Saleya is a beautiful setting for a charming market. Its origins date back to the time when the town's fortifications were being extended, in the 16th century, and its present-day appearance to the 18th. It is a place to stroll, to see, and be seen.

It is on the Cours Saleya that the flower market is held, the largest flower market in Nice. The street overflows with the tons of vegetables and flowers brought by farmers, market gardeners, and traders every Tuesday and Thursday, from six in the morning until six in the evening. The astonishing variety of produce here is as fresh as can be, and the growers aim for the highest quality. The bistro counters and café terraces are full of life.

The dryness of the summers in the hinterland of Nice and Provence in general means that it has never been easy to grow the flowers that so characterize the town. Glasshouses were built to house the more vulnerable types, and the carnation is one such fortunate flower. Louis XIV, who liberally adorned his palace at Versailles with carnations, had them sent direct from Nice. However, despite having blossomed in many a buttonhole, the carnation has not always enjoyed such favor; it has been accused of possessing evil powers, and its cultivation has at times suffered as a result of its ill repute. Nice nevertheless saw the carnation in a positive light. Many flower growers

Another of Nice's claims to fame is the market on the renowned Cours Saleya. The produce here ensures that there is no lack of inspiration when it comes to lunch.

set about developing cultivation methods and improving the varieties available. By the turn of the 20th century there were in existence two new strains: one with enormous blooms and one perpetually flowering type. The unquestioned star of the Cours Saleya, the carnation is troubled by one rival, the rose. It, too, is cultivated in Nice's glasshouses; it, too, can soften the heart of many a lover of flowers.

The market on the Cours Saleya is probably the most important meeting place for the region's florists and flower growers. These florists and flower growers, incidentally, provide 80 percent of the fresh flowers

Nice is also known as the "capital of flowers." The flower market is not to be missed.

used for the magnificent decorations of the carnival procession. An average of 20 floats parade through the streets of the town every year, and every one is decorated with about 5,000 marguerites, irises, carnations, gladioli, roses, gerberas, mimosa blossoms, and dozens more, that are worked into mosaics of astounding beauty.

Louis XIV loved carnations. He always used to have the flowers sent from Nice to Paris, which was at that time a lengthy and demanding journey.

A bouquet need not always be of roses. The most beautiful bunches of flowers, luxuriant or delicate, can be bought inexpensively in the market.

"Mesclun"

Mesclun, sometimes written *mesclum*, means "mixed." The name comes from the local dialect word *mescla*, "to mix." The mixture in question is an extremely tasty salad, often served to accompany an assorted cheese platter in good restaurants.

This *mesclun* salad was a specialty once only found in Nice. It is now more widely exported. It consists of a mixture of young shoots, chosen for their delicate flavor and picked when the leaves have barely sprouted. Ingredients include *roquette* (arugula, rocket, or hedge mustard), *pourpier* (purslane), *oseille* (sorrel), *pissenlit* (dandelion leaves), and *laitue feuille de chêne* (oak leaf lettuce).

In times past, the inhabitants of the Nice area used to collect wild herbs and plants. Simply by going out into the meadows, they were able to gather tasty morsels such as *cresson de fontaine* (watercress), arugula, *persil* (parsley). Gradually the idea developed of planting salad herbs that they could harvest.

The market gardeners prepare the soil in the fields and glasshouses in a particular way. They enrich it with humus, and scatter the seeds of each variety separately. Three to four weeks later the tender leaves are ready to be picked. If the leaves are snipped off rather than pulled up, the shoots can regrow.

Mesclun is now stocked in the chill cabinets of most French supermarkets. The mixture may vary: arugula for its spicy hotness, a few sprigs of chervil for their aniseed flavor, some corn salad for its refreshing taste, radicchio for its rich red color, all selected according to each diner's individual choice and the meal it is to accompany.

Mesclun has moved ever further up the popularity scales in recent years, and is one of the most expensive types of salad on the French market. It often forms the basis for the creation of original combinations, served as *hors d'oeuvre* to start the meal. The dish needs no more addition than a few slivers of Parmesan, or pine nuts, chopped black olives, walnuts, goat cheese, or of course glorious slices of truffle. There is no end to the variations used to dress and accompany it.

Freshness is all

Salad is synonymous with crisp, green freshness. When purchasing, look for shiny, firm leaves. The plant should have a heart that is still tightly packed. A little soil at the base does no harm, and in fact helps keep the plant moist.
The best place to keep salad is in the drawer in the bottom of the refrigerator. Salad should be eaten as quickly as possible. A suggestion: Why not serve it with herbs such as oregano, parsley, and chives?

A brief salad guide

Trévise (Radicchio): small, firm, red and white heads with a slightly bitter flavor

Scarole (escarole): a flat-leaved endive with a bright yellow heart and slightly bitter taste

Mâche (corn salad, lamb's lettuce): tender, refreshing, and full of vitamins

Laitue (lettuce): mild in flavor, with a slight sweetness depending on variety

Endive (Belgian endive or witloof): Pale-colored spikes with crisp, slightly bitter leaves. Used for salad or cooked as a vegetable

Roquette (arugula, rocket): dark green, longish leaves with a faintly peppery taste

Feuille de chêne (oak leaf lettuce): has more flavor than normal lettuce, and a faint walnut aroma

Frisée (curly endive): narrow, toothed leaves. Outer leaves are green and inner ones yellow. Flavor is pleasantly bitter

Cerfeuil (chervil): a delicate herb with a sweet flavor reminiscent of aniseed

Romaine (Cos or sweet romaine lettuce): very crisp with a slight bitterness

Pissenlit (dandelion): a wild plant with a fresh, bitter flavor. Needs to be eaten young

Pourpier (purslane): small, crisp, and succulent leaves with a slight walnut flavor

Some typical dishes from Nice

Nice not only has its world famous carnival; it is equally famous for its cuisine, with its delicious flavors and sun-drenched appeal. The proximity to Italy is unmistakable. Classic specialties not to be missed include ravioli, sardines, and *poche de veau* (stuffed slices of breast of veal) all stuffed with Swiss chard, a vegetable for which Nice is known. There are also such delights as *pissaladière* (anchovy tart), *tian de courgette ou de courge* (a baked dish of zucchini or marrow), *bagna cauda* (dip for raw vegetables), *daube* (braised meat), *morue* (dried cod), and sweet specialties like *ganses* (small, sweet, deep fried cakes made with flour) and

beignets pommes-raisins secs (doughnuts with apples and raisins).

Sausages include the wonderful little *pérugina* type, flavored with caraway, delicious with some *févettes* (fava beans). Add a drink of pastis, and vacation time seems here indeed.

Porchetta is something of a bone of contention. This is sucking pig, stuffed, reshaped, and sold in slices. It is reputedly a dish from over the Alps in Italy, but one that Nice also claims as its own culinary invention.

Salade niçoise
Salada nissarda
Salad in the style of Nice

Serves 8

Scant ½ lb/200 g cucumber	
5 oz/150 g *mesclun*	
(or mixed salad)	
1 lb/500 g tomatoes	
Scant ½ lb/100 g celery hearts	
14 oz/400 g fresh purple artichoke hearts	
6 oz/160 g green bell pepper	
Scant ¼ lb/100 g scallions	
1 lb 6 oz/600 g small fresh fava beans	
½ lb/250 g radishes (elongated shape)	
1 clove of garlic, peeled	
7 oz/200 g tuna in olive oil	

8–12 leaves of basil, chopped finely

4 hard boiled eggs, quartered

16 anchovy fillets

⅓ cup/50 g black Nice olives

Scant ½ cup/100 ml olive oil

Freshly ground pepper

Red wine vinegar

Wash the vegetables. Slice the cucumber thinly, sprinkle with salt, and drain. Clean the radishes, and leave the fine leaves on. Rub a salad bowl with garlic, and line with *mesclun*. Quarter the tomatoes, and place on top. Sprinkle with salt.

Thinly slice the white part of the celery, the artichoke hearts, the bell pepper, and the scallions. Shell the fava beans. Arrange with the cucumber on top of the tomatoes. Season with salt. Crumble the tuna into fairly generously

sized pieces, and add. Add the basil and the pieces of egg. Decorate with the anchovies and olives.

At the last moment, dress with olive oil, red wine vinegar, and pepper. Toss the salad to mix, in front of the guests. It is best served at room temperature.

Recipe: Udotsi

Tourte de blettes
La tourta de blea
Swiss chard tart

Serves 8

For the base

Generous 1 lb/500 g all-purpose flour	
2 eggs	
Generous 1 cup/250 g butter	
⅞ cup/200 g sugar	
A pinch of salt	

For the filling

generous ¼ cup/30 g raisins	
1 tbsp/15 ml rum	
Generous 2 lb/2 kg Swiss chard with fine stems (pale-colored chard if possible)	
⅔ cup/150 g sugar	
2 eggs	
½ cup/50 g freshly grated Emmental or Gruyère cheese	
3 ½ oz/100 g pine nuts	
3 ½ tbsp/50 ml marc (from Provence)	
2 tbsp olive oil	
1 tbsp pastis	
10 oz/300 g apples	
⅛ cup/30 g sugar	
Confectioners' sugar	

Soak the raisins in the rum. To make the base, sift the flour onto the work surface and make a well in the center. Break the eggs into this. Soften and add the butter, along with the sugar and salt. Mix with the hands until the dough is smooth, but do not knead. Add a few drops of water if necessary. Leave the dough to rest.

Meanwhile prepare the filling. Remove the stems and ribs from the chard. (These can be used for another dish.) Slice the green part of the leaves into strips. Wash until the water no longer discolors green. This repeated rinsing removes the bitter flavor. Finally, squeeze out the leaves by hand, reserving the juice. Mix the chard with ⅔ cup of sugar, the eggs, grated cheese, drained raisins, pine nuts, marc, olive oil, and pastis.

Divide the dough into two portions. Roll out the first about ⅛ inch/3–4 mm thick, and use it to line a greased and floured shallow baking pan. Prick the base all over with a fork. Preheat the oven to 350 °F/180 °C.

Peel and core the apples, and slice thinly. Spread the filling on the base in a layer ¾ inch/2 cm thick. Pour half the reserved chard juice over this, then layer the apple slices on top. Roll out the second portion of dough and place on top of the pie. Fold over and seal the edges, so that the filling is entirely enclosed. Prick the top all over with a fork. Bake in the preheated oven for 40 minutes. The *tourte* is cooked when the edges draw away from the baking pan. Remove the *tourte* from the oven and sprinkle the top with sugar. When cool, it may be sprinkled with confectioners' sugar if wished.

Recipe: Udotsi

Gnocchis
Lu gnoc nissart
Gnocchi

Serves 8

4 lb 6 oz/2 kg potatoes
Generous 1 lb/500 g all-purpose flour
3 egg yolks
2 tbsp/30 ml olive oil
Freshly ground pepper
Butter
1½ cups/150 g freshly grated Parmesan

Wash the potatoes, and boil them in their skins. Drain them when cooked, peel them while still hot, and mash them. Mix the flour, egg yolks, oil, and pepper with the mashed potato. Mix until smooth and even, but do not knead the mixture any more than is necessary.

Divide the potato mixture into four. On a floured board, shape each portion by hand to a roll about ½ inch/1 cm in diameter. Cut into pieces about ¾ inch/2 cm long. Shape each into a dumpling and score each side with the tines of a fork in traditional gnocchi fashion.

Bring some salted water to a boil, and add the gnocchi. Lift them out as soon as they rise to the surface. Drain, and transfer to a warmed dish.

Serve the gnocchi immediately, with butter and sage or with a sauce, and sprinkled with grated cheese.

The main ingredients that constitute ratatouille are fresh, typically Mediterranean vegetables, such as zucchini and eggplant.
Red and green bell peppers add color. These should be cut in half and cored, then sliced.

Olive oil adds flavor, along with lightly browned onions and garlic. Eggplants and bell peppers also taste better if lightly sautéed first.
The tomatoes are added after the zucchini. It is best to use tomatoes that are very ripe.

Ratatouille niçoise
Ratatouia nissarda
Ratatouille in the style of Nice

Serves 8

½ large bulb/30 g of garlic
14 oz/400 g white onions
2 lb 10 oz/1.2 kg small, long zucchini
2 lb 10 oz/1.2 kg eggplants
1 ¼ lb/600 g red and green bell peppers
1 ½ tbsp/25 ml olive oil
2 lb 10 oz/1.2 kg ripe tomatoes
Salt and freshly milled pepper
1 bouquet garni (thyme, bay, flat-leaf parsley with stalk, and celery leaves)
10 leaves of basil, chopped

Peel the onions. Prepare the vegetables by slicing off the ends of the zucchini and eggplants, washing and coring the bell peppers, and dicing all (separately).
Heat the olive oil in a skillet, and sauté each type of vegetable in turn until golden. Drain in a sieve, and transfer to a casserole or saucepan (with a lid).
Skin the tomatoes. Remove the inner part of the fruit, including the seeds. Cut the firm flesh into pieces, and then add to the other vegetables.
Peel and crush the garlic and add. Season with salt and pepper, and add the bouquet garni. Cover the vegetables with butter paper, put on the lid, and simmer for 40–45 minutes, preferably in the oven at 250–300 °F/120–150 °C.
Add the basil, and serve.

Recipe: Udotsi

349

Small stores selling freshly baked *socca* can be found at the roadside throughout Nice.

socca is baked until golden, then cut into pieces ready to be eaten.

"Socca"

Socca has been the workmen's traditional early morning snack. It can be bought and eaten, standing, at street stalls all over Nice. It is a type of flat bread made from chickpeas (garbanzo beans) and olive oil, cooked on a copper hotplate set over a wood fire, or baked in the oven. It is a specialty that really has to be tried – though it is a little hot to handle! Eaten while hot and freshly cooked, *socca* is served well seasoned, and has a texture that is at the same time soft and crisp. Nicely golden, occasionally even a little burned here and there, it goes well with a glass of chilled rosé. When demand has exceeded supply, patience may be needed while waiting for fresh stocks to arrive from the kitchens. The fresh *socca* is brought ready prepared by "dispatch riders" on motorcycles with a trunk, this trunk is specially adapted to carry the huge flat bread.

Pan bagnat is a more satisfying snack than *socca*, but just as popular. It occupies an essential place in the cuisine of Nice.

Another popular snack in Nice is *pan bagnat*, a generously filled sandwich whose invention harks back to the idea that a salad can be eaten more quickly and conveniently if it is inserted between two pieces of bread.

"Poutine" and "nonnat"

There is a tiny fried fish that has the power to make mouths water in Nice. At the beginning of spring, the *poutine* arrives on the fishmongers' displays, and a diminutive taste of the sea finds its way into local cooking pots.

Poutine and *nonnat* are popular local specialties. The first mainly consists of sardines, as well as young shad; the second are young sprats. The fishermen cast especially fine-meshed nets during the spawning season, and if the currents are in their favor, they can catch a few kilos of young fish. This makes the catch a fine and expensive specialty. The fish are put into boiling water and poached. Both *poutine* and *nonnat* are sometimes served with a dressing of olive oil and lemon juice poured over them in a thin stream, or may be eaten in an omelet, or pastry crust.

Pan bagnat, pain mouillé
Soaked bread

Serves 1

1 small, flat loaf of sour dough or mixed grain bread (5–8 in/15–20 cm diameter)
1 clove of garlic
2 tomatoes (one very ripe)
1 generous tbsp/20 ml olive oil
2 tsp/10 ml vinegar
Salt and freshly milled pepper
5 radishes
1 scallion
1 hard boiled egg
A few small fresh fava beans
1 small purple artichoke
½ green bell pepper, cut into strips
2 leaves of basil, chopped
5–6 pitted black olives
1 ½ oz/40 g tuna in olive oil and/or 2 anchovy fillets

Cut the bread horizontally in half, and hollow out the center. Rub with garlic if liked. Saturate with the ripe tomato, the olive oil, and the vinegar. Season with salt and pepper. Arrange the remaining ingredients in the hollow of the lower half of the bread as follows: thinly slice the tomato, egg, radishes, and scallion. Remove the beans from the pod and add. Slice the artichoke heart thinly and layer on top of the rest. Top with the strips of bell pepper, the basil, olives, tuna, and anchovies. Season with salt and pepper, and replace the lid. Press down to compress the salad.
Pan bagnat tastes still better if it is allowed to stand in the sun for a moment before eating. The warmth brings out the flavor of the olive oil.

The Wines of Bellet: Bellissimi!

The area of production of Bellet is as small as it is ancient; within an Appellation d'Origine Contrôlée region totaling 650 hectares (about 1,600 acres), the area capable of cultivation is just 50 hectares (120 acres). It lies within the bounds of Nice, and its origins go back to the time when Marseille was founded. The sandy loam of its terraced vineyards are blessed with 2,700 hours of sunshine a year, with rainfall and a favorable microclimate, and sea breezes to cool the heat of summer. All these advantages mean that the grapes here ripen slowly and well.

Yields per hectare are low, well below the permitted 40 hl/ha (2.35 tons/acre), but these yields guarantee quality. This is the aim of the 14 highly tradition-conscious winegrowers of Bellet, who of course harvest the grapes by hand.

The main grape variety used for the white wines is Rolle, which has close connections with the area around Nice. Other varieties are Ugni Blanc and Chardonnay. The wines have a beautiful, glowing color undimmed by aging. When young, they have a pear and white blossom aroma; their bouquet after aging in optimum conditions is mainly of toasted almonds and quince, and they have a long finish. They are consumed when lightly chilled, to bring out their fruity character, and are best drunk as an aperitif before a meal or to accompany fish dishes.

The rosés are soft, with a golden shimmer and a bouquet of roses and rose hips. They harmonize well with the cuisine of Nice, with other Mediterranean food, and exotic dishes; they are best drunk at between 50 and 54 °F (10 and 12 °C).

The red wines are made from Braquet and Folle Noire (Fuella) grapes (both varieties that have almost died out, though they were once found all over the area

A dashing setting for a noble wine: the Château de Bellet.

around Nice) together with smaller proportions of Grenache and Cinsault. They have a characteristic intense aroma of wild roses, a spiciness and dryness, and good keeping qualities. When young, they should be drunk fairly cold, at 59–61 °F (15–16 °C), when they are a good partner for fish and seafood. Aged, they should be drunk at room temperature, as an accompaniment to game birds or cheese.

Little if any of the wines of Bellet are exported, since the quantities produced are so small. The wine is very different from its southern French neighbors, so the opportunity of tasting it on site makes a journey to the Nice area well worth while.

Golden bottle labels for a regal wine. This is a wine best appreciated amid its own local country and climate.

The Clot dou Baile estate was awarded a gold medal in Paris in 1988 for a white wine made entirely from the Rolle grape. This winery produces excellent wines of all three types, which age well. The rosés are exceptionally fine and delightful.

At Château de Bellet, the red wines – about 8,000 bottles a year – are matured for 18 months in oak barriques. The quality of these wines, too, is remarkable, and they also keep well, making them a good investment for the connoisseur.

The winemakers of Bellet observe strict regulations and production methods. The first of these is to harvest the grapes by hand.

The winemakers are concerned with the quality of the wine they produce. The size of the yield – lower than the permitted maximum – pales into insignificance beside that.

Monaco

The principality of Monaco is an independent enclave just ¾ square mile (195 ha) in size, within the French département of Alpes-Maritimes. The old town stands on a rock, and the terraced business quarter of Condamine overlooks the harbor. Beside these and the villa district of Fontvieille lies Monte Carlo, basking in the splendor of its magnificent villas.

The principality of Monaco is omnipresent in the events of our times, enjoying an international reputation that keeps it in the reports of one gossip columnist after another. Its ruling prince married an American film star, and it is a place that sought to make dreams come true; a place that is today no more than a dream. When Prince Rainier III, ruler of Monaco since 1949, married Grace Kelly, a star whose films included some by Alfred Hitchcock, their wedding attracted worldwide attention and typified the glossy, sentimental romance. Everyday reality is different and more ordinary – though Monaco still sees itself as a paradise, and this is undoubtedly true, that paradise is more in the nature of a tax haven.

The principality numbers 30,000 inhabitants, of whom only 5,000 are native Monegasque. The ever more utopian wish to become a

Arrival in the realm of luxurious living: The "Hôtel de Paris" is the traditional abode of the aristocratic and rich visitors who come to Monaco.

The French word "le rocher" (the rock) means "Monaco" to the people of the region.

resident is surrounded by an almost Kafkaesque maze of regulations governing naturalization; every inch of soil is worth its weight in gold.

Monaco is a place that loves rich people, who enjoy life to the full and fill the private beaches and exclusive bars. This resplendent tiny country has the largest gambling city in Europe, luxury hotels, casinos, cabarets, a Sporting Club patronized by the biggest American stars, luxury boutiques, a huge, ultra-modern center for thalassotherapy, 23 tennis courts, a Formula 1 racing track, and hotels that are almost fully booked all year round. Millions of tourists a year visit Monaco. Coffee and banana splits are suitably highly priced.

Yet the sights of Monaco – the changing of the *garde des carabiniers* outside the prince's palace, the amazing tropical garden, and the exceptional Oceanographic Museum – make a visit to this world of the rich and beautiful well worth while. The visitor should not miss the casino, that luxurious gaming temple with its Renaissance room and monumental Bohemian glass chandeliers, or the "Café de Paris" with its impressive 10,764 square foot (1,000 m²) sliding roof that opens to reveal the starry skies over Monaco. A stroll through the hall of the "Hôtel de Paris" is to be recommended, to see the magnificent marble, wood carving, and other décor.

Wandering through Monte Carlo – an expensive pastime! – may tempt the visitor toward a table in the exclusive restaurant "Le Louis XV," enticing as a culinary setting and a most appetizing inducement.

The rock stands guard over the scene, as a vantage point from which the old town and the palace command the sea. There on the heights, streets bounded by arcades shelter a brightly colored, lively market dealing in the fish, flowers, and fruit that are so typical of the Mediterranean coast.

"Le Louis XV"

The "Louis XV" is situated inside the "Hôtel de Paris," an illustrious building erected in 1864. The hotel and the restaurant, dating back to the beginning of the 20th century, are decorated with costly woodwork and furnishings. Liveried servants park the limousines of the elegant guests. Above this ambience of magnificence and excess, there linger the echoes of a period when first the English aristocracy, then that of Europe, transformed the hotels into palaces, the streets lined with pine trees into boulevards, the wild coves into private beaches, the tiny harbors into arenas for the display of yachts, and the Côte d'Azur into the Riviera. Inside the "Louis XV," the gaze of the onlooker is constantly directed toward beautiful and extraordinary sights. Even if some Sun King were to alight here, he would attract no particular attention.

The *grand siècle* has left its mark, at the same time aristocratic and bourgeois, edged with gold and flooded with light. Every element of the décor, each item of crockery,

Beneath the crystal chandeliers is the perfect place to enjoy a glass of champagne in luxury.

Even the cutlery at the "Louis XV" exudes elegance and class. Nothing is left to chance.

All that glisters might be gold! The "Louis XV" offers a splendid trip into the world of gastronomy.

The table is laid with the greatest attention to detail, an appropriate setting for Alain Ducasse's creations.

Franck Cerruti, head cook of the "Louis XV," turns the produce into delicious dishes.

competes with the next. Frescoes on the ceiling, circular portraits of bewigged courtesans along the walls, enormous mirrors and tall marble clocks, their obstinate hands permanently poised at midday as if to stop the onward march of time. The tables are set with silver cutlery and crystal glassware on white tablecloths; around them plush, heavy chairs.

Footsteps are silenced by the flowered carpet; impeccable service accompanies the excursion into the land of gastronomy. The intoxication intensifies. The "Louis XV" has at its disposal the outstanding cellar of the "Hôtel de Paris": 300,000 bottles, and 621 different wines, among them some great and rare vintages, some almost unaffordably expensive.

Alain Ducasse

Often described by fellow chefs as masterly and a model for his profession, Alain Ducasse transforms any restaurant in which he works into a temple of gastronomy. He is enthusiastic about Provence and its culinary richness, and uses none but the best ingredients from its local producers and markets as the starting point for his refined, elegant, highly creative cuisine. He also has a gift for spotting young talent, attracting to his restaurant the chefs of tomorrow. They share his convictions as to the key to good cooking: "One criterion: fla vor. One demand: quality. One judge: the chef."

In 1987, when he took over management of the kitchens of the "Louis XV," he made no secret of his ambition to achieve three star rating in the Michelin Guide, the gastronomes' bible. This was tantamount to trying to make it into one of the finest restaurants in the world. It took him just three years to achieve his aim.

In the 1,507 square feet (140 m²) of the kitchen area, there is an atmosphere of methodical and organized industry at the broiler, in the smokery, in the fish and butchery sections, and in the chocolate production area. Head cook Franck Cerruti, who strives to emulate Alain Ducasse, transforms the raw ingredients with their southern French flavors and aromas into a skillful blend of exquisite taste. Alain Ducasse, sometimes in the company of a few friends, tastes the results in a tiny dining room set up in the middle of the kitchen. Six video screens enable him to see everything that is happening in the cooking area while he devotes his attention to his guests.

The cellars of the "Hôtel de Paris" contain veritable treasures. The wines and brandies are the very pinnacle of fine taste.

Légumes des jardins de Provence mijotés à la truffe noire écrasée huile d'olive de Ligurie, aceto balsamico et gros sel gris

Vegetables from the gardens of Provence cooked with chopped black truffle, Ligurian olive oil, balsamic vinegar, and gray sea salt

Serves 4

16 carrots with leaves
8 radishes
16 turnips with leaves
2 bulbs of fennel
8 scallions
Generous 1 lb/500 g fava beans
3 ½ tbsp/50 ml olive oil
8 tbsp/100 g butter
2 ½ cups/600 ml vegetable stock
3 ½ tbsp/50 ml chicken stock
8 artichokes
Juice of ½ lemon
Generous 1 lb/500 g peas
7 oz/200 g green beans
8 spears of asparagus
Fine grained salt
White pepper
1 oz/30 g chopped truffle
2 tbsp balsamic vinegar
Coarse gray sea salt (preferably moist, organic type)

Wash and trim the carrots, radishes, turnips, and fennel. Sauté them separately, ideally in separate saucepans, using 2 tbsp of the olive oil and 3 tbsp of the butter in all. Transfer all to a single saucepan, add 3 ½ tbsp of the vegetable stock as well as the chicken stock, and cook until done. Remove the vegetables.

Remove the stalks and outer leaves from the artichokes, as well as the tips of the leaves. Boil in 2 cups of the vegetable stock to which some lemon juice has been added.

Clean the remaining vegetables and shell the fava beans. Use only the tips of the asparagus. Boil each type of vegetable separately in well salted, vigorously boiling water. When cooked, drain and rinse immediately under running cold water.

Transfer all the vegetables to two flame-proof casseroles or saucepans, and add the remaining stock and olive oil, and the chopped truffle. Season with salt and with pepper.

Heat through thoroughly, then carefully stir in the remaining butter. Pour over the balsamic vinegar.

Place the vegetables on deep plates to serve, pouring over the truffle-flavored butter from the cooking pans. Sprinkle with the gray sea salt.

MENTON

The French Riviera reaches its easternmost border in a mood of balmy ease at Menton. The town lies drowsily in apparently unending sunshine, shaded by palm trees, cypresses, eucalyptus, and the refreshing retreat of its idyllic gardens.

The legend and history of the lemon

A French jury of journalists meets every year to award, with the utmost seriousness, the *prix orange* and the *prix citron*. The first of these awards honors the personality who has been most pleasant and sympathetic in their dealings with the press; the second is for the person who has been the opposite. The orange is credited with all the virtues of sweetness, leaving the lemon to bear the reproach of sourness. The time may be right to redress the balance. Unattractive as the lemon may appear, it is full of fine qualities.

There is a story that when Adam and Eve were forced out of Eden, Eve took with her a golden fruit. Adam was afraid of incurring Divine wrath, and ordered her to throw it away. Eve was charmed by the Bay of Garavan, because it reminded her of her lost Garden of Eden. So she buried the fruit there – at a place that, today, is called Menton.

Menton lies at the farthest end of the Côte d'Azur. Italy begins just beyond. The church tower of Saint-Michel, built in 1701, stands high above the roofs of the town.

The true history of the lemon is a different tale: On their arrival in this area, the Romans brought the lemon with them from the Near East, where it was used to a mild climate. They planted it here, and it flourished in the local calcareous soils and the microclimate of Menton. The lemon and its companion, the orange, took over the surrounding hillsides, clothing them in their evergreen foliage, dotted with orange and yellow, and filled the air with their incomparable scent. The success of the citrus has been so great that, in 1929, Menton was the largest producer of lemons in Europe with 100,000 trees. In the same year, the first exhibition of citrus fruit took place in the Riviera Hotel, the hotel that prompted the first *fête du citron* (the lemon festival) in 1934. This has grown into a festival unique of its kind in the world, with folkloristic carnival processions, and huge floats representing a particular theme, composed of some 130 tons (120 tonnes) of citrus fruits. The parade passes along the Promenade du Soleil, accompanied by music and dance groups and flag-waving performers, until well into the night, promising interest and entertainment. The closing extravaganza is a large firework display on the beach. Every year, the *fête du citron* attracts over 400,000 visitors from across Europe. When they have had their fill of festivities, they visit the Palais Carnolès, the former residence of the princes of Monaco. The

What could be sweeter and juicier than an orange ripened under the sun of Menton?

palace has an unusual collection of fruit, numbering well over 400 varieties, including about 100 citrus fruits such as pomelos, citrons, kumquats, clementines, and other species, some extremely rare. In the early years of the last century, Menton earned its livelihood from the export of its best citrus fruits. The cargoes of *messinoises* set sail for the American continent – 30,000 boxes holding 360 fruits each. The fruits were individually wrapped in tissue paper, which absorbed the scent of the lemons, and was kept long after the fruit had been eaten, for the children to play with. The remaining fruit, of lesser quality, was sent to the chemical industry. Citrus production also served to supply various crafts. For example, the peel was widely used

Menton is famous for its lemons. A lemon festival is held every year, devoted to a particular theme, such as "The World of Walt Disney."

There are no limits to the imagination: The *fête du citron*, which has become world famous, features both innovative and traditional themes that offer constant surprises.

to provide essences for confectioners, and the wood to make luxury furniture. Cultivation and production of lemons has declined considerably as a result of hard winters during the last 60 years, in particular the winter of 1956, and a fungal disease that attacked the orchards in southern France during the first half of the 1940s.

Menton today produces 55 tons (50 tonnes) of citrus fruit a year, of outstanding quality. The *quatre saison* variety, which is available all year round, is exceptionally aromatic. The zest is not very bitter, so ideal – unsprayed, of course – for use in flavoring cakes.

Harvest times for the other four varieties produced in Menton follow each other in succession through the seasons. *Primofiore* is harvested between October and December, *limoni* from December to May, *verdeli* in the summer, and *mayolino* or *bianchetto* are gathered in the autumn.

When buying lemons, it is best to choose medium sized or smaller fruits, as these are usually juicier and have more flavor. Greenish coloration here and there does not indicate the degree of ripeness. Treatment with pesticides while the citrus fruits are growing is necessary for the protection of the plant, so it is against the law to use any designations such as "untreated."

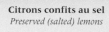

Citrons confits au sel
Preserved (salted) lemons

8 unwaxed lemons	
8 tbsp coarse salt	
4 bay leaves	
1 tsp coriander	
1 tsp red pepper	

Clean and dry a glass jar large enough to hold 8 lemons. Place it in a slow oven for a few minutes.

Blanch the lemons for about 20 seconds. Brush clean, rinse, and dry them carefully. Cut partially through each lemon, starting at the tip and stopping about ½ inch/1 cm from the bottom. Make a second similar cut to divide the lemon into quarters, but so that the sections remain attached to each other. Salt the inside. Pack the lemons closely in the sterilized glass jar, interspersed with the bay leaves. Sprinkle the remaining spices over them. Cover completely with lukewarm water. Put the lid on the jar, and leave the lemons in a dark place at room temperature for one month. Lemons preserved in this way will keep in the refrigerator for a further two months.

The lemons can be preserved in lemon juice instead. In that case, the water is replaced with lemon juice. Another method is to bottle them in olive oil. For this, the lemons are sliced first, and steeped in salt for 12 hours to remove the moisture.

In both cases, the bottling liquid can be used to flavor salads, vegetables, and broiled meat.

A brief guide to lemons

Verna: An all-year variety from Spain. It has a very yellow rind and juicy flesh.

Interdonato: This variety originates from Sicily. It has a hint of acidity, and a long, smooth shape. It is only available from the end of August until the end of October.

Lisbon: This comes from California, and has few pips. It is only available in the first five months of the year in Europe.

Lime: This green citrus fruit from the tropics is wonderfully juicy, and perfect for punches and fruit cups.

The cook should always have lemons to hand. They can be used to flavor sauces, fish, and poultry, and they also taste good with grated carrots. They are much used in oriental cookery. An example is the use of preserved lemons in *tajine*, a dish made in a similar way to couscous, or in a dish of oriental fried vegetables.

Being rich in vitamins, they are an indispensable ingredient for breakfast juices. Their fragrance and refreshing quality makes them ideal for salad dressings, for desserts, or for appetizers.

Vitamin-rich lemons

Like all citrus fruits, lemons are both a good source of fiber and a matchless source of vitamin C in winter. Vitamin C is water-soluble. It promotes the body's own defenses, hastens wound healing, and helps build healthy connective tissue, bones, and teeth. Frequent colds and tiring easily are sure signs of a lack of vitamin C. Smokers and those undergoing periods of stress have an increased vitamin C requirement.

Grapefruit: has a slight bitterness, and is smaller than a pomelo.

Valencia orange: there are many varieties of oranges.

Citron: the rind is candied and used in baking.

Lime: limes are frost tender, however they are juicy and flavorsome.

Kumquat: a slightly bitter miniature orange with a thin, edible skin.

Lemon: acid fruits with a high vitamin C content; rich in minerals and trace elements.

Limequat: a cross between the tender lime and the kumquat, which is hardier.

Pomelo: thick, yellow or pink peel, and a bittersweet, slightly acid flavor.

APPENDIX

Glossary

Affinage: In cheese, the ripening of the cheese, until it reaches optimum eating condition. Wine: aging in the bottle

Affineur: A dealer in cheese who buys young cheeses and matures them in his own cellar

Aïoli: A garlic mayonnaise; indispensable in Provence eaten with cold meat or vegetables, and as an accompaniment to appetizers

Anchoïade: Anchovy purée made with olive oil and capers

Appellation d'Origine Contrôlée: Highest designation of quality, awarded in France by the National Institute for the Designations of Origin of Wines and Eaux-de-Vie

Bastides: Name for the fortified farmhouses that are characteristic of Provence

Bodega: A typically Provençal small café

Bouquet garni: A bunch of flavoring herbs, consisting of parsley, thyme, and bay

Bouquet: The aroma of a wine that has developed and matured

Brouillade: Name of a truffle and scrambled egg dish very popular in Provence

Cabanons: Originally small huts used by fishermen as storm shelters. Now often adapted into weekend leisure accommodation

Camelles: Heaps of salt built up in the *salines*

Course camarguaise: A contest between man and bull for entertainment in an arena. The bull is not killed

Crème fraîche: A matured cream with a mildly sharp flavor and velvety texture. Used to enrich and bind sauces, and in sweet or savory dishes. See page 223 (bottom right panel) for alternative

Cuvée: The term used for champagne or wine in which the final product is blended from several different barrels

Dégustation: Wine-tasting to discover the character and bouquet of the wine

Fines herbes: Mixture of chopped herbs, comprising parsley, tarragon, chervil, and chives

Foie gras: Consists of enlarged goose or duck liver

Garrigue: Type of vegetation typical of the Mediterranean: A species-rich range of plants flourishing in the protection of shrubs and low trees: juniper, rosemary, thyme, sage, tree heath, broom, and rock rose

Herbes de Provence: Collective term for thyme, rosemary, bay, and summer savory or marjoram

Hors d'oeuvre: Collective term for hot or cold first course dishes

Mas: Traditional house in Provence (formerly, farmhouse; now increasingly a rustic villa)

Maceration: Soaking of fruit, herbs, or other ingredients in alcohol

Pena: Orchestra that consists of brass and percussion instruments

Pétanque: A game – a type of *boules*

Phylloxera: A louse that destroys vines. Often refers to the large-scale attack that devastated vines in the latter half of the 19th century

Pistou: Seasoning paste of basil and olive oil

Rabasse: Provençal name for the truffle

Razeteurs: Participants in a *course camarguaise*

Saline: Area set aside for reclaiming salt for cooking from natural salt water by evaporation

Sansouire: Salt "steppes" of the Camargue

Sardinade: Sociable get-together in *cabanons*, when usually sardines are grilled

Tannins: Tannins in wine come from the skins and stems of the grapes, and act as natural preservatives

Tapenade: Olive purée with anchovies and capers

Vin de Pays: Country wines, usually with not more than ten percent alcohol and produced by agricultural cooperatives

Vin doux naturel (VDN): "Naturally sweet wine" – a special category of sweet and dessert wines from southern France, e.g. Muscat and Rasteau wines

Bibliography

General

Bildatlas Provence,
Durch das Rhonetal bis an das Mittelmeer:
Orange, Avignon, Arles, Camargue und Marseille
sowie das Hinterland. Hamburg 2001.

Provence: Côte d'Azur, Rhône-Alps,
Euro-regional map.
GeoCenter International Ltd 1992.

Culinaria France,
ed. André Dominé, Photographs by Günter Beer.
Königswinter 2004.

Knoblauch, Kräuter und Oliven,
Specialties of Provençal cuisine, Monique Lichtner.
Weingarten 1992.

Das Land um Orange,
Destinations ancient and modern, J. Reiher
Rüsselsheim 1999.

The Most Beautiful Villages of Provence,
Text by Michael Jacobs, Photographs by Hugh Palmer.
London c.1994.

Provence/Côte d'Azur,
Baedekers Allianz Reiseführer Ostfildern 2005.

Provence, Art, Architecture, Landscape,
ed. Rolf Toman, Photographs by Achim Bednorz,
Text by Christian Freigang. Königswinter 2005.

Literary Writings

Blue Boy,
(Jean le Bleu) Jean Giono. London 1948.

Cézanne in der Provence,
Evmarie Schmitt. Munich 2001.

Encore Provence,
Peter Mayle. London 2000.

The End of a Dream,
Reminiscences of the French Jura and Haute Provence,
Gael Elton Mayo. London 1993 (orig. publ. 1987).

The Garden of Eden,
Ernest Hemingway. London 1987 (orig. publ. New
York 1986).

Hotel Pastis,
Peter Mayle. London 2004.

Hymne an die Provence,
Norbert Kustos. Munich 1999.

Letters from my Windmill,
(Lettres de mon Moulin), Alphonse Daudet.
Harmondsworth; New York: Penguin 2001.

Die Leute von Port Madeleine,
Village tales from Provence, Klaus Harpprecht.
Reinbek 2000.

Mit Rilke durch die Provence,
Irina Frowen (ed.) Frankfurt/Main 1998.

My Father's Glory; My Mother's Castle: Marcel
Pagnol's Memories of Childhood,
(Souvenirs d'Enfance: La Gloire de mon Père; Le
Château de ma Mère) Marcel Pagnol. London 1991
(transl. R. Barisse. Orig. publ. as The Days were too
Short London 1960).

Provence,
Lawrence Durrell. New York 1994.

Les Sermons de Marcel Pagnol,
Moving sermons from Provence, Marcel Pagnol. Basses-
Alpes 1993.

A Troubadour's Testament,
James Cowan. Boston 1998.

Der Trüffelsucher,
Gustaf Sobin. Berlin 2001.

Van Gogh's Provence,
Text by Berndt Küster. Hamburg 1999

Verborgenes im Lavendel,
Background and foreground facts in Provence.
Impressions from the turbulent history of a grandiose
landscape, Herbert G. Scholz Rüsselsheim 1996.

The Water of the Hills: Jean de Florette; Manon
of the Springs,
(L'Eau des Collines) Marcel Pagnol. London 1989.

A Year in Provence,
Peter Mayle. London 2000.

Index of Place Names

Recipe Index

ABBREVIATIONS AND QUANTITIES

1 oz = 1 ounce = 28 grams
1 lb = 1 pound = 16 ounces
1 cup = 8 ounces *
1 cup = 8 fluid ounces = 250 milliliters (liquids)
2 cups = 1 pint (liquids)
8 pints = 4 quarts = 1 gallon (liquids)
1 g = 1 gram = $\frac{1}{1000}$ kilogram
1 kg = 1 kilogram = 1000 grams = 2¼ lb
1 l = 1 liter = 1000 milliliters (ml) = approx 34 fluid ounces
125 milliliters (ml) = approx 8 tablespoons = ½ cup
1 tbsp = 1 level tablespoon = 15-20 g * = 15 milliliters (liquids)
1 tsp = 1 level teaspoon = 3-5 g * = 5 ml (liquids)

Where measurements of dry ingredients are given in spoons, this always refers to the dry ingredient as described in the wording immediately following, e.g. 1 tbsp chopped onions BUT: 1 onion, peeled and chopped.

*The weight of dry ingredients varies significantly depending on the density factor, e.g. 1 cup flour weighs less than 1 cup butter.
Quantities in ingredients have been rounded up or down for convenience, where appropriate. Metric conversions may therefore not correspond exactly.
It is important to use either American or metric measurements within a recipe.

Quantities in recipes
Recipes serve four people, unless stated otherwise.
Exception: Recipes for drinks (quantities given per person).

GENERAL INDEX

Addresses

Nougat Le Chaudron d'Or p. 15
BP 171 26204 – Montélimar Cedex
Tel.: 04 75 01 03 95
Fax: 04 75 53 08 75
Factory tour and tasting

La table de Nicole route de Grignan p. 16 ff.
26230 – Valaurie
Tel.: 04 75 98 52 03
Fax: 04 75 98 58 45

La Beaugravière p. 24 f.
Nationale 7
84430 – Mondragon
Tel.: 04 90 40 82 54
Fax: 04 90 40 91 01

Moulin Dozol Autrand p. 30
26110 – Nyons
Tel.: 04 75 26 02 52
Fax: 04 75 26 02 52
Mill visits by prior arrangement

Musée de l'olivier p. 30
avenue des tilleuls
26110 – Nyons
Tel.: 04 75 26 12 12

Le Vieux Moulin p. 30
26110 – Mirabel aux Baronnies
Tel.: 04 75 27 12 02
Fax: 04 75 27 19 92
Mill visits by prior arrangement

Le caveau de Gigondas p. 46 ff.
de la mairie
84190 – Gigondas
Tel.: 04 90 65 82 29
Open all year

Le Domaine de Cabasse p. 38 f.
84110 – Séguret
Tel.: 04 90 46 91 12
Fax: 04 90 46 94 01

Domaine de Deurre
R.N. 94
26110 – Vinsobres
Tel.: 04 75 27 62 66

Mas de Gourgonnier
13890 – Mouriès
Tel.: 04 90 47 50 45

Mas de la Dame p. 60
13520 – Les Baux de provence
Tel.: 04 90 54 32 24

Mas Sainte Berthe
13520 – Les Baux de Provence
Tel.: 04 90 54 39 01

Domaine Hauvette
13210 – Saint-Rémy-de-Provence
Tel.: 04 90 92 03 90

Château d'Estoublon Mogador p. 61 f.
Route de Maussane /
13990-Fontvieille
Tel.: 04 90 54 64 00

Domaine de la Vallongue
BN n° 4- 13810 -Eygallières
Tel.: 0 49 09 59 70

Domaine des Terres Blanches p. 61
RD 99- 13210 –
Saint-Rémy-de Provence
Tel.: 04 90 95 91 66

Domaine de Lauzières p. 60 f.
13890 – Mouriès
Tel.: 04 90 47 62 88

Château Romanin
13210 – Saint-Rémy-de-Provence
Tel.: 04 90 92 45 87

Domaine Dalmeran
13103 – Saint Etienne du Grès
Tel.: 04 90 49 05 98

Domaine Milan
"La Tuilière Vieille"
13210 – Saint Rémy-de-Provence
Tel.: 04 90 92 12 52

Moulin Jean-Marie Cornille p. 62
Coopérative oléicole de la Vallée
des Bauxrue Charloun-Rieu
13520 – Maussane-les-Alpilles
Tel.: 04 90 54 32 27

Moulin des Pénitents p. 62 f.
Coopérative oléicole du Plan
et des Mées
04190 Les Mées
Tel.: 04 92 34 07 67

La Balméenne p. 62
avenue Jules-Ferry
84190 Beaumes-de-Venise
Tel.: 04 90 62 94 15

La Régalido p. 64
13990 – Fontvieille en Provence
Tel.: 04 90 54 60 22
Fax: 04 90 54 64 29

Mas Doù Juge p. 86 f.
c/o Roger et Renée Granier
Quartier Pin Fourcat

Route du Bac Sauvage
13460 – Saintes Marie de la Mer
Tel.: 04 66 73 51 45
Fax: 04 66 73 51 42

La Confiserie du Mont-Ventoux p. 110
288, avenue Notre Dame de Santé
84200 Carpentras
Tel.: 04 90 63 05 25

La Prévôté p. 114
4, rue Jean-Jacques Rousseau
84800 – Isle sur la Sorgue
Tel.: 04 90 38 57 29

Au Pierrôt Blanc p. 116 f
55, rue des Marchands
84400 – Apt
Tel.: 04 90 74 12 48

Bernard Mathys p. 120
Le Chêne
84400 Gargas (par Apt)
Tel.: 04 90 04 84 64

Château la Canorgue p. 126 f.
Route du Pont-Julien
84480 – Bonnieux
Tel.: 04 90 75 81 01

Château Val Joanis p. 127 f
84120 – Pertuis
Tel.: 04 90 79 20 77

Château de Mille p. 129
Conrad Pinatel & fils
84400 – Apt
Tel.: 04 90 74 11 94

Château de l'Isolette p. 129
Luc Pinatel
84400 – Apt
Tel.: 04 90 74 16 70

Auberge des Seguins p. 130 f.
84480 Buoux
Tel.: 04 90 74 19 89

Le Moulin de
Lourmarin p. 132 ff.
84160 Lourmarin
Tel.: 04 90 68 06 69

Super Taff p. 138 ff.
rue Henri de Savourin
84160 – Lourmarin

Le Clos de la Violette p. 141 ff.
10, avenue de la Violette
Tel.: 04 42 23 30 71

Les calissons
d'Entrecasteaux p. 150 f.
2, rue d'Entrecasteaux
13100 – Aix-en-Provence
Tel.: 04 42 27 15 02

Les santons Fouque p. 156
65, cours Gambetta -route de Nice
13100 – Aix-en-provence
Tel.: 04 42 26 33 38

Château Simone p. 158 f.
13 590 Meyreuil
Tel.: 04 42 66 92 58

Distilleries et Domaines p. 166
de Provence
04300 – Forcalquier
Tel.: 04 92 75 00 58

Fromagerie de Banon p. 168 f.
Route de Carniol
04150 – Banon
Tel.: 04 92 73 25 03

Maurice Melchio p. 172 f.
04150 – Banon
Tel.: 04 92 73 23 05

La Bonne Etape p. 178 ff.
Pierre & Jany Gleize
04160 Château Arnoux
Tel.: 04 92 64 00 09

Musée de la Lavande p. 187
route de Gordes
Tel.: 04 90 76 91 23
Closed January/February
Prieuré de Salagon p. 188
04300 – Mane
Tel.: 04 92 75 19 93

Le Grand Rubren p. 194 ff.
1, rue de Savoie BP – 27
04400 – Barcelonnette
Tel.: 04 92 81 44 00

Le Miramar p. 216 ff.
12, quai du port
13000-Marseille
Tel.: 04 91 91 10 40

Le Moulin Bleu p. 228
7, cours du 11 Novembre
13190 – Allauch
Tel.: 04 91 68 17 86

Clos d'Albizzi p. 234
Chemin Saint Vincent
13260 – Cassis
Tel.: 04 40 11 14 3

Clos Sainte-Madeleine p. 235
Avenue de Revestel
13714 – Cassis Cedex
Tel.: 04 42 01 70 28

Domaine de la Ferme
Blanche p. 232
RN 559, 13714 – Cassis Cedex
Tel.: 04 42 01 73 94

Château Pradeaux p. 236 f.
Quartier Les Pradeaux
83270 – Saint-Cyr-sur-Mer
Tel.: 04 94 32 10 21

Château de Pibarnon p. 237 f.
Comtes de Saint-Victor
83740 – La Cadière d'Azur
Tel.: 04 94 90 12 73

Domaine de Souviou p. 238
La Laidière
Sainte-Anne-d'Evenos BP 101
83330 – Evenos
Tel.: 94 90 37 07

L'Ile Rousse p. 240 f.
Centre Thalasso Héliovital Thalgo
17, bd Louis Lumière
83150 – Bandol
Tel.: 04 94 29 33 00

Hostellerie Bérard p. 242 ff.
83740 – La Cadière d'Azur
Tel.: 04 94 90 11 43

Kiwi Lacour p. 254 ff.
Domaine du Fenouillet
83400 – Hyères
Tel.: 04 94 65 13 26

Le Mas du Langoustier p. 258 f.
Ile de Porquerolles
Tel.: 04 94 58 30 09

Domaine Ott p. 268 ff.
Route du Fort de Brégançon
83250 – La Londe-des-Maures
Tel.: 04 94 01 53 53

Château Rasque p. 270
Route de Draguignan
83460 – Taradeau
Tel.: 04 94 73 31 72

Domaine de Richeaume p. 270
Chemin Départemental 57B
13114 – Puyloubier
Tel.: 04 42 66 31 27

Domaine Réal Martin p. 271
Route de Barjols
83143 – Le Val
Tel.: 04 94 86 40 90

Château Minuty
D 61 – 83580 Gassin
Tel.: 04 94 56 12 09

Domaine Gavoty p. 271
Domaine du Grand Campdumy
83340 – Cabasse
Tel.: 04 94 69 72 39

**Commanderie de
Peyrassol** p. 271
RN 7 – 83340 – Flassans
Tel.: 04 94 69 71 02

Maison des Vins de p. 274
Côtes de Provence, RN – 7
83460 – Les Arcs-sur-Argens
Tel.: 04 94 99 50 10

Le Bacchus Gourmand p. 276 f.
Maison des Vins RN 7
83460 – Les Arcs-sur-Argens
Tel.: 04 94 47 48 47

**Maison des Vins Coteaux
Varois** p. 273
Abbaye de la Celle
83170 – La Celle
Tel.: 04 94 69 33 18

Bruno p. 280
Campagne Mariette
83510 – Lorgues
Tel.: 04 94 85 93 93

Massif des Maures p. 282 ff.
Les ruchers des Maures
83340 – Les Mayons
Tel.: 04 94 60 01 80

Robert Bedot p. 296 f.
Les Combrettes
Quartier des Quatre-Chemins
83520 – Roquebrune-sur-Argens
Tel.: 04 94 45 44 33

La Villa des Lys p. 302 ff.
Hôtel Majestic
14, la Croisette
06400 – Cannes
Tel.: 04 92 98 77 00

Abbaye de Lérins p. 312
Ile Saint Honorat, BP – 157
06406 – Cannes Cedex
Tel.: 04 92 99 54 10
Renseignements bateaux:
Tel.: 04 92 98 71 30

Les Vieux Murs p. 314 ff.
Promenade Amiral-de-Grasse
06600 – Antibes
Tel.: 04 93 34 06 73

Parfumerie Fragonard p. 319
20, Boulevard Fragonard
06130 – Grasse
Tel.: 04 93 36 44 65

Confiserie Florian p. 322 ff.
Pont du Loup
06140 – Tourrettes-sur-Loup
Tel.: 04 93 59 32 91

Patisserie-Confiserie Auer
p. 334 ff.
7, rue Saint-François-de-Paule
06000 Nice
Tel.: 04 93 80 33 13

Château de Bellet p. 353
440, chemin de Saquier
06200 – Saint-Roman-de Bellet
Tel.: 04 93 37 81 57

Clot Dou Baile p. 353
277, chemin du Saquier
06200 – Nice-St-Roman de Bellet
Tel.: 04 93 29 85 87

**Le Louis XV / Alain Ducasse
Hôtel de Paris** p. 355 ff.
Place du Casino / Monte-Carlo
MC 98000 Monaco
Tel.: 377 92 16 30 01

Acknowledgements

The publishers would like to express their thanks to everyone who has given their kind support and assistance, including those individuals who are not known to the publishers by name, but who have contributed to the project. The author and editor thanks in particular those who helped her in her researches. This book in its present form would not have been possible without the kind assistance of everyone in the restaurant kitchens, the wine cellars of the region, and the café terraces, who provided information about their work, their country, and its traditions. Their views have been represented as accurately as possible. Thanks are also due to the photographers of the TERRA and Image du Sud agencies, to the photographer Françoise Pagès, and adviser André Dominé.

Picture Credits

All photographs by: Karin Hessmann, Cologne

except:

©**Artothek,** Peissenberg. Photograph: Hans Hinz: "Mont St. Victoire", Paul Cézanne, oil on canvas, 60 x 72 cm, 1904/1906, Kunstmuseum Basel, Basel p. 145 © **Beaujard, Bernard:** 92 top right, 93 top left © **Château d'Estoublon,** Fontvieille: 61 three illustrs. bottom © **Château de Versailles et de Trianon:** Marie-Caroline de Bourbon-Sicile, Duchesse de Berry (1798–1830), Painting by Sir Thomas Lawrence (1769–1830), Photograph: Bernard-RMN, Paris p. 107 © **CIVPV,** Photograph: François ou Mouial. 263 top, Photograph: P. Mouial: 267 bottom right © **Cine Foto Provence:** 158 © **Confiserie Florian,** Pont-du-Loup: 323, 324, 325 © **Corbis/Picture Press:** 72, 82, Photograph: Gail Mooney, 93 bottom center, Photograph: J.K. Benda: 240 © **Domaine de Cabasse,** Séguret, photo: Eliophot. Six.: 43 left © **Domaine Ott,** photo: Eliophot. Six.: 268, 269 top right © **Dominé, André,** Trilla: 86, 87, 93 top right © **Duranti, Chris:** 328, 329 © **Franken, Owen:** 17 Two recipe illustrs. bottom, 20, 21 © **Hostellerie Bérard,** La Cadière d'Azur: 242 bottom, 243, 244 bottom © **Hulton Getty:** 264, 318 bottom © **Image du Sud** Saint Laurent du Var, Photographs: Zintzmeyer: 8, 26, 33 large illustr., 34 left, 185 bottom center, 364, 365, Photographs: Rozet: 10, 12, 14, 185 left and top center, Photographs: Wacongne: 28 top left, 283, both illustrs. center, Photographs: Lautier: 28 top center, 283 top left, Photograph: Palomba: 28 top right, Photographs: Cosson: 28 second row left, 283 top right, bottom right, Photographs: Ajuria: 28 bottom right, 336 top left, 363 bottom left, Photographs: Tréal: 40, 41, 345, Photographs: Julien: 55 top right, 246 top, Photographs: Le Studio, 55 left and top center, 175, 321 center right, bottom left, 363 bottom right, Photograph: Lucas: 56, Photograph: Scott: 67 bottom right, Photographs: Débru: 70, 76, 79, 84 top left, 97 free illustr. bottom left, 151 free illustr. top right, Photograph: Teissier: 83, Photograph: Rebours: 148 left, Photograph: Martinetti: 185 bottom right, Photographs: Genar: 185 second row right, bottom left, Photograph: Moyard: 185 second row center, Photograph: Richoux: 189 right, Photograph: Pillon: 201 bottom, Photographs: Sounier: 283 bottom left, 285,